ALSO BY THE EDITORS AT AMERICA'S TEST KITCHEN

The Complete Mediterranean Cookbook

Cook's Science

Bread Illustrated

Master of the Grill

Kitchen Hacks

What Good Cooks Know

100 Recipes: The Absolute Best Ways to Make the True Essentials

The Best of America's Test Kitchen (2007–2017 Editions)

The Complete America's Test Kitchen TV Show Cookbook 2001–2017

The New Family Cookbook

The Complete Vegetarian Cookbook

The Complete Cooking for Two Cookbook

The America's Test Kitchen Cooking School Cookbook

The Cook's Illustrated Meat Book

The Cook's Illustrated Baking Book

The Cook's Illustrated Cookbook

The Science of Good Cooking

The New Best Recipe

Soups, Stews, and Chilis

The America's Test Kitchen Quick Family Cookbook

The America's Test Kitchen Healthy Family Cookbook

The America's Test Kitchen Family Baking Book

THE COOK'S ILLUSTRATED ALL-TIME BEST SERIES

All-Time Best Appetizers

All-Time Best Soups

THE AMERICA'S TEST KITCHEN LIBRARY SERIES

Vegan for Everybody

Naturally Sweet

Foolproof Preserving

Paleo Perfected

The How Can It Be Gluten-Free Cookbook: Volume 2

The How Can It Be Gluten-Free Cookbook

The Best Mexican Recipes

The Make-Ahead Cook

Healthy Slow Cooker Revolution

Slow Cooker Revolution Volume 2: The Easy-Prep Edition

Slow Cooker Revolution

The Six-Ingredient Solution

Pressure Cooker Perfection

The America's Test Kitchen D.I.Y. Cookbook

Pasta Revolution

THE COOK'S COUNTRY SERIES

Cook It in Cast Iron

Cook's Country Eats Local

The Complete Cook's Country TV Show Cookbook

FOR A FULL LISTING OF ALL OUR BOOKS

CooksCountry.com

AmericasTestKitchen.com

PRAISE FOR OTHER AMERICA'S TEST KITCHEN TITLES

"Another winning cookbook from ATK. . . . The folks at America's Test Kitchen apply their rigorous experiments to determine the facts about these pans."
BOOKLIST ON *COOK IT IN CAST IRON*

Selected as an Amazon Best Books of 2015 in the Cookbooks and Food Writing Category
AMAZON ON *THE COMPLETE VEGETARIAN COOKBOOK*

"An exceptional resource for novice canners, though preserving veterans will find plenty here to love as well."
LIBRARY JOURNAL (STARRED REVIEW) ON *FOOLPROOF PRESERVING*

"A terrifically accessible and useful guide to grilling in all its forms that sets a new bar for its competitors."
PUBLISHERS WEEKLY (STARRED REVIEW) ON *MASTER OF THE GRILL*

"A beautifully illustrated, 318-page culinary compendium showcasing an impressive variety and diversity of authentic Mexican cuisine."
MIDWEST BOOK REVIEW ON *THE BEST MEXICAN RECIPES*

"The 21st-century *Fannie Farmer Cookbook* or *The Joy of Cooking*. If you had to have one cookbook and that's all you could have, this one would do it."
CBS SAN FRANCISCO ON *THE NEW FAMILY COOKBOOK*

"The sum total of exhaustive experimentation . . . anyone interested in gluten-free cookery simply shouldn't be without it."
NIGELLA LAWSON ON *THE HOW CAN IT BE GLUTEN-FREE COOKBOOK*

"This book upgrades slow cooking for discriminating, 21st-century palates—that is indeed revolutionary."
THE DALLAS MORNING NEWS ON *SLOW COOKER REVOLUTION*

"The go-to gift book for newlyweds, small families, or empty nesters."
ORLANDO SENTINEL ON *THE COMPLETE COOKING FOR TWO COOKBOOK*

"Some 2,500 photos walk readers through 600 painstakingly tested recipes, leaving little room for error."
ASSOCIATED PRESS ON *THE AMERICA'S TEST KITCHEN COOKING SCHOOL COOKBOOK*

"A one-volume kitchen seminar, addressing in one smart chapter after another the sometimes surprising whys behind a cook's best practices. . . . You get the myth, the theory, the science, and the proof, all rigorously interrogated as only America's Test Kitchen can do."
NPR ON *THE SCIENCE OF GOOD COOKING*

"This encyclopedia of meat cookery would feel completely overwhelming if it weren't so meticulously organized and artfully designed. This is *Cook's Illustrated* at its finest."
THE KITCHN ON *THE COOK'S ILLUSTRATED MEAT BOOK*

"This book is a comprehensive, no-nonsense guide . . . a well-thought-out, clearly explained primer for every aspect of home baking."
THE WALL STREET JOURNAL ON *THE COOK'S ILLUSTRATED BAKING BOOK*

"The perfect kitchen home companion. . . . The practical side of things is very much on display . . . cook-friendly and kitchen-oriented, illuminating the process of preparing food instead of mystifying it."
THE WALL STREET JOURNAL ON *THE COOK'S ILLUSTRATED COOKBOOK*

"There are pasta books . . . and then there's this pasta book. Flip your carbohydrate dreams upside down and strain them through this sieve of revolutionary, creative, and also traditional recipes."
SAN FRANCISCO BOOK REVIEW ON *PASTA REVOLUTION*

"Further proof that practice makes perfect, if not transcendent. . . . If an intermediate cook follows the directions exactly, the results will be better than takeout or Mom's."
THE NEW YORK TIMES ON *THE NEW BEST RECIPE*

ONE-PAN WONDERS

**Fuss-Free Meals for
Your Sheet Pan, Dutch Oven,
Skillet, Roasting Pan,
Casserole, and Slow Cooker**

BY THE EDITORS
AT AMERICA'S TEST KITCHEN

CONTENTS

WELCOME TO AMERICA'S TEST KITCHEN

This book has been tested, written, and edited by the folks at America's Test Kitchen, a very real 2,500-square-foot kitchen located just outside of Boston. It is the home of *Cook's Illustrated* magazine and *Cook's Country* magazine and is the Monday-through-Friday destination for more than 60 test cooks, editors, and cookware specialists. Our mission is to test recipes over and over again until we understand how and why they work and until we arrive at the "best" version.

We start the process of testing a recipe with a complete lack of preconceptions, which means that we accept no claim, no technique, and no recipe at face value. We simply assemble as many variations as possible, test a half-dozen of the most promising, and taste the results blind. We then construct our own recipe and continue to test it, varying ingredients, techniques, and cooking times until we reach a consensus. As we like to say in the test kitchen, "We make the mistakes so you don't have to." The result, we hope, is the best version of a particular recipe, but we realize that only you can be the final judge of our success (or failure). We use the same rigorous approach when we test equipment and taste ingredients.

All of this would not be possible without a belief that good cooking, much like good music, is based on a foundation of objective technique. Some people like spicy foods and others don't, but there is a right way to sauté, there is a best way to cook a pot roast, and there are measurable scientific principles involved in producing perfectly beaten, stable egg whites. Our ultimate goal is to investigate the fundamental principles of cooking to give you the techniques, tools, and ingredients you need to become a better cook. It is as simple as that.

To see what goes on behind the scenes at America's Test Kitchen, check out our social media channels for kitchen snapshots, exclusive content, video tips, and much more. You can watch us work (in our actual test kitchen) by tuning in to *America's Test Kitchen* or *Cook's Country from America's Test Kitchen* on public television or on our websites. Listen in to America's Test Kitchen Radio (ATKradio.com) on public radio to hear insights that illuminate the truth about real home cooking. Want to hone your cooking skills or finally learn how to bake—with an America's Test Kitchen test cook? Enroll in one of our online cooking classes. If the big questions about the hows and whys of food science are your passion, join our *Cook's Science* experts for a deep dive. However you choose to visit us, we welcome you into our kitchen, where you can stand by our side as we test our way to the best recipes in America.

facebook.com/AmericasTestKitchen

twitter.com/TestKitchen

youtube.com/AmericasTestKitchen

instagram.com/TestKitchen

pinterest.com/TestKitchen

google.com/+AmericasTestKitchen

AmericasTestKitchen.com

CooksIllustrated.com

CooksCountry.com

CooksScience.com

OnlineCookingSchool.com

Introduction

One-pan recipes make some pretty big promises. From "dump and stir" to "set it and forget it," this branch of home cookery promises meals that minimize effort and yield unbelievable results. Here in the test kitchen, we saw one-pan recipes as the ultimate challenge. After all, what's the point of serving a whole meal from a single vessel if it doesn't taste good? And why confine yourself to one pan if it makes a recipe harder than it was in the first place? So, with a clear goal in mind, we set out to streamline our favorite dishes (and think up a host of new ones) for an inspiring range of satisfying meals—from speedy stir-fries to slow-cooked roasts—without shortchanging flavor, texture, or overall impact.

During recipe development, we took "one-pan" quite literally. Each chapter centers on a different vessel to show the range of its possibilities, and aside from using a few mixing bowls, a food processor, or, in one case, a second sheet pan for a layer of insulation, these meals are truly single-pan. While you may want to serve a salad or loaf of bread alongside some of these dishes, the majority of our recipes are self-contained meals that will please everyone at the table.

To reduce hands-on time, we cut out excess steps where we could, and discovered new ways to bring old favorites to the table. Take our Modern Beef Pot Pie (page 45): Where once you had to roll out a pie crust, we top off our meaty filling with slices of Parmesan-crusted bread (it doesn't hurt that it's a visual stunner to boot). Or check out our Easy Baked Mac and Cheese (page 236): We make passing up the blue box painless, with pasta that cooks right in its sauce and uses pantry standbys to produce a supremely cheesy treat right in a casserole dish.

When it came to selecting vessels, we looked for new ways to use the pots and pans we rely on every day, always trying to capitalize on each vessel's strengths. For instance, we deployed the wide surface area and sturdy build of our favorite sheet pan to brown both steak and veggies for fajitas, and turned to the high-sided, tight-sealing Dutch oven for clams that warm through on a bed of Israeli couscous. (We share plenty of useful tricks and our expert equipment picks—selected after rigorously testing the top models on the market—at the start of each chapter.)

After simmering, sautéing, broiling, and roasting hundreds of meals, we've come up with a collection of recipes that deserve a place in your regular dinner rotation. Whether you're looking for a cheesy, bubbling lasagna for a busy Tuesday night or a smoky-sweet bacon-wrapped pork loin for a special gathering, this book delivers modern, streamlined meals you'll want to make seven days a week.

WEEKNIGHT FRIENDLY

Keep an eye out for this icon—it will direct you to those recipes that take an hour or less, or to slow-cooker recipes that will cook over the course of a typical workday.

The Six Tenets of One-Pan Cooking

1 Keep the Ingredient List Short but Flavorful

To simplify our one-pan meals, we made every effort to strip down the ingredient lists to the hard-hitting items, and this is where our test kitchen know-how really shined. Umami elevators like tomato paste, minced anchovies, and soy sauce brought supersavory taste (and no fishy flavor from the anchovies, believe it or not) to many recipes. Turning to chicken broth as our cooking liquid yielded full-flavored rice, grains, and pasta every time. We also used a single ingredient multiple ways wherever possible, like adding both kimchi and its brine to a dead-easy Korean stir-fry. And we didn't shy away from convenience items like frozen peas or canned tomatoes: These everyday products deliver on fresh, bright flavor year-round.

Eggplant and Sweet Potato Curry
Tomato paste gives this vegetarian dish some meaty oomph, page 174.

Beef Taco Bake
Canned refried beans and spicy Ro-tel tomatoes deliver authentic taco flavor, page 228.

Bacon-Wrapped Pork Loin with Roasted Red Potatoes and Peach Sauce
Strips of crisp bacon insulate the pork and the drippings flavor the potatoes, page 261.

2 Bring Your Flavors to Life

There's no denying the virtues of a well-stocked spice rack, and for this book, we brought everything from oregano and thyme to chili powder and garam masala into rotation in pursuit of the perfect flavor profile. However, for these potent seasonings to make a real impression, we knew simply stirring them in wouldn't suffice. Blooming spices, whether on a stovetop or in the microwave, releases their aromatic oils that can suffuse an entire dish. By simply heating spices in oil, butter, or the juices rendered from browned meat or chicken, we immediately (and effortlessly) elevated their flavors.

Indian-Style Chicken Curry
Warming curry powder and garam masala with the aromatics brings their exotic flavors to life, page 173.

Roast Turkey Breast with Herb Stuffing and Cranberry Sauce
Fresh sage and thyme bloomed in melted butter give the stuffing a supersavory identity, page 265.

Pork Chops with Chile Rice and Peanuts
We used the residual juices from the browned chops to bloom oregano, ancho chile powder, and coriander in tomato paste for a rich base, page 30.

3 Team Up with Your Microwave

From blooming aromatics to parcooking potatoes to cooking up a simple sauce, our microwave was pivotal in enabling us to avoid having to reach for (and later wash) a second pan. It also proved an essential time-saver, helping us keep our recipe prep as efficient as possible. And when we wanted to top off a pasta dish with extra crunch, or coat chicken or pork with a crackling crust, briefly microwaving panko bread crumbs with a little oil was enough to turn pale boxed bread crumbs golden and crisp.

Sausage Lasagna with Spinach and Mushrooms
Sweating mushrooms in the microwave eliminates any lasagna-sogging moisture, page 239.

Pesto Chicken with Fennel and Tomato Couscous
Zapping sliced fennel with garlic and oil starts melding the base's flavors while softening the fennel's crunch, page 277.

Thai Curry Rice with Cod
The world's easiest red curry sauce comes together in the microwave, ready to drizzle over our fish, page 69.

4 Cook in Stages

As many of us learned early on from Easy-Bake Oven letdowns, no great dishes were ever made by just dumping everything together and letting it cook. Often, turning out a perfectly cooked protein plus sides means tailoring your technique or seasoning to suit each component—and that's precisely what many of these recipes demanded to keep their flavors distinct. When we wanted to pair a tender fish fillet with crisp potatoes, or hearty root vegetables with delicate greens, staggering the cooking times was essential. A bonus: While one food cooked we could turn our attention to making a flavorful sauce.

5 Create Two Cooking Environments in One Vessel

Some of our most significant aha! moments came when pondering how our vessels could cook two ways at once— how we could, for example, simmer a rich stew while steaming a side of green vegetables. Approaching our recipes this way introduced some unexpected items into the mix, as we created a vessel within a vessel—or above it. A wire rack, a steamer basket, the Dutch oven's lid, and skewers all allowed us to execute more than one cooking technique at a time, and we were wowed by the results.

6 Finish with a Flourish

While getting a homemade meal on the table every night is an achievement in itself, we never want to skimp on presentation. More often than not, our favorite way to finish off a dish is with a fresh flourish, be that a sprinkling of chopped cilantro or a bright drizzle of vinaigrette. Particularly when a meal veers toward hearty, slow-cooked flavors (think robust root vegetables, a hefty cut of beef, or creamy scalloped potatoes), we seek out a way to lighten things up. For many of the recipes in this book, the last step involves whisking together a quick, flavorful sauce, sprinkling on some fresh herbs, or passing lemon wedges at the table. These small touches work wonders for both the flavor and the visual appeal of our meals.

Roasted Salmon, Broccoli, and Potatoes with Whole-Grain Mustard Sauce
To maximize the potatoes' roasting time, we swapped out the cooked broccoli for the salmon partway through roasting, page 85.

Peruvian Roast Chicken with Swiss Chard and Sweet Potatoes
The sweet potatoes get lots of browning time before the chicken is added, then chard takes its turn, cooking in the pan juices, page 253.

Spiced Pork Tenderloin with Couscous
Superflavorful couscous cooks in the liquid left from the seasoned pork, page 278.

Chicken Stew with Cheddar Biscuits
You will never guess how we managed to bake up a batch of biscuits alongside a bubbling chicken stew, page 157.

Spicy Shrimp Skewers with Cheesy Grits
We threaded shrimp onto skewers and lay them across the low sides of a casserole dish. The shrimp cooked through in the oven's dry heat as our cheesy grits baked below, page 207.

Smothered Pork Chops with Broccoli
A steamer basket holds the broccoli high and dry so it can cook above the saucy chops, page 141.

Roast Pork Loin with Sweet Potatoes and Cilantro Sauce
A citrusy cilantro vinaigrette gives this rich roast some brightness, page 254.

Lentils and Rice with Yogurt Sauce and Crunchy Toasted Almonds
We give this hearty vegetarian dish a lift with a cool, citrusy yogurt sauce, page 181.

New York Strip Steaks with Crispy Potatoes and Parsley Sauce
These thick, beefy strip steaks get a fresh finish with a chimichurri-style sauce, page 54.

THE SKILLET

WEEKNIGHT FRIENDLY

Sausage Lasagna

The Skillet Your Kitchen Workhorse

The skillet is the most versatile tool in your one-pan arsenal. Performing well on the stovetop and in the oven, this vessel is as capable of delivering a deep sear on steaks as it is of poaching eggs or braising delicate fish. Here's how we put our skillets to work in preparing one-pan meals.

From Stovetop to Oven

Because this vessel excels both on the stovetop and in the oven, we could harness the direct heat of the range before moving food to the oven for gentler, steadier cooking. For one-pan cooking, this meant we could deliver a deep sear or concentrate the flavors of a filling on the stovetop before moving seamlessly into the oven to bake through.

Simmer Directly in the Sauce

Think skillet cooking rules out pasta? Think again. The relatively low sides of a skillet forced us to think creatively when it came to dishes that typically cook in abundant liquid (often involving one pot for boiling water and a separate pan for sauce). Whether cooking pasta, simmering beef, or poaching chicken, we started out with just the right amount of flavorful cooking liquid to cook our food without spilling over, allowing it to reduce gradually into a concentrated, perfectly thickened sauce.

Work in Stages

A crowded pan causes food to steam rather than brown, so when a good sear was important, it was critical to cook ingredients in stages. This process was key to building and preserving flavor and cooking each component to its ideal state. Whether we were browning chicken breasts before cooking them through in steamy rice (thereby banning bland chicken), wilting bok choy before searing salmon (and guarding against a fishy-flavored vegetable side), or turning the juices into a pan sauce, this technique served us well.

Preheat Properly

Browning builds flavor, but only when your skillet is good and hot. While developing our skillet recipes, we kept a close eye on the oil—monitoring its appearance as the skillet heats up is the best way to gauge when it's time to start cooking. Hot oil that creates faint waves in web-like patterns (we call it shimmering) is perfect for sautéing onions and vegetables that would burn at a hotter temperature. Just-smoking oil (with small wisps of smoke escaping the surface) is best for creating well-crusted meat, chicken, and other foods that need more heat to develop browning.

Equipping Your Kitchen

Nonstick Skillet
The Smooth Operator

Slick and inexpensive, nonstick skillets are a must-have for one-pan cooking. They're perfect for stir-frying, cooking delicate foods like fish and eggs, preparing pasta and rice dishes, and turning out pork or poultry dishes not requiring a pan sauce. The coating will show wear no matter how careful you are, so we focused our exhaustive equipment testing on pans under $50. Our winner has a metal utensil-safe surface and an ovensafe handle. Our favorite: **OXO Good Grips Non-Stick 12" Open Frypan** ($39.99).

Traditional Skillet
The Classic

A good traditional skillet will last a lifetime if you treat it right. In our tests, we preferred models with low, flaring sides for quick evaporation. This skillet's surface promotes excellent browning because food adheres slightly, creating caramelized bits (called fond) that are the foundation for great flavor. Our winning 12-inch skillet fits eight chicken pieces without crowding and holds ample vegetables, grains, and meat for a satisfying one-pan meal. Look for fully clad models with layers of aluminum and stainless steel. Our favorite: **All-Clad 12-Inch Stainless Fry Pan** ($154.95).

BONUS BUYS
Carbon-Steel Skillet
The MVP

With all of the best qualities of traditional, nonstick, and even cast-iron skillets in a single vessel, this restaurant kitchen mainstay is worth the hype—if you're willing to put in a little work. This specialty skillet requires seasoning and careful upkeep, but our tests proved that well-maintained carbon steel will be as slippery as your favorite nonstick skillet while delivering a deep, even sear to rival a traditional pan. Our favorite: **Matfer Bourgeat Black Steel Round Frying Pan, 11 7/8"** ($44.38).

Sauté Pan
The Fan Favorite

Great for shallow braising and frying, wilting heaps of greens, or cooking food right in its sauce, this high-sided pan has its virtues but is hardly essential equipment. Despite the name, these pans aren't great at sautéing, but they can deliver deep browning. Look for a model with balanced weight and a tight-fitting lid. Our favorite: **All-Clad Stainless 3-Quart Tri-Ply Sauté Pan** ($224.95).

COVER IT UP

Many of our recipes require some time with the pan covered, but our winning nonstick and traditional skillets are sold without lids. We recommend having a 12-inch ovensafe lid with a heat-resistant handle at the ready.

UNSTUFFED SHELLS WITH BUTTERNUT SQUASH AND LEEKS

SERVES 4 TO 6   TOTAL TIME: 1 HOUR 15 MINUTES

WHY THIS RECIPE WORKS Cheesy jumbo stuffed shells have undeniable appeal, but preboiling and stuffing individual shells can be an ordeal. We set out to make an unstuffed version in which the pasta cooked directly in the sauce. We quickly found the right ratio of liquid to shells to ensure perfectly cooked noodles, but finding the ideal amount of vegetables proved trickier. Cooking butternut squash and leeks in a creamy sauce promised a hearty vegetarian meal, but if we used too much of either vegetable, the skillet was prone to overflowing; too little and the servings looked meager. We settled on 1½ pounds of squash and 1 pound of leeks. Cooking them briefly before adding the pasta and liquid deepened their flavors and ensured that the pasta and squash would finish cooking at the same time. Instead of stuffing the shells, we sprinkled a little Parmesan cheese and dolloped a rich lemon-ricotta mixture over everything before sliding the skillet back in the oven to brown and melt the cheesy toppings. You can substitute large or medium shells, ziti, farfalle, campanelle, or orecchiette for the jumbo shells here. The skillet will be very full when you add the shells in step 3 (stir gently to start), but will become more manageable as the liquid evaporates and the shells become more malleable. You will need a 12-inch ovensafe nonstick skillet for this recipe.

 8 ounces (1 cup) whole-milk ricotta cheese
 2 ounces Parmesan cheese, grated (1 cup)
 1 teaspoon grated lemon zest
    Salt and pepper
 1 tablespoon extra-virgin olive oil
1½ pounds butternut squash, peeled, seeded, and cut into ½-inch pieces (5 cups)
 1 pound leeks, white and light green parts only, halved lengthwise, sliced thin, and washed thoroughly
 2 garlic cloves, minced
    Pinch cayenne pepper
 ¼ cup dry white wine
 4 cups water
 1 cup heavy cream
12 ounces jumbo pasta shells
 2 tablespoons chopped fresh basil

1 Adjust oven rack to middle position and heat oven to 375 degrees. Combine ricotta, ½ cup Parmesan, lemon zest, ¼ teaspoon salt, and ¼ teaspoon pepper in bowl; cover and refrigerate until needed.

2 Heat oil in 12-inch ovensafe nonstick skillet over medium heat until shimmering. Add squash, leeks, and ½ teaspoon salt and cook until leeks are softened, about 5 minutes. Stir in garlic and cayenne and cook until fragrant, about 30 seconds. Add wine and cook until almost completely evaporated, about 1 minute.

3 Stir in water and cream, then add pasta. Increase heat to medium-high and cook at vigorous simmer, stirring gently and often, until pasta is tender and liquid has thickened, about 15 minutes.

4 Season with salt and pepper to taste. Sprinkle remaining ½ cup Parmesan over top, then dollop evenly with ricotta mixture. Transfer skillet to oven and bake until Parmesan is melted and spotty brown, about 5 minutes. Remove skillet from oven (skillet handle will be hot). Let cool for 10 minutes, then sprinkle with basil and serve.

SPANAKOPITA

SERVES 4   TOTAL TIME: 1 HOUR 30 MINUTES

WHY THIS RECIPE WORKS Spanakopita is a Greek spinach-and-cheese pie with a crisp phyllo shell. This meal had a lot of one-pan promise, but simplifying the crust was a challenge. The traditional method of buttering or oiling and stacking sheets of phyllo dough creates flaky layers, but this seemed too labor-intensive. Instead, we sprayed sheets of phyllo with olive oil spray, crumpled each into a ball, and placed them on the filling. This created plenty of surface area without tedious layering, plus it didn't matter if a sheet tore. As for the filling, we used our skillet to drive off any remaining moisture from the thawed spinach so our crust wouldn't steam in the oven. A mix of feta and ricotta cheeses added briny flavor and rich, creamy texture, while scallions, mint, and dill delivered an herbal backbone. Phyllo dough is also available in larger 18 by 14-inch sheets; if using, cut them in half to make 14 by 9-inch sheets. Don't thaw the phyllo in the microwave; let it sit in the refrigerator overnight or on the counter for 4 to 5 hours. You will need a 10-inch ovensafe nonstick skillet for this recipe.

 1 tablespoon unsalted butter
20 ounces frozen chopped spinach,
     thawed and squeezed dry
 ¼ teaspoon salt
 ¼ teaspoon pepper
 3 garlic cloves, minced
 ⅛ teaspoon ground nutmeg
 ⅛ teaspoon cayenne pepper
 8 ounces feta cheese, crumbled (2 cups)
 6 ounces (¾ cup) whole-milk ricotta cheese
 4 scallions, sliced thin
 2 large eggs, lightly beaten
 ¼ cup minced fresh mint
 2 tablespoons minced fresh dill
20 (14 by 9-inch) phyllo sheets, thawed
     Olive oil spray

1 Adjust oven rack to lower-middle position and heat oven to 375 degrees. Melt butter in 10-inch nonstick skillet over medium heat. Add spinach, salt, and pepper and cook until mixture is dry, about 4 minutes. Stir in garlic, nutmeg, and cayenne and cook until fragrant, about 30 seconds. Transfer mixture to large bowl and let cool slightly, about 5 minutes.

2 Stir feta, ricotta, scallions, eggs, mint, and dill into cooled spinach mixture until well combined. Spread mixture evenly into now-empty skillet.

3 Working with 1 sheet phyllo at a time, lay flat on clean counter and spray liberally with oil spray. Crumple oiled phyllo into 2-inch ball and place on top of spinach mixture in skillet.

4 Transfer skillet to oven and bake until phyllo is golden brown and crisp, about 25 minutes, rotating skillet halfway through baking. Remove skillet from oven (skillet handle will be hot). Let cool for 10 minutes before serving.

TOPPING SPANAKOPITA WITH PHYLLO DOUGH

1 Using your hands, gently crumple oiled sheet of phyllo into 2-inch ball.
2 Place crumpled phyllo ball on top of spinach mixture.

BAKED SHRIMP AND ORZO WITH FETA AND TOMATOES

SERVES 4   TOTAL TIME: 1 HOUR 15 MINUTES

WHY THIS RECIPE WORKS Creamy orzo and tender shrimp form the basis of this simple, satisfying Greek-style pasta. To build in plenty of Mediterranean flavor, we started by sautéing chopped onion and red bell pepper, softening them before adding in minced garlic and oregano. To guarantee perfectly cooked shrimp and pasta, we settled on a combined stovetop-oven cooking method. Sautéing the orzo in the aromatics unlocked its toasty notes, and crumbled saffron threads, though not traditional, introduced a sunny hue and warm, complex flavor. We then stirred in chicken broth and the drained juice from a can of diced tomatoes; as the orzo cooked to al dente, its released starch (similar to a risotto) created a sauce with a subtly creamy texture. To prevent the shrimp from overcooking, we stirred them right into the orzo, along with the reserved tomatoes and frozen peas, and transferred the skillet to the oven to cook through gently. A sprinkling of feta before baking reinforced the dish's Greek flavors and promised an appealing browned, cheesy crust. Make sure that the orzo is al dente, or slightly firm to the bite; otherwise it may overcook in the oven. If using smaller or larger shrimp, the cooking times may vary accordingly. You can leave the shrimp tails on, if desired. The small amount of saffron makes a big difference to the flavor and look of the dish, so be sure to include it. You will need a 12-inch ovensafe nonstick skillet for this recipe.

1 pound extra-large shrimp (21 to 25 per pound), peeled, deveined, and tails removed
   Salt and pepper
1 tablespoon extra-virgin olive oil
1 red onion, chopped fine
1 red bell pepper, stemmed, seeded, and cut into ½-inch pieces
4 garlic cloves, minced
2 teaspoons minced fresh oregano or ½ teaspoon dried
2 cups (12 ounces) orzo
   Pinch saffron threads, crumbled
3 cups chicken broth
1 (14.5-ounce) can diced tomatoes, drained with juice reserved
½ cup frozen peas
3 ounces feta cheese, crumbled (¾ cup)
2 scallions, sliced thin
   Lemon wedges

1 Adjust oven rack to middle position and heat oven to 375 degrees. Pat shrimp dry with paper towels and season with salt and pepper; cover and refrigerate until needed.

2 Heat oil in 12-inch ovensafe nonstick skillet over medium heat until shimmering. Add onion and bell pepper and cook until vegetables are softened, 5 to 7 minutes. Stir in garlic and oregano and cook until fragrant, about 30 seconds. Stir in orzo and saffron and cook, stirring often, until orzo is lightly browned, about 4 minutes.

3 Stir in broth and reserved tomato juice, bring to simmer, and cook, stirring occasionally, until orzo is al dente, 10 to 12 minutes.

4 Stir in shrimp, tomatoes, and peas, then sprinkle feta evenly over top. Transfer skillet to oven and bake until shrimp are cooked through and feta is lightly browned, about 20 minutes.

5 Remove skillet from oven (skillet handle will be hot). Sprinkle scallions over top and serve with lemon wedges.

TURKEY MEATBALLS WITH LEMONY RICE

SERVES 4   TOTAL TIME: 1 HOUR 15 MINUTES

WHY THIS RECIPE WORKS For a satisfying skillet meal full of tender turkey meatballs and perfectly seasoned rice, we sought a simple approach that would let these two mild-mannered components really shine. A bread crumb–egg panade gave the meatballs a tender texture, and stirring sliced scallion greens, parsley, and lemon zest into the mix added plenty of freshness and character. We rolled and refrigerated the meatballs to set them up, then browned them in oil to build their flavor. We then used the meatballs' rendered fat to toast the rice, giving the grains a meaty dimension before adding in aromatics. Chicken broth promised rice with rich flavor, while lemon juice and zest added citrusy brightness. We let the browned meatballs finish cooking directly in the rice, absorbing some of the flavorful cooking liquid at the same time. The rice and meat finished up simultaneously, and a sprinkling of nutty Parmesan, scallions, and parsley and a squeeze of lemon made for a perfect finish. You will need a 12-inch skillet with a tight-fitting lid for this recipe. Turn the meatballs gently as they brown in step 2 so they don't break. Be sure to use ground turkey, not ground turkey breast (also labeled 99 percent fat-free), in this recipe.

2 slices hearty white sandwich bread, torn into 1-inch pieces

1¼ pounds ground turkey

1 large egg

6 scallions, white and green parts separated and sliced thin

3 tablespoons minced fresh parsley

1 tablespoon grated lemon zest plus 2 tablespoons juice, plus lemon wedges for serving
   Salt and pepper

2 tablespoons extra-virgin olive oil

1½ cups long-grain white rice

3 garlic cloves, minced

3¼ cups chicken broth

1 ounce Parmesan cheese, grated (½ cup)

1 Pulse bread in food processor to fine crumbs, 10 to 15 pulses; transfer to large bowl. Add turkey, egg, 2 tablespoons scallion greens, 2 tablespoons parsley, 1½ teaspoons lemon zest, ½ teaspoon salt, and ½ teaspoon pepper and mix with your hands until thoroughly combined. Divide mixture into 20 portions, roll into meatballs, and transfer to plate. Refrigerate meatballs for at least 15 minutes, or up to 1 day.

2 Heat oil in 12-inch nonstick skillet over medium-high heat until shimmering. Cook meatballs until well browned all over, 5 to 7 minutes. Transfer meatballs to paper towel–lined plate.

3 Add rice to fat left in skillet and cook over medium-high heat, stirring often, until edges of rice begin to turn translucent, about 1 minute. Add scallion whites, garlic, and ½ teaspoon salt and cook until fragrant, about 1 minute. Add broth, lemon juice, and remaining 1½ teaspoons lemon zest and bring to boil.

4 Return meatballs to skillet, cover, and reduce heat to low. Cook until rice is tender and meatballs are cooked through, about 20 minutes. Remove from heat and let sit, covered, for 5 minutes. Sprinkle with Parmesan, remaining scallion greens, and remaining 1 tablespoon parsley. Serve with lemon wedges.

LEMONY CHICKEN WITH SPINACH AND POTATOES

SERVES 4   TOTAL TIME: 45 MINUTES

WHY THIS RECIPE WORKS For a fuss-free chicken dinner packed with fresh flavor, we set our sights on turning out perfectly cooked breasts and effortless vegetables to match. Searing the chicken breasts in oil imparted some flavorful browning as the meat cooked through. We halved small, tender fingerling potatoes, which cooked quickly in the microwave while the chicken was browning. To give the spuds some crispness, we browned them cut side down in the residual chicken juices, then stirred in lemon juice, butter, garlic, and thyme for a complex, savory taste. Baby spinach wilts readily and works well with citrusy flavors, so we stirred it in at the very end to complement our lemony potatoes. We served our spinach and potatoes topped with the browned chicken breasts, drizzling everything with oil and lemon juice and sprinkling on crumbled goat cheese for a tangy, rich finish. Baby arugula or baby kale can be substituted for the baby spinach if desired. You will need a 12-inch nonstick skillet for this recipe.

WEEKNIGHT FRIENDLY

1 pound fingerling potatoes, unpeeled, halved lengthwise

3 tablespoons extra-virgin olive oil
Salt and pepper

4 (6- to 8-ounce) boneless, skinless chicken breasts, trimmed

3 tablespoons lemon juice

1 tablespoon unsalted butter

3 garlic cloves, minced

1 teaspoon minced fresh thyme or ¼ teaspoon dried

3 ounces (3 cups) baby spinach

2 ounces goat cheese, crumbled (½ cup)

1 Toss potatoes with 1 tablespoon oil and ¼ teaspoon salt in bowl. Cover and microwave, stirring occasionally, until potatoes are tender, about 7 minutes; drain well.

2 Meanwhile, pat chicken dry with paper towels and season with salt and pepper. Heat 1 tablespoon oil in 12-inch nonstick skillet over medium-high heat until just smoking. Add chicken and cook until browned and registers 160 degrees, about 6 minutes per side. Transfer to plate and tent loosely with aluminum foil.

3 Add potatoes, cut side down, to fat left in skillet and cook until golden brown, about 3 minutes. Stir in 2 tablespoons lemon juice, butter, garlic, thyme, and ¼ teaspoon pepper and cook until fragrant, about 30 seconds. Stir in spinach and cook until just wilted, about 30 seconds.

4 Transfer potato mixture to platter, top with chicken, and drizzle with remaining 1 tablespoon lemon juice and remaining 1 tablespoon oil. Sprinkle with goat cheese and serve.

PAN-SEARED SALMON WITH LENTILS AND CHARD

SERVES 4   TOTAL TIME: 1 HOUR

WHY THIS RECIPE WORKS Salmon and braised lentils is a classic pairing in French home cooking. In the course of streamlining the cooking process, we also took this dish one step further by adding Swiss chard to get a complete meal full of rich, earthy flavor. Sautéing chopped onion, garlic, and thyme created a flavorful base for the lentils. We used chicken broth as our cooking liquid for plenty of rich flavor, and a squeeze of lemon juice offered some bright contrast while also encouraging the lentils to hold their shape during cooking. As soon as the lentils were tender, we removed them and browned the salmon in the skillet, using just a little oil to create a crisp skin on the fillets. Preparing the chard was as simple as chopping the leaves (discarding the fibrous, bitter stems), stirring them into the rewarmed lentils, and allowing the leaves to wilt. You can use either skin-on or skinless salmon here; some tasters loved the crisp cooked salmon skin. You will need a 12-inch nonstick skillet with a tight-fitting lid for this recipe.

3   tablespoons unsalted butter
1   onion, chopped fine
2   garlic cloves, minced
¼   teaspoon minced fresh thyme or pinch dried
     Salt and pepper
3   cups chicken broth
1   cup brown lentils, picked over and rinsed
1   teaspoon lemon juice, plus lemon wedges for serving
4   (6-ounce) center-cut, skin-on salmon fillets, 1½ inches thick
1   tablespoon vegetable oil
12 ounces Swiss chard, stemmed and chopped

1 Melt 2 tablespoons butter in 12-inch nonstick skillet over medium-high heat. Add onion, garlic, thyme, and ¼ teaspoon salt and cook, stirring often, until onion begins to brown, about 5 minutes. Stir in broth, lentils, and lemon juice and bring to boil. Reduce heat to low, cover, and cook until lentils are tender, 25 to 30 minutes.

2 Uncover and cook, stirring often, until most liquid has evaporated, about 2 minutes. Season with salt and pepper to taste, transfer to bowl, and cover to keep warm.

3 Pat salmon dry with paper towels and season with salt and pepper. Wipe out skillet with paper towels, add oil, and heat over medium-high heat until just smoking. Carefully lay salmon in skillet, skin side up, and cook until well browned on first side, 4 to 6 minutes.

4 Flip salmon over, reduce heat to medium, and cook until center is still translucent when checked with tip of paring knife and registers 125 degrees (for medium-rare), 3 to 6 minutes. Transfer salmon to clean plate, tent loosely with aluminum foil.

5 Add lentil mixture to now-empty skillet and cook over medium-high heat until hot, about 4 minutes. Stir in chard and remaining 1 tablespoon butter and cook until chard is wilted, 2 to 3 minutes. Serve with salmon and lemon wedges.

PARMESAN CHICKEN WITH WARM ARUGULA, RADICCHIO, AND FENNEL SALAD

SERVES 4 TOTAL TIME: 1 HOUR

WHY THIS RECIPE WORKS With its crisp coating and juicy, tender meat, Parmesan chicken is a surefire crowd-pleaser and a guaranteed win for any weeknight dinner. Pasta is a classic pairing, but we were more interested in a fresh, vegetable-heavy side that would brighten up our savory breaded chicken and wouldn't involve another pan. So, after the chicken cutlets had finished cooking through, we took advantage of the preheated skillet to soften thinly sliced fennel and halved cherry tomatoes. We tossed the cooked vegetables in a simple vinaigrette of minced shallot, Dijon mustard, white wine vinegar, and extra-virgin olive oil. Adding raw radicchio and baby arugula to the cooked vegetables added crunch and a light bitterness that paired well with the sweetness of the fennel and contrasted perfectly with rich, juicy chicken. Use the large holes of a box grater to shred the Parmesan. Sprinkle with additional shredded Parmesan before serving, if desired. You will need a 12-inch nonstick skillet for this recipe.

WEEKNIGHT FRIENDLY

½ cup all-purpose flour

2 large eggs

1 cup panko bread crumbs

3 ounces Parmesan cheese, shredded (1 cup)

6 (4-ounce) chicken cutlets, ½ inch thick, trimmed
   Salt and pepper

10 tablespoons extra-virgin olive oil

1 tablespoon white wine vinegar

1½ teaspoons minced shallot

½ teaspoon Dijon mustard

1 fennel bulb, stalks discarded, bulb halved, cored, and sliced thin

12 ounces cherry tomatoes, halved

½ head radicchio (5 ounces), cored and sliced thin

2 cups baby arugula

1 Adjust oven rack to middle position and heat oven to 200 degrees. Spread flour in shallow dish. Beat eggs in second shallow dish. Combine panko and Parmesan in third shallow dish. Pat chicken dry with paper towels and season with salt and pepper. Working with 1 cutlet at a time, dredge in flour, dip in egg, then coat with panko mixture, pressing gently to adhere.

2 Heat 3 tablespoons oil in 12-inch nonstick skillet over medium heat until shimmering. Add 3 cutlets and cook until chicken is tender, golden brown, and crisp, about 4 minutes per side. Transfer to paper towel–lined platter and transfer to oven to keep warm. Wipe out skillet with paper towels and repeat with 3 tablespoons oil and remaining 3 cutlets.

3 Whisk vinegar, shallot, mustard, ¼ teaspoon salt, and pinch pepper together in large bowl. Whisking constantly, slowly drizzle in 3 tablespoons oil until emulsified.

4 Wipe out skillet with paper towels. Heat remaining 1 tablespoon oil in now-empty skillet over medium heat until shimmering. Add fennel and cook until softened and just beginning to brown, about 5 minutes; transfer to bowl with vinaigrette.

5 Add tomatoes to now-empty skillet and cook until softened, about 2 minutes; transfer to bowl with vinaigrette. Add radicchio and arugula to bowl with vinaigrette and gently toss to combine. Season with salt and pepper to taste and serve with chicken.

BRAISED HALIBUT WITH CARROTS AND CORIANDER

SERVES 4   TOTAL TIME: 45 MINUTES

WEEKNIGHT FRIENDLY

WHY THIS RECIPE WORKS Though an often-overlooked method for cooking fish, braising is gentle and forgiving, all but guaranteeing moist, succulent fish. And it's easy enough to add vegetables to the mix for a simple one-pan meal. We started with fillets of firm-fleshed halibut. To avoid overcooking the part that would be submerged in liquid, we precooked one side of the fillets in butter, intending to flip them over for braising. Sweet carrots and shallots were a natural pairing for this mild fish; we softened them in the skillet before pouring in white wine. Coriander reinforced the wine's flavor and complemented the shallots perfectly. With the carrots buffering the pan's direct heat, we returned the fish to the skillet raw side down, covered the pan, and let the fish and vegetables cook gradually and take on the braising liquid's bright flavors. Everything was ready after 10 minutes. Preparing a lush sauce was as easy as reducing the cooking liquid (adding some lemon for zing). A sprinkling of fresh cilantro made for a lively presentation. We prefer to prepare this recipe with halibut, but a similar firm-fleshed white fish, such as striped bass or sea bass, that is between ¾ and 1 inch thick can be substituted. To ensure that your fish cooks evenly, purchase fillets that are similarly shaped and uniformly thick. You will need a 12-inch skillet with a tight-fitting lid for this recipe.

4 (6- to 8-ounce) skinless halibut fillets, ¾ to 1 inch thick
  Salt and pepper
6 tablespoons unsalted butter
1 pound carrots, peeled and shaved with vegetable peeler lengthwise into ribbons
4 shallots, halved and sliced thin
½ teaspoon ground coriander
¾ cup dry white wine
1½ teaspoons lemon juice, plus lemon wedges for serving
1 tablespoon minced fresh cilantro

1 Sprinkle halibut with ½ teaspoon salt. Melt butter in 12-inch skillet over low heat. Place halibut in skillet skinned side up, increase heat to medium, and cook, shaking pan occasionally, until butter begins to brown (fish should not brown), 3 to 4 minutes. Using spatula, carefully transfer halibut to large plate, raw side down.

2 Add carrots, shallots, coriander, and ½ teaspoon salt to skillet and cook, stirring frequently, until vegetables begin to soften, 2 to 4 minutes. Add wine and bring to gentle simmer. Place halibut, raw side down, on top of vegetables. Cover skillet and cook, adjusting heat to maintain gentle simmer, until halibut registers 135 to 140 degrees, 10 to 14 minutes. Remove skillet from heat and, using 2 spatulas, transfer halibut and vegetables to serving platter or individual plates. Tent loosely with aluminum foil.

3 Cook liquid left in skillet over high heat until sauce is thickened, 2 to 3 minutes. Remove pan from heat, stir in lemon juice, and season with salt and pepper to taste. Spoon sauce over halibut and sprinkle with cilantro. Serve immediately with lemon wedges.

Variations

BRAISED HALIBUT WITH LEEKS AND MUSTARD
Substitute 1 pound leeks, white and light green parts only, halved lengthwise, sliced thin, and washed thoroughly, for carrots and shallots. Substitute 1 teaspoon Dijon mustard for coriander. Reduce lemon juice to 1 teaspoon and substitute parsley for cilantro.

BRAISED HALIBUT WITH FENNEL AND TARRAGON
Substitute 2 fennel bulbs, stalks discarded, bulbs halved, cored, and sliced thin, for carrots. Omit coriander and reduce lemon juice to 1 teaspoon. Substitute tarragon for cilantro.

CURRIED VEGETABLE COUSCOUS AND CHICKEN WITH LIME-YOGURT SAUCE

SERVES 4   TOTAL TIME: 45 MINUTES

WHY THIS RECIPE WORKS Couscous cooks in the time it takes to set the table, making it the perfect base for a weeknight meal. In addition to being fast and easy to cook, it also absorbs lots of flavor from its cooking liquid. With couscous in mind, we devised a simple, full-flavored curry packed with vegetables and paired it with chicken breasts for an easy-prep, no-fuss protein. We seared the breasts on one side, giving the chicken some color and creating a flavorful fond, and then set them aside to turn our focus to the vegetables. Cauliflower is a classic addition to curry, but for even more hearty flavor we used Swiss chard as well. After blooming and stirring in curry powder and garlic, we added chicken broth, nestled the chicken on top, covered the pan, and let everything simmer. Once the chicken was cooked through, we removed it and stirred in the couscous, allowing it to steam and soak up the flavorful curry. Raisins plumped right in the couscous promised a sweet, juicy contrast. Served with a cool lime-yogurt sauce, this meal was as flavor-packed as it was simple. Be sure to use chicken breasts that are roughly the same size to ensure even cooking. You will need a 12-inch skillet with a tight-fitting lid for this recipe.

WEEKNIGHT FRIENDLY

¼ cup plain whole-milk yogurt

2 teaspoons lime juice

Salt and pepper

4 (6- to 8-ounce) boneless, skinless chicken breasts, trimmed

2 tablespoons extra-virgin olive oil

1 onion, chopped fine

½ head cauliflower (1 pound), cored and cut into 1-inch florets

1 pound Swiss chard, stemmed and cut into 1-inch pieces

2 teaspoons curry powder

2 garlic cloves, minced

1¼ cups chicken broth

1 cup couscous

¼ cup raisins

2 tablespoons minced fresh cilantro

1 Whisk yogurt, lime juice, ¼ teaspoon salt, and ¼ teaspoon pepper together in bowl; cover and refrigerate until serving. Pat chicken dry with paper towels and season with salt and pepper. Heat 1 tablespoon oil in 12-inch skillet over medium-high heat until just smoking. Add chicken and cook until golden brown on 1 side, 4 to 6 minutes; transfer to plate.

2 Add remaining 1 tablespoon oil to now-empty skillet and heat over medium heat until shimmering. Add onion and ¼ teaspoon salt and cook until onion is softened, about 5 minutes. Stir in cauliflower. Add chard, a handful at a time, and cook until wilted, about 2 minutes. Stir in curry powder and garlic and cook until fragrant, about 30 seconds. Stir in broth and nestle chicken, browned side up, into skillet, along with any accumulated juices. Bring to simmer, then reduce heat to medium-low, cover, and simmer gently until chicken registers 160 degrees, about 10 minutes.

3 Transfer chicken to plate, tent loosely with aluminum foil, and let rest while preparing couscous. Stir couscous and raisins into vegetable-broth mixture. Cover, remove from heat, and let stand for 5 minutes.

4 Fluff couscous mixture with fork and season with salt and pepper to taste. Arrange chicken on top of couscous mixture, then drizzle with yogurt mixture and sprinkle with cilantro before serving.

BROWN RICE AND BEANS WITH CORN AND CHERRY TOMATO SALSA

SERVES 4 TO 6   TOTAL TIME: 1 HOUR 30 MINUTES

WHY THIS RECIPE WORKS The sustaining combination of rice and beans is a staple in many cuisines, but often it's served as a side dish to accompany a protein. We felt a few additions could transform rice and beans into a satisfying vegetarian meal. And instead of dirtying several pots to cook the rice and beans separately, we set out to make the meal in one skillet. Most recipes we found used white rice, but we liked the hearty texture and robust flavor of brown. Because of the greater surface area in a skillet, we found that we had to adjust our usual liquid-to-rice ratio: We needed a full 4 cups of broth to cook 1 cup of brown rice. To give our dish more heft, we added 1½ cups of corn to the skillet, sautéing it briefly to give it a toasty flavor, then added garlic, cumin, and a pinch of cayenne for depth. Using canned black beans instead of dried kept things simple; we stirred them in partway through cooking so they would soften slightly and warm through without breaking down entirely. For a fresh, bright finish, we created a quick salsa of cherry tomatoes, scallions, cilantro, and lime juice. You will need a 12-inch nonstick skillet with a tight-fitting lid for this recipe.

2 tablespoons extra-virgin olive oil
1 onion, chopped fine
  Salt and pepper
1½ cups frozen corn, thawed and patted dry
1 cup long-grain brown rice
4 garlic cloves, minced
1 teaspoon ground cumin
  Pinch cayenne pepper
4 cups vegetable broth
2 (15-ounce) cans black beans, rinsed
12 ounces cherry tomatoes, quartered
5 scallions, sliced thin
¼ cup minced fresh cilantro
1 tablespoon lime juice

1 Heat 1 tablespoon oil in 12-inch nonstick skillet over medium-high heat until shimmering. Add onion and ¼ teaspoon salt and cook until onion is softened and beginning to brown, 5 to 7 minutes. Stir in corn and cook until lightly browned, about 4 minutes. Stir in rice, garlic, cumin, and cayenne and cook until fragrant, about 30 seconds.

2 Stir in broth and bring to simmer. Cover, reduce heat to medium-low, and simmer gently, stirring occasionally, for 25 minutes.

3 Stir in beans. Cover and simmer, stirring occasionally, until liquid is absorbed and rice is tender, about 30 minutes. Season with salt and pepper to taste.

4 Combine remaining 1 tablespoon oil, tomatoes, scallions, cilantro, and lime juice in bowl and season with salt and pepper to taste. Spoon tomato mixture over rice and beans and serve.

TEX-MEX CHICKEN AND RICE

SERVES 4 TOTAL TIME: 45 MINUTES

WHY THIS RECIPE WORKS For chicken and rice with Southwestern flair, we looked for a way to add a touch of authentic heat and brightness without a laundry list of ingredients. To keep things simple, we added a can of black beans to the rice mixture, which lent color and richness. For distinct south-of-the-border flavor, we added a can of Ro-tel tomatoes: The blend of tomatoes and green chiles added not only acidity but also just the right amount of heat. To temper a little of that heat, we stirred ½ cup of shredded Monterey Jack cheese right into the rice mixture and sprinkled another cup over the top. We broiled the whole dish to melt and brown the cheese, but tasters weren't satisfied: They clamored for crunch. We sprinkled on crushed tortilla chips before broiling, then finished the dish with a couple of tablespoons of cilantro. Be sure to use chicken breasts that are roughly the same size to ensure even cooking. If you can't find Ro-tel tomatoes, substitute ¾ cup canned diced tomatoes, drained, and 1 tablespoon of chopped canned green chiles. You will need a 12-inch broiler-safe skillet with a tight-fitting lid for this recipe. The skillet will be fairly full once you add the browned chicken in step 2, so you may want to consider using a straight-sided skillet or sauté pan if you have one.

WEEKNIGHT FRIENDLY

4 (6- to 8-ounce) boneless, skinless chicken breasts, trimmed
Salt and pepper
1 tablespoon vegetable oil
3½ cups chicken broth
1½ cups long-grain white rice
1 (10-ounce) can Ro-tel Original Diced Tomatoes & Green Chilies
1 (15-ounce) can black beans, rinsed
6 ounces Monterey Jack cheese, shredded (1½ cups)
4 ounces tortilla chips or Fritos corn chips, crushed
2 tablespoons minced fresh cilantro

1 Pat chicken dry with paper towels and season with salt and pepper. Heat oil in 12-inch broiler-safe skillet over medium-high heat until just smoking. Add chicken and cook until golden brown on 1 side, 4 to 6 minutes; transfer to plate.

2 Add broth, rice, tomatoes and their juice, beans, and ¼ teaspoon salt to now-empty skillet, scraping up any browned bits. Nestle chicken, browned side up, into skillet, along with any accumulated juices. Bring to simmer, then reduce heat to medium-low, cover, and simmer gently until chicken registers 160 degrees, about 10 minutes.

3 Transfer chicken to plate, tent loosely with aluminum foil, and let rest while finishing rice. Stir rice mixture to recombine, then cover and cook until liquid is absorbed and rice is tender, 5 to 10 minutes. Meanwhile, adjust oven rack 6 inches from broiler element and heat broiler.

4 Stir ½ cup Monterey Jack into rice, then season with salt and pepper to taste. Arrange chicken on top of rice, then sprinkle with tortilla chips and remaining 1 cup Monterey Jack. Broil until golden brown, about 3 minutes. Remove skillet from oven (skillet handle will be hot). Sprinkle with cilantro and serve.

PORK CHOPS WITH CHILE RICE AND PEANUTS

SERVES 4   TOTAL TIME: 1 HOUR

WHY THIS RECIPE WORKS The addictive blend of honey, lime, chile, and spices that flavors this pork chop and rice dish is inspired by the chile-lime peanuts sold by street vendors throughout Mexico. We started by cutting small slits through the pork chops' fat to ensure they lay flat during cooking. We seared just one side to develop some browning without overcooking the chops, then sautéed onion, garlic, seasonings, and tomato paste before adding broth. Simmering both pork chops and rice in this liquid infused each with flavor, and once the chops were cooked we removed them and let the rice finish cooking. A quick vinaigrette of cilantro, lime zest, lime juice, oil, and honey delivered a tangy-sweet finish to the dish, and folding chopped peanuts into the rice added even more flavor and great crunch. You will need a 12-inch skillet with a tight-fitting lid for this recipe.

4 (6- to 8-ounce) boneless pork chops, ¾ to 1 inch thick, trimmed
  Salt and pepper
3 tablespoons extra-virgin olive oil
1 onion, chopped fine
3 garlic cloves, minced
1 tablespoon tomato paste
1 tablespoon minced fresh oregano or 1 teaspoon dried
1 teaspoon ancho chile powder
¼ teaspoon ground coriander
  Pinch cayenne pepper
1½ cups long-grain white rice
4 cups chicken broth
¼ cup minced fresh cilantro
1 tablespoon honey
2 teaspoons grated lime zest plus 3 tablespoons juice (2 limes)
⅓ cup unsalted dry-roasted peanuts, chopped

1 Cut 2 slits, about 2 inches apart, through fat on edges of each chop. Pat chops dry with paper towels and season with salt and pepper. Heat 1 tablespoon oil in 12-inch skillet over medium-high heat until just smoking. Brown chops well on 1 side, about 5 minutes; transfer to plate.

2 Pour off all but 1 tablespoon fat from skillet. Add onion and cook until softened, about 5 minutes. Stir in garlic, tomato paste, oregano, chile powder, coriander, and cayenne; cook until fragrant, about 30 seconds. Stir in rice to coat with spices, then stir in broth.

3 Nestle chops, browned side up, into skillet, along with any accumulated juices. Bring to simmer, then reduce heat to medium-low, cover, and simmer gently until chops register 145 degrees, 6 to 8 minutes.

4 Transfer chops to cutting board, tent loosely with aluminum foil, and let rest while finishing rice. Stir rice mixture to recombine, then cover and cook until liquid is absorbed and rice is tender, 10 to 15 minutes. Meanwhile, whisk remaining 2 tablespoons oil, 2 tablespoons cilantro, honey, lime zest and juice, and ⅛ teaspoon salt together in bowl.

5 Off heat, gently fold peanuts and remaining 2 tablespoons cilantro into rice and season with salt and pepper to taste; transfer to platter. Slice chops into ½-inch-thick slices and arrange over rice on platter. Drizzle honey-lime vinaigrette over pork and serve.

PREPARING A PORK CHOP

To prevent pork chops from curling during cooking, cut 2 slits, about 2 inches apart, through fat on edges of each chop.

BARBECUED PORK CHOPS WITH SUCCOTASH SALAD

SERVES 4   TOTAL TIME: 45 MINUTES

WHY THIS RECIPE WORKS For a fun barbecue dinner made indoors, we made our job easy by using superflavorful store-bought barbecue sauce. Thickly coating our boneless pork chops, the sauce guaranteed some juicy meat. We simmered the chops directly in the sauce for flavor and ease and then served that syrupy sauce alongside our chops, which gave them a caramelized, almost-grilled flavor. As a fresh and complementary side, we took succotash up a notch by making it into a salad. We sautéed some corn to give it some char. When it was toasted to sweet perfection, we added lima beans to warm them through and then tossed both with baby spinach, bell pepper, lime juice, and chives for a side salad with bright tang. Because fresh lima beans can be difficult to find, we used frozen lima beans for a fresher taste and shorter cooking time. As for the corn, kernels scraped from fresh ears tasted much sweeter than frozen, and they gave the succotash nice crunch.

WEEKNIGHT FRIENDLY

4 (6- to 8-ounce) boneless pork chops, ¾ to 1 inch thick, trimmed
   Salt and pepper
3 tablespoons extra-virgin olive oil
1 cup barbecue sauce
¼ cup water
4 ears corn, kernels cut from cobs
2 cups frozen lima beans
1 red bell pepper, stemmed, seeded, and chopped
4 ounces (4 cups) baby spinach
2 tablespoons lime juice
2 tablespoons minced fresh chives

1 Cut 2 slits, about 2 inches apart, through fat on edges of each chop. Pat chops dry with paper towels and season with salt and pepper. Heat 1 tablespoon oil in 12-inch skillet over medium-high heat until just smoking. Cook chops until well browned on 1 side, about 6 minutes.

2 Reduce heat to medium. Pour barbecue sauce and water in skillet, flip chops, and cook until meat registers 145 degrees, 8 to 10 minutes. Transfer chops to serving platter. Pour remaining sauce from skillet into bowl for serving. Wipe out skillet.

3 Heat 1 tablespoon oil in now-empty skillet until shimmering. Add corn and cook for 3 minutes without stirring. Stir in lima beans and cook until warmed through, about 2 minutes. Transfer to large bowl.

4 Add bell pepper, spinach, lime juice, chives, remaining 1 tablespoon oil, ½ teaspoon salt, and ¼ teaspoon pepper to bowl with corn and toss to coat. Serve with pork chops and barbecue sauce.

SWEET POTATO HASH

SERVES 4 TOTAL TIME: 45 MINUTES

WHY THIS RECIPE WORKS To put a sweet twist on traditional potato hash, we looked to swap out regular spuds for sweet potatoes and boost the flavor with a backbone of chili powder. Unfortunately, our first attempts resulted in a very soft, mushy hash—sweet potatoes don't boast the same starchiness as russets, so they don't retain their shape as well once cooked. We got better results by mixing in some russets with the sweet potatoes; the russets softened and crumbled, binding the hash together. To speed things up, we parcooked the potatoes in the microwave until tender, then moved them to the skillet to brown and crisp. We rounded out the flavors with onion, garlic, thyme, and a dash of hot sauce, plus heavy cream for richness. To make our hash a hearty meal, we poached eight eggs right in the hash. This hash was such a hit that we decided to develop a red flannel hash variation, mottled with sweet, vibrant beets. If you notice that the potatoes aren't getting brown in step 3, turn up the heat (but don't let them burn). You will need a 12-inch nonstick skillet with a tight-fitting lid for this recipe.

12 ounces russet potatoes, peeled and cut into ¼-inch pieces

12 ounces sweet potatoes, peeled and cut into ¼-inch pieces

2 tablespoons vegetable oil
Salt and pepper

1 onion, chopped fine

2 garlic cloves, minced

½ teaspoon minced fresh thyme or ¼ teaspoon dried

½ teaspoon chili powder

⅓ cup heavy cream

¼ teaspoon hot sauce

8 large eggs

1 Toss russet and sweet potatoes with 1 tablespoon oil, ½ teaspoon salt, and ¼ teaspoon pepper in bowl. Cover and microwave until potatoes are translucent around edges, 5 to 8 minutes, stirring halfway through microwaving.

2 Meanwhile, heat remaining 1 tablespoon oil in 12-inch nonstick skillet over medium-high heat until shimmering. Add onion and cook until softened and lightly browned, 5 to 7 minutes.

3 Stir in garlic, thyme, and chili powder and cook until fragrant, about 30 seconds. Stir in hot potatoes, cream, and hot sauce. Using back of spatula, gently pack potatoes into pan and cook undisturbed for 2 minutes. Flip hash, a portion at a time, and lightly repack into pan. Repeat flipping process every few minutes until potatoes are nicely browned, 6 to 8 minutes.

4 Off heat, make 4 shallow indentations (about 2 inches wide) in surface of hash using back of spoon. Crack 2 eggs into each indentation and season with salt and pepper. Cover and cook over medium-low heat until egg whites are just set and yolks are still runny, 5 to 10 minutes. Serve.

Variation

SWEET POTATO RED FLANNEL HASH

Note that the beets will not brown like the potatoes; they will burn if the pan gets too dry.

Reduce russet potatoes and sweet potatoes to 8 ounces each. Microwave 8 ounces beets, peeled and cut into ¼-inch pieces, with potatoes. Add ¼ teaspoon Worcestershire sauce to skillet with cream and hot sauce.

FLANK STEAK TACOS WITH CHARRED CORN SALSA

SERVES 4   TOTAL TIME: 45 MINUTES

WHY THIS RECIPE WORKS   Steak tacos are usually reserved for the summer, when you can sear the meat over a blazing hot grill, giving it a charred crust that many consider the best part of the dish. To bring that delicious charred flavor indoors, we cranked up the heat on our skillet. Cutting the steak into four strips increased the meat's surface area, giving us plenty of perfectly charred crust. It also gave us more tasty browned bits in the skillet, which we used to our advantage. We cooked some sliced red onion and a poblano chile, a traditional accompaniment to steak tacos called *rajas*, in the same skillet, where they absorbed the flavors of the beef. To add even more charred flavor to our tacos, we then used the skillet to toast corn for a smoky salsa, which we seasoned with jalapeño, lime juice, and cilantro, the perfect finish to our non-grilled grilled dinner. Warm tortillas by stacking them on a plate, covering with a damp dish towel, and microwaving for 60 to 90 seconds. Serve with your favorite taco toppings. You will need a 12-inch nonstick skillet for this recipe.

WEEKNIGHT FRIENDLY

1 tablespoon ground cumin
  Salt and pepper
1 (1½- to 1¾-pound) flank steak, trimmed and cut lengthwise (with grain) into 4 equal pieces
3 tablespoons vegetable oil
1 red onion, three-quarters sliced thin, one-quarter chopped fine
1 poblano chile, stemmed, seeded, and sliced thin
1½ cups frozen corn, thawed
1 jalapeño chile, stemmed, seeded, and minced
2 tablespoons lime juice
1 tablespoon minced fresh cilantro
12 (6-inch) corn tortillas, warmed

1 Combine cumin, 1 teaspoon salt, and ½ teaspoon pepper in bowl. Pat steak dry with paper towels and season with cumin mixture. Heat 2 tablespoons oil in 12-inch nonstick skillet over medium-high heat until just smoking. Lay steak pieces in skillet, spaced slightly apart, and cook, without moving, until lightly browned on first side, about 3 minutes. Flip steaks and cook until lightly browned on second side, about 3 minutes.

2 Flip steaks and cook, flipping as needed to ensure even browning, until well browned and meat registers 120 to 125 degrees (for medium-rare), 2 to 3 minutes. Transfer steaks to cutting board, tent loosely with aluminum foil, and let rest.

3 Heat remaining 1 tablespoon oil in now-empty skillet over medium heat until shimmering. Add sliced onion and poblano and cook, stirring occasionally, until softened and just beginning to brown, 6 to 8 minutes; transfer to bowl.

4 Add corn to now-empty skillet and cook, without stirring, until lightly charred, about 3 minutes. Stir corn and cook until tender, about 1 minute. Transfer corn to separate bowl and stir in chopped onion, jalapeño, lime juice, cilantro, ¾ teaspoon salt, and ½ teaspoon pepper.

5 Slice steak thinly against grain and serve with warm tortillas, poblano mixture, and corn salsa.

CUTTING FLANK STEAK FOR TACOS

1 Using chef's knife, cut steak lengthwise (with grain) into 4 equal pieces.
2 Once cooked, slice steak thinly against grain.

CHIPOTLE BEEF CHILI BOWLS WITH LIME-CILANTRO CREMA

SERVES 4   TOTAL TIME: 1 HOUR 15 MINUTES

WHY THIS RECIPE WORKS Looking to make enough chili for one night's dinner without hauling out a heavy pot, we pulled out our skillet. We would use it to make both the chili and the rice, cooking in stages, for a meal with minimal fuss. We toasted and simmered the rice, flavoring it with lime zest and juice to brighten it up, and transferred it directly to individual serving bowls, which we kept warm in a low oven. While the rice cooked, we prepared our ingredients for a quick but flavorful chili. Treating ground beef with salt and baking soda ensured it would remain moist and tender, even with a short cooking time. Blooming garlic, cumin, and chipotle chile powder boosted their potency for fast flavor. Soon enough, our chili bowls were ready for filling, and a simple lime-cilantro crema gave them an authentic finish. You will need a 12-inch nonstick skillet with a tight-fitting lid for this recipe. Serve with pickled jalapeños, shredded cheese, and diced avocado.

½ cup sour cream

¼ cup minced fresh cilantro

2 teaspoons grated lime zest plus 3 tablespoons juice (2 limes)

Salt and pepper

1 pound 90 percent lean ground beef

2 tablespoons water plus 2 cups water

¼ teaspoon baking soda

2 tablespoons vegetable oil

1 cup long-grain white rice

1 onion, chopped fine

1 red bell pepper, stemmed, seeded, and chopped

2 garlic cloves, minced

1 tablespoon ground cumin

2 teaspoons chipotle chile powder

1 (15-ounce) can tomato sauce

1 (15-ounce) can black beans, rinsed

1 cup frozen corn, thawed

1 Adjust oven rack to middle position, place 4 individual serving bowls on rack, and heat oven to 200 degrees. Whisk sour cream, 2 tablespoons cilantro, 1 teaspoon lime zest, 1 tablespoon lime juice, and ¼ teaspoon salt together in bowl; cover and refrigerate until serving. Toss beef with 2 tablespoons water, baking soda, ¼ teaspoon salt, and pinch pepper in bowl until thoroughly combined; let sit for 20 minutes.

2 Meanwhile, heat 1 tablespoon oil in 12-inch nonstick skillet over medium heat until shimmering. Add rice and cook, stirring often, until edges begin to turn translucent, about 2 minutes. Add remaining 2 cups water and ½ teaspoon salt and bring to boil. Cover, reduce heat to low, and simmer until liquid is absorbed and rice is tender, about 20 minutes.

3 Remove rice from heat, add remaining 1 teaspoon lime zest and remaining 2 tablespoons juice, and fluff gently with fork to incorporate. Portion cooked rice into warmed serving bowls, cover with aluminum foil, and keep warm in oven.

4 Heat remaining 1 tablespoon oil in now-empty skillet over medium heat until shimmering. Add onion and bell pepper and cook until just beginning to brown, 5 to 7 minutes. Add beef, breaking up pieces with wooden spoon, and cook until no longer pink, 6 to 8 minutes.

5 Stir in garlic, cumin, and chile powder, and cook until fragrant, about 1 minute. Stir in tomato sauce, beans, corn, and 1 teaspoon salt, and cook until slightly thickened, about 3 minutes. Spoon chili over rice in bowls, sprinkle with remaining 2 tablespoons cilantro, and serve with lime-cilantro crema.

PORK TAMALE PIE

SERVES 4 TO 6   TOTAL TIME: 1 HOUR 15 MINUTES

WHY THIS RECIPE WORKS Inspired by Mexican tamales but a lot less labor-intensive, a good tamale pie is loaded with juicy meat and vegetables and topped with a golden cornmeal crust—a perfect one-pan meal. To create a well-seasoned filling, we browned ground pork, then added scallion whites, chili powder, and oregano, letting their flavors intensify in the rendered fat. Canned black beans, diced tomatoes, and frozen corn made the meal heartier, and pepper Jack cheese added extra spice and richness. We prepared an easy cornbread topping, fortified with the tang of buttermilk and the bite of scallion, to spread over the filling before baking. The result was a crunchy, corny topping that paired perfectly with the spicy filling. Don't use coarse-ground cornmeal in this recipe. You will need a 10-inch ovensafe skillet for this recipe.

¼ cup vegetable oil

1 pound ground pork

6 scallions, white and green parts separated and sliced thin

2 tablespoons chili powder

1 tablespoon minced fresh oregano or 1 teaspoon dried
Salt and pepper

1 (15-ounce) can black beans, rinsed

1 (14.5-ounce) can diced tomatoes

1 cup frozen corn

½ cup chicken broth

4 ounces pepper Jack cheese, shredded (1 cup)

¾ cup (3¾ ounces) all-purpose flour

¾ cup (3¾ ounces) cornmeal

¾ teaspoon baking powder

¼ teaspoon baking soda

¾ cup buttermilk

1 large egg

1 Adjust oven rack to middle position and heat oven to 400 degrees. Heat 1 tablespoon oil in 10-inch ovensafe skillet over medium-high heat until just smoking. Add pork and cook, breaking up meat with wooden spoon, until just beginning to brown, 5 to 7 minutes.

2 Stir in scallion whites, chili powder, oregano, and ¼ teaspoon salt and cook until fragrant, about 1 minute. Stir in beans, tomatoes and their juice, corn, and broth. Bring to simmer and cook until mixture has thickened slightly, 5 to 7 minutes.

Off heat, stir in pepper Jack until well combined. Season with salt and pepper to taste. (Filling can be refrigerated for up to 1 day; return to simmer and add broth to loosen sauce if necessary.)

3 Whisk flour, cornmeal, baking powder, baking soda, scallion greens, and ¾ teaspoon salt together in large bowl. In separate bowl, whisk buttermilk, egg, and remaining 3 tablespoons oil until smooth. Stir buttermilk mixture into flour mixture until just combined.

4 Spread cornmeal batter evenly over filling in skillet. Transfer skillet to oven and bake until topping is golden brown and toothpick inserted into center comes out clean, about 20 minutes, rotating skillet halfway through baking.

5 Remove skillet from oven (skillet handle will be hot). Let cool for 10 minutes before serving.

MAKING TAMALE PIE

Using rubber spatula, spread cornmeal batter evenly over meat mixture in skillet.

SAUSAGE LASAGNA

SERVES 6   TOTAL TIME: 1 HOUR 30 MINUTES

WHY THIS RECIPE WORKS We wanted a big, bubbling lasagna made with minimal effort (and minimal dishes). We built a bold sauce by sautéing onion, garlic, and red pepper flakes before cooking the sausage in the sauce and adding tomatoes, simmering to meld their flavors. With our sauce at the ready, we assembled the lasagna, layering sauce, a rich ricotta-egg mixture, no-boil lasagna noodles (broken and shingled to suit the round vessel), and plenty of Parmesan and mozzarella. We topped the lasagna with extra cheese and slid it into the oven. Soon enough our beautifully browned, perfectly cooked lasagna was ready to serve. Do not use nonfat ricotta or fat-free mozzarella here. You will need a 12-inch ovensafe nonstick skillet for this recipe.

3 (14.5-ounce) cans whole peeled tomatoes
2 tablespoons extra-virgin olive oil
1 onion, chopped fine
   Salt and pepper
3 garlic cloves, minced
¼ teaspoon red pepper flakes
1 pound hot or sweet Italian sausage, casings removed
12 ounces (1½ cups) whole-milk ricotta cheese
1 large egg yolk
1 teaspoon minced fresh thyme or ¼ teaspoon dried
8 ounces mozzarella cheese, shredded (2 cups)
¼ cup grated Parmesan cheese
12 no-boil lasagna noodles, broken in half
3 tablespoons chopped fresh basil

1 Adjust oven rack to middle position and heat oven to 375 degrees. Pulse tomatoes and their juice in food processor until coarsely ground, about 10 pulses.

2 Heat oil in 12-inch ovensafe nonstick skillet over medium heat until shimmering. Add onion and ½ teaspoon salt and cook until onion is softened and lightly browned, 5 to 7 minutes. Stir in garlic and pepper flakes and cook until fragrant, about 30 seconds. Add sausage and cook, breaking up meat with wooden spoon, until no longer pink, about 5 minutes. Stir in processed tomatoes, bring to simmer, and cook until sauce is thickened slightly, about 10 minutes; transfer to bowl.

3 In second bowl, combine ricotta, egg yolk, thyme, ½ teaspoon salt, and ½ teaspoon pepper. Combine mozzarella and Parmesan in third bowl.

4 Spread ¾ cup sauce over bottom of now-empty skillet. Shingle 7 noodle halves around edge of skillet and place 1 noodle half in center. Dollop one-third of ricotta mixture over noodles, then top with one-quarter mozzarella mixture and one-third remaining sauce (in that order). Repeat layering process of noodles, ricotta mixture, mozzarella mixture, and sauce twice more. Top with remaining mozzarella mixture. (Lasagna can be held at room temperature for 2 hours before baking.)

5 Transfer skillet to oven and bake until cheese is golden brown and lasagna is bubbling around edges, 30 to 40 minutes, rotating skillet halfway through baking. Remove skillet from oven (skillet handle will be hot). Let cool for 10 minutes, then sprinkle with basil and serve.

MAKING SKILLET LASAGNA

Shingle 7 noodle halves around edge of skillet and place 1 noodle half in center.

MODERN BEEF POT PIE

SERVES 4 TO 6   TOTAL TIME: 2 HOURS

WHY THIS RECIPE WORKS Beef pot pie is as comforting a meal as there is, but very often the thought of making a pie crust stops us in our tracks. To satisfy our craving for crust—but with less fuss—we pondered easy yet delicious alternatives. We considered topping the beef filling with bread crumbs, but ultimately landed on slices of crusty bread drizzled with oil, salt, pepper, and a little Parmesan cheese. The underside of the bread absorbed some of the pot pie's juices, while the cheesy top browned and crisped under the broiler. We loved the contrast of the crunchy topping with the juicy filling, but as the bread absorbed some of the sauce it turned the filling dry. Increasing the amount of beef broth was an easy fix. As for the filling, chuck-eye roast proved the best option for a tender, beefy pot pie, as it features great marbling at a low price. This cut lent wonderful flavor and richness to the sauce. Parsley and peas added a little freshness and color to our easy and delicious beef pot pie. You will need a 12-inch broiler-safe skillet with a tight-fitting lid for this recipe.

2 pounds boneless beef chuck-eye roast, pulled apart at seams, trimmed, and cut into ¾-inch pieces
  Salt and pepper
3 tablespoons vegetable oil
4 carrots, peeled and cut into ½-inch pieces
8 ounces cremini mushrooms, trimmed and quartered
1 onion, chopped fine
2 tablespoons tomato paste
4 garlic cloves, minced
3 tablespoons all-purpose flour
½ cup red wine
2½ cups beef broth
1 cup frozen peas
1 (18-inch) baguette, sliced ½ inch thick, ends discarded
1 ounce Parmesan cheese, grated (½ cup)
2 tablespoons minced fresh parsley

1 Adjust oven rack to middle position and heat oven to 400 degrees. Pat beef dry with paper towels and season with salt and pepper. Heat 1 tablespoon oil in 12-inch broiler-safe skillet over medium-high heat until just smoking. Add beef and cook until well browned on all sides, 7 to 10 minutes; transfer to bowl.

2 Add carrots, mushrooms, and onion to fat left in skillet and cook over medium heat until softened and lightly browned, 5 to 7 minutes. Stir in tomato paste and garlic and cook until fragrant, about 30 seconds. Stir in flour and cook for 1 minute.

3 Stir in wine and cook until almost completely evaporated, about 2 minutes. Slowly stir in broth, scraping up any browned bits and smoothing out any lumps. Bring to simmer, then stir in browned beef and any accumulated juices. Cover, transfer skillet to oven, and cook until beef is tender, about 1 hour, stirring once halfway through cooking. (Filling can be refrigerated for up to 1 day; return to simmer and add broth to loosen sauce if necessary.)

4 Remove skillet from oven (skillet handle will be hot). Adjust oven rack 8 inches from broiler element and heat broiler. Stir peas into beef mixture and season with salt and pepper to taste.

5 Brush bread with remaining 2 tablespoons oil, season with salt and pepper, and shingle around edge of skillet, leaving center open. Sprinkle Parmesan over bread. Broil until cheese is melted and bread is browned, about 2 minutes. Remove skillet from oven (skillet handle will be hot). Let cool for 5 minutes, then sprinkle with parsley and serve.

CHICKEN POT PIE

SERVES 4 TO 6   TOTAL TIME: 1 HOUR 45 MINUTES

WHY THIS RECIPE WORKS Everyone loves chicken pot pie, but from poaching the chicken to blanching the vegetables to rolling out the crust, it requires a lot of work. We wanted to simplify this savory pie without sacrificing its homey flavors by preparing it in a skillet. Poaching the chicken breasts directly in the sauce enabled us to use boneless breasts, and instead of fussing with homemade pie dough, we turned to a convenient (and even flakier) alternative: store-bought puff pastry. We rolled the dough out to a 12-inch square, draped it over the skillet, cut a few vent holes in the center, and brushed on an egg wash for deep browning. Our streamlined pie baked to a beautiful golden hue in just 30 minutes. To thaw frozen puff pastry, let it sit either in the refrigerator for 24 hours or on the counter for 30 minutes to 1 hour. Be sure to use chicken breasts that are roughly the same size to ensure even cooking. You will need a 12-inch ovensafe skillet for this recipe.

4 tablespoons unsalted butter
4 carrots, peeled and sliced ¼ inch thick
2 celery ribs, cut into ¼-inch pieces
1 onion, chopped fine
  Salt and pepper
1 teaspoon minced fresh thyme or ¼ teaspoon dried
6 tablespoons all-purpose flour
2 cups chicken broth
1½ pounds boneless, skinless chicken breasts, trimmed
½ cup frozen peas
¼ cup heavy cream
3 tablespoons minced fresh parsley
1 tablespoon dry sherry
1 (9½ by 9-inch) sheet puff pastry, thawed
1 large egg, lightly beaten with 2 tablespoons water

1 Adjust oven rack to middle position and heat oven to 400 degrees. Melt butter in 12-inch ovensafe skillet over medium heat. Add carrots, celery, onion, ¼ teaspoon salt, and ¼ teaspoon pepper and cook until vegetables are softened, about 5 minutes. Stir in thyme and cook until fragrant, about 30 seconds. Stir in flour and cook for 2 minutes. Slowly whisk in broth, scraping up any browned bits and smoothing out any lumps, and bring to simmer.

2 Nestle chicken into skillet. Reduce heat to low to maintain gentle simmer, cover, and cook until chicken registers 160 degrees and sauce has thickened, 15 to 20 minutes, flipping chicken halfway through cooking.

3 Transfer chicken to cutting board, let cool slightly, then shred into bite-size pieces. Stir shredded chicken, peas, cream, parsley, and sherry into skillet. Season with salt and pepper to taste. (Filling can be refrigerated for up to 1 day; return to simmer and add broth to loosen sauce if necessary.)

4 On clean, lightly floured counter, roll puff pastry into 12-inch square. Loosely roll dough around rolling pin, then gently unroll it over filling in skillet, letting excess dough hang over edge. Cut four 2-inch oval-shaped vents in center of dough, then brush dough with egg mixture. Bake until crust is golden brown and filling is bubbling, 30 to 35 minutes, rotating skillet halfway through baking.

5 Remove skillet from oven (skillet handle will be hot). Let cool for 10 minutes before serving.

TOPPING A POT PIE WITH PUFF PASTRY

1 Loosely roll dough around rolling pin and then gently unroll over filling, letting excess dough hang over edge.
2 Cut four 2-inch oval-shaped vents in center of dough, then brush dough with egg mixture.

CLASSIC CHICKEN AND RICE WITH CARROTS AND PEAS

SERVES 4   TOTAL TIME: 1 HOUR

WHY THIS RECIPE WORKS To serve up superior chicken and rice, we opted out of convenience items like canned soup and instant rice in favor of fresher (but no less convenient) flavors. We prepared the quick-cooking chicken breasts first, simply seasoning them with salt and pepper and searing them on one side for some flavorful browning. Hoping to avoid the mushy texture and bland taste of instant rice (a common choice for this simple dish), we selected long-grain rice, which stays tender and flavorful over long cooking times. Sautéing the rice in aromatics helped keep the grains distinct and creamy when we poured in the chicken broth. We finished cooking the chicken right in the rice, removing it from the skillet as soon as it cooked through, and then we let the rice continue to simmer gently, absorbing the flavorful liquid. Frozen peas—typically sweeter and certainly more convenient than fresh—offered bright bursts of flavor, and fresh lemon and parsley perked everything up. Be sure to use chicken breasts that are roughly the same size to ensure even cooking. You will need a 12-inch skillet with a tight-fitting lid for this recipe. The skillet will be fairly full once you add the browned chicken in step 2, so you may want to consider using a straight-sided skillet or sauté pan if you have one. Fresh basil, chives, tarragon, or cilantro can be substituted for the parsley.

4 (6- to 8-ounce) boneless, skinless chicken breasts, trimmed
   Salt and pepper
2 tablespoons vegetable oil
1 onion, chopped fine
1½ cups long-grain white rice
3 garlic cloves, minced
   Pinch red pepper flakes
4 carrots, peeled and sliced on bias ½ inch thick
3½ cups chicken broth
1 cup frozen peas
2 tablespoons lemon juice
1 tablespoon minced fresh parsley

1 Pat chicken dry with paper towels and season with salt and pepper. Heat oil in 12-inch skillet over medium-high heat until just smoking. Add chicken and cook until golden brown on 1 side, 4 to 6 minutes; transfer to plate.

2 Add onion and ½ teaspoon salt to fat left in skillet and cook until softened, about 5 minutes. Stir in rice, garlic, and pepper flakes and cook until fragrant, about 30 seconds. Stir in carrots, then stir in broth, scraping up any browned bits.

3 Nestle chicken, browned side up, into skillet, along with any accumulated juices. Bring to simmer, then reduce heat to medium-low, cover, and simmer gently until chicken registers 160 degrees, about 10 minutes.

4 Transfer chicken to cutting board, tent loosely with aluminum foil, and let rest while finishing rice. Stir rice mixture to recombine, then cover and cook until liquid is absorbed and rice is tender, 5 to 10 minutes.

5 Off heat, sprinkle with peas, cover, and let warm through, about 2 minutes. Sprinkle with lemon juice and gently fluff rice mixture with fork. Slice chicken into ½-inch-thick slices and arrange on top of rice. Sprinkle with parsley and serve.

CHICKEN SAUSAGE WITH BRAISED RED CABBAGE AND POTATOES

SERVES 4 TO 6   TOTAL TIME: 1 HOUR 15 MINUTES

WHY THIS RECIPE WORKS This fresh take on sausage and cabbage captures the flavor of an all-day braise in under an hour and a half. Precooked chicken sausage, browned for a quick flavor boost, kept things easy, and braising cabbage in cider with grated apple, bay leaves, and thyme offered complexity and kept the texture intact. Returning the sausage to the skillet partway through cooking helped marry the dish's sweet, salty, and tart flavors. A hit of cider vinegar rounded things out, and small red potatoes (1 to 2 inches in diameter) cooked quickly in the microwave (if your potatoes are larger, be sure to quarter them). We also browned them in the skillet to quickly crisp them. Chicken sausage is available in a variety of flavors; feel free to substitute any flavor that you think will pair well with this dish. You will need a 12-inch skillet with a tight-fitting lid for this recipe. The skillet will be very full once you add the cabbage in step 3, but will become more manageable as the cabbage wilts.

1½ pounds small red potatoes, unpeeled, halved
¼ cup vegetable oil
    Salt and pepper
1½ pounds cooked chicken-apple sausage
 1 onion, halved and sliced thin
 1 head red cabbage (2 pounds), cored and shredded
1½ cups apple cider
 1 Granny Smith apple, peeled and grated
 2 bay leaves
1½ teaspoons minced fresh thyme or ½ teaspoon dried
 2 tablespoons cider vinegar
 2 tablespoons minced fresh chives

1 Toss potatoes with 1 tablespoon oil, ¼ teaspoon salt, and ¼ teaspoon pepper in bowl. Cover and microwave, stirring occasionally, until potatoes are tender, about 5 minutes; drain well.

2 Meanwhile, heat 1 tablespoon oil in 12-inch skillet over medium heat until shimmering. Add sausage and brown on all sides, about 5 minutes; transfer to platter.

3 Add onion and ½ teaspoon salt to fat left in skillet and cook over medium heat until onion is softened, about 5 minutes. Stir in cabbage, cider, apple, bay leaves, and thyme. Cover and cook until cabbage is softened, about 15 minutes.

4 Nestle sausage into vegetables, cover, and cook until cabbage is very tender, 8 to 10 minutes. Uncover and simmer until liquid is almost evaporated, 2 to 3 minutes. Transfer sausage to platter and discard bay leaves. Stir vinegar into vegetables and season with salt and pepper to taste. Transfer vegetables to platter with sausage and tent with aluminum foil.

5 Add remaining 2 tablespoons oil to now-empty skillet and heat over medium heat until shimmering. Add potatoes, cut side down, and cook until browned, 2 to 5 minutes. Transfer to platter with sausage and cabbage, sprinkle with chives, and serve.

SHREDDING CABBAGE

1 Cut cabbage into quarters, then trim and discard hard core.
2 Separate cabbage into leaves and stack and flatten them. Use chef's knife to cut each stack into thin shreds.

ROASTED CHICKEN AND STUFFING

SERVES 4   TOTAL TIME: 2 HOURS

WHY THIS RECIPE WORKS To enjoy holiday-caliber roast chicken and stuffing without dirtying a mountain of pots and pans, we roasted the bird atop the stuffing ingredients in a skillet. Not only did this method streamline the process, but it allowed the chicken juices to flavor the stuffing—something you don't get when cooking the two separately. We started by sautéing a classic base of chopped onions and minced celery, which we seasoned with sage and thyme. We then put the chicken—brushed with a flavorful herb butter—on top of the vegetables and scattered bread cubes all around the bird, allowing them to toast and soak up the flavorful juice as the chicken roasted. Once the chicken was cooked through and resting, a quick stir and some broth moistened the stuffing, tying the dish together. You can find Italian bread in the bakery section of your grocery store. You will need a 12-inch ovensafe skillet with a tight-fitting lid for this recipe.

1   (4-pound) whole chicken, giblets discarded
6   tablespoons unsalted butter
2   tablespoons minced fresh sage
2   tablespoons minced fresh thyme
    Salt and pepper
2   onions, chopped fine
2   celery ribs, minced
7   ounces Italian bread, cut into ½-inch cubes (6 cups)
⅓   cup chicken broth

1 Adjust oven rack to lower-middle position and heat oven to 375 degrees. Pat chicken dry with paper towels. Melt 4 tablespoons butter in small bowl in microwave, about 45 seconds. Stir in 1 tablespoon sage, 1 tablespoon thyme, 1 teaspoon salt, and ½ teaspoon pepper. Brush chicken with herb butter.

2 Melt remaining 2 tablespoons butter in 12-inch ovensafe skillet over medium heat. Add onions, celery, ½ teaspoon salt, and ½ teaspoon pepper and cook until vegetables are softened, about 5 minutes. Add remaining 1 tablespoon sage and remaining 1 table-spoon thyme and cook until fragrant, about 1 minute. Off heat, place chicken, breast side up, on top of vegetables. Arrange bread cubes around chicken in bottom of skillet.

3 Transfer skillet to oven and roast until breasts register 160 degrees and thighs register 175 degrees, about 1 hour, rotating skillet halfway through roasting.

4 Remove skillet from oven (skillet handle will be hot). Carefully transfer chicken to plate and let rest while finishing stuffing. Stir bread and vegetables in skillet to combine; cover and let stand for 10 minutes.

5 Stir broth and any accumulated chicken juices into stuffing to combine. Warm stuffing, uncovered, over low heat until heated through, about 3 minutes. Remove from heat, cover, and let sit while carving chicken. Transfer chicken to carving board, carve, and serve with stuffing.

SCATTERING BREAD CUBES FOR STUFFING

Arrange ½-inch cubes of Italian bread around chicken in bottom of skillet.

NEW YORK STRIP STEAKS WITH CRISPY POTATOES AND PARSLEY SAUCE

SERVES 4   TOTAL TIME: 45 MINUTES

WHY THIS RECIPE WORKS We wanted a steakhouse-worthy dinner that was simple enough to be a weeknight treat. Inspired by the bright, garlicky flavors of Argentinean chimichurri, we created a bold parsley sauce by quickly processing fresh parsley with olive oil, red onion, and red wine vinegar. Adding four garlic cloves promised plenty of kick, and red pepper flakes delivered a bit of pleasant heat. With our sauce ready, we seared our beefy, well-marbled strip steaks in a hot skillet until well browned. Cooking the steaks to medium-rare kept the meat moist and tender. For a perfectly crisp side of potatoes, we cut red potatoes into wedges and jump-started their cooking in the microwave. Using the meaty juices left behind in the skillet, we imparted some flavorful browning onto the wedges, giving them an appealing golden hue and crisp bite. Drizzled with our punchy, verdant parsley sauce, these perfectly seared steaks could give those on any steakhouse menu a run for their money. You will need a 12-inch nonstick skillet for this recipe.

Parsley Sauce

- 1 cup fresh parsley leaves
- ½ cup extra-virgin olive oil
- ¼ cup chopped red onion
- ¼ cup red wine vinegar
- 2 tablespoons water
- 4 garlic cloves, minced
- 1 teaspoon salt
- ¼ teaspoon red pepper flakes

Steak and Potatoes

- 1½ pounds red potatoes, unpeeled, cut into 1-inch wedges
- ¼ cup vegetable oil
- Salt and pepper
- 2 (1-pound) boneless strip steaks, 1½ to 1¾ inches thick, trimmed and halved crosswise

1 **For the parsley sauce** Process all ingredients in food processor until finely chopped and well combined, about 20 seconds; set aside for serving.

2 **For the steak and potatoes** Toss potatoes with 1 tablespoon oil, ¼ teaspoon salt, and ⅛ teaspoon pepper in bowl. Cover and microwave, stirring occasionally, until potatoes begin to soften, 5 to 7 minutes; drain well.

3 Meanwhile, heat 1 tablespoon oil in 12-inch non-stick skillet over medium-high heat until just smoking. Pat steaks dry with paper towels and season with salt and pepper. Lay steaks in skillet and cook until well browned on first side, 3 to 5 minutes.

4 Flip steaks, reduce heat to medium, and cook until meat registers 120 to 125 degrees (for medium-rare), 5 to 7 minutes. Transfer steaks to cutting board, tent with aluminum foil, and let rest while finishing potatoes.

5 Add remaining 2 tablespoons oil to now-empty skillet and heat over medium heat until shimmering. Add potatoes and cook, stirring occasionally, until well browned, about 10 minutes. Slice steak into ½-inch-thick slices, drizzle with sauce, and serve with potatoes.

TERIYAKI STIR-FRIED BEEF WITH GREEN BEANS AND SHIITAKES

SERVES 4   TOTAL TIME: 45 MINUTES

WHY THIS RECIPE WORKS A wok may be the customary stir-fry vessel, but the flat surface of a nonstick skillet imparts better browning on a home stovetop. We started by slicing flank steak thin, marinating it in soy sauce and sugar, and seared it in batches for optimal browning. Green beans and meaty shiitakes, browned first and steamed to finish, provided nice contrast. Mashing fresh ginger and garlic in the center of the pan unlocked more authentic flavor before we added back the beef and tossed everything with a sweet, gently spicy sauce. To make the beef easier to slice, freeze it for 20 minutes. You can substitute 1 tablespoon white wine or sake mixed with 1 teaspoon sugar for the mirin. Stir-fries cook quickly, so have everything prepped before you begin cooking. You will need a 12-inch nonstick skillet with a tight-fitting lid for this recipe. Serve with rice.

WEEKNIGHT FRIENDLY

1 (1-pound) flank steak, trimmed and cut into 2-inch-wide strips with grain, then sliced against grain into ⅛-inch-thick slices

¼ cup soy sauce

1 teaspoon plus 2 tablespoons sugar

½ cup chicken broth

1 tablespoon mirin

1 teaspoon cornstarch

¼ teaspoon red pepper flakes

3 garlic cloves, minced

1 tablespoon grated fresh ginger

2 tablespoons vegetable oil

8 ounces shiitake mushrooms, stemmed and cut into 1-inch pieces

12 ounces green beans, trimmed and halved

¼ cup water

3 scallions, cut into 1½-inch pieces, white parts quartered lengthwise

1 Toss beef with 2 tablespoons soy sauce and 1 teaspoon sugar in bowl and let sit, stirring occasionally, for at least 10 minutes or up to 1 hour. Meanwhile, whisk remaining 2 tablespoons soy sauce, remaining 2 tablespoons sugar, broth, mirin, cornstarch, and pepper flakes in second bowl. In third bowl, combine garlic, ginger, and 1 teaspoon oil.

2 Drain beef, discarding liquid. Heat 1 teaspoon oil in 12-inch nonstick skillet over high heat until just smoking. Add half of beef in single layer and cook, without stirring, for 1 minute. Stir beef and cook until browned, 1 to 2 minutes; transfer beef to clean bowl. Repeat with 1 teaspoon oil and remaining beef. Rinse and dry skillet.

3 Add remaining 1 tablespoon oil to now-empty skillet and heat over high heat until just smoking. Add mushrooms and cook until starting to brown, about 2 minutes. Add green beans and cook, stirring often, until spotty brown, 3 to 4 minutes. Add water, cover, and cook until green beans are crisp-tender, 2 to 3 minutes.

4 Uncover and push vegetables aside to clear center of skillet. Add garlic-ginger mixture to clearing and cook, mashing with spatula, until fragrant, 15 to 20 seconds. Stir garlic-ginger mixture into vegetables. Stir in beef, along with any accumulated juices, and scallions. Whisk sauce to recombine, then add to skillet. Cook, stirring constantly, until thickened, about 30 seconds. Serve.

KOREAN BEEF AND KIMCHI STIR-FRY

SERVES 4   TOTAL TIME: 45 MINUTES

WHY THIS RECIPE WORKS For a simple Korean-inspired stir-fry, we called on kimchi to do double duty, bringing a vegetable component to the dish while also flavoring it with tangy heat. After browning sliced flank steak in hot oil (in batches to avoid steaming), we added kimchi and a bit of its brine to the skillet, warming it before tossing in bean sprouts for a crunchy contrast to the soft pickled cabbage. Clearing a space in the center, we mashed minced garlic and grated ginger against the skillet's hot surface to quickly bloom their flavors and fragrances before incorporating them into the vegetables. We returned the beef to the pan and added a simple sauce of chicken broth, soy sauce, sugar, and sesame oil (plus cornstarch for body), stirring to coat the meat and vegetables. Sliced scallions added freshness to our supersimple dinner. You can find kimchi, a spicy Korean pickled vegetable condiment, in the refrigerated section of Asian markets and in some well-stocked supermarkets. Cut large pieces of kimchi into bite-size pieces before stir-frying. To make the beef easier to slice, freeze it for 20 minutes. Stir-fries cook quickly, so have everything prepped before you begin cooking. You will need a 12-inch nonstick skillet for this recipe. Serve with rice.

Sauce

- ½ cup chicken broth
- 2 tablespoons soy sauce
- 1 tablespoon sugar
- 2 teaspoons cornstarch
- 1 teaspoon toasted sesame oil

Stir-Fry

- 3 garlic cloves, minced
- 1 tablespoon grated fresh ginger
- 2 tablespoons vegetable oil
- 1 (1-pound) flank steak, trimmed and cut into 2-inch-wide strips with grain, then sliced against grain into ⅛-inch-thick slices
- 1 cup drained cabbage kimchi plus 1 tablespoon kimchi liquid
- 4 ounces (2 cups) bean sprouts
- 5 scallions, cut into 1½-inch pieces, white parts quartered lengthwise

1 **For the sauce** Whisk all ingredients together in bowl.

2 **For the stir-fry** Combine garlic, ginger, and 1 teaspoon oil in bowl.

3 Heat 1 teaspoon oil in 12-inch nonstick skillet over high heat until just smoking. Add half of beef in single layer and cook, without stirring, for 1 minute. Stir beef and cook until browned, 1 to 2 minutes; transfer to clean bowl. Repeat with 1 teaspoon oil and remaining beef.

4 Add remaining 1 tablespoon oil to now-empty skillet and return to high heat until just smoking. Add kimchi and kimchi liquid and cook until warmed through, about 2 minutes. Stir in bean sprouts.

5 Push vegetables aside to clear center of skillet. Add garlic-ginger mixture to clearing and cook, mashing with spatula, until fragrant, 15 to 20 seconds. Stir garlic-ginger mixture into vegetables.

6 Stir in beef, along with any accumulated juices, and scallions. Whisk sauce to recombine, then add to skillet. Cook, stirring constantly, until thickened, about 30 seconds. Serve.

SESAME PORK CUTLETS WITH WILTED NAPA CABBAGE SALAD

SERVES 4 TOTAL TIME: 45 MINUTES

WHY THIS RECIPE WORKS Crisp pan-fried pork cutlets make a great centerpiece for an easy weeknight meal, but too often they turn out bland and soggy. To avoid this, we breaded our cutlets, updating the traditional flour, egg, and bread crumb formula with an untraditional ingredient: sesame seeds. Using a whopping ⅔ cup of seeds ensured the crust had ample sesame flavor and kept it extra-crisp. To complement the savory chops, we made a warm, soft, Asian-style salad, which came together in a snap: We browned garlic and ginger in a blend of vegetable and sesame oils, then added cabbage and carrot, wilting the cabbage leaves slightly. Matchsticks of pear contributed crunch and a touch of sweetness, a perfect contrast to the pork cutlets. We like using Asian pear in this recipe for its bright crispness, but Bosc or Anjou pears will also work. You will need a 12-inch nonstick skillet with a lid for this recipe.

WEEKNIGHT FRIENDLY

⅔ cup all-purpose flour

2 large eggs

1 cup panko bread crumbs

⅔ cup sesame seeds

8 (4-ounce) boneless pork chops, trimmed and pounded to ½-inch thickness
  Salt and pepper

⅓ cup plus 1 tablespoon vegetable oil

1½ teaspoons toasted sesame oil

2 garlic cloves, minced

1 teaspoon grated fresh ginger

1 small head napa cabbage (1½ pounds), cored and shredded

1 carrot, peeled and shredded

1 Asian pear, peeled, halved, cored, and cut into 2-inch matchsticks

¼ cup fresh cilantro leaves

3 tablespoons rice vinegar

1 Spread flour in shallow dish. Beat eggs in second shallow dish. Combine panko and sesame seeds in third shallow dish.

2 Pat pork dry with paper towels and season with salt and pepper. Working with 1 cutlet at a time, dredge in flour, dip in egg, then coat with sesame–panko mixture, pressing gently to adhere.

3 Heat ⅓ cup vegetable oil in 12-inch nonstick skillet over medium-high heat until shimmering. Carefully place 4 cutlets in skillet and cook until golden brown and crisp on first side, 2 to 3 minutes. Flip cutlets and cook until second side is golden brown and crisp, 2 to 3 minutes. Transfer to paper towel–lined plate and repeat with remaining 4 cutlets.

4 Add remaining 1 tablespoon vegetable oil and sesame oil to now-empty skillet and heat over medium heat until shimmering. Add garlic and ginger and cook until fragrant, about 30 seconds. Add cabbage and carrot, cover, and cook until just wilted, stirring occasionally, about 5 minutes. Off heat, add pear, cilantro, and rice vinegar and toss to combine. Season with salt and pepper to taste and serve with pork.

CASHEW PORK WITH SNOW PEAS, CARROTS, AND GINGER

SERVES 4 TOTAL TIME: 45 MINUTES

WEEKNIGHT FRIENDLY

WHY THIS RECIPE WORKS For a fresh riff on Chinese takeout, we started with mild pork tenderloin, rich cashews, and sweet snow peas. Coating strips of pork in cornstarch sealed in the meat's moisture and promised to cling to thick sauce. Toasting the cashews deepened their buttery flavor, and adding them just before serving preserved their crunch. We seared the pork for some flavorful browning, then set it aside to cook our snow peas. Blooming garlic and ginger in the skillet unlocked their aromas before we poured in chicken broth, mirin, soy sauce, and cornstarch to create our sauce. We returned the pork and cashews to the skillet and tossed everything together. Spooned over rice, our easy stir-fry delivered big flavor in every bite. You can substitute ¼ cup white wine or sake mixed with 4 teaspoons sugar for the mirin. You will need a 12-inch nonstick skillet for this recipe. Serve with rice.

½ cup raw cashews, chopped
1 cup chicken broth
¼ cup mirin
¼ cup soy sauce
3 tablespoons cornstarch
6 garlic cloves, minced
1 tablespoon grated fresh ginger
3 tablespoons vegetable oil
1 (16-ounce) pork tenderloin, trimmed
8 ounces snow peas, strings removed
2 carrots, peeled and cut into 2-inch-long matchsticks

1 Toast cashews in 12-inch nonstick skillet over medium heat until golden, about 5 minutes; transfer to plate. Meanwhile, whisk broth, mirin, soy sauce, and 1 tablespoon cornstarch together in bowl. In separate bowl, combine garlic, ginger, and 1 teaspoon oil.

2 Cut pork crosswise into ½-inch-thick slices, then cut each slice into ½-inch-thick strips. Toss pork with 1 tablespoon oil in large bowl, then add remaining 2 tablespoons cornstarch and toss to coat.

3 Heat 2 teaspoons oil in now-empty skillet over medium-high heat until just smoking. Add half of pork in single layer and cook, without stirring, for 1 minute. Stir pork and cook until browned, 1 to 2 minutes;

transfer to clean bowl. Repeat with 2 teaspoons oil and remaining pork.

4 Add remaining 1 teaspoon oil, snow peas, and carrots to now-empty skillet and cook until snow peas are bright green, about 1 minute. Push vegetables aside to clear center of skillet. Add garlic-ginger mixture to clearing and cook, mashing with spatula, until fragrant, 15 to 20 seconds. Stir garlic-ginger mixture into vegetables.

5 Whisk sauce to recombine, then add to skillet. Cook, stirring constantly, until thickened, about 2 minutes. Add pork, along with any accumulated juices, and cashews to skillet and cook until heated through, about 1 minute. Serve.

CUTTING PORK FOR STIR-FRY

1 Using sharp knife, cut pork tenderloin crosswise into ½-inch-thick slices.
2 Then cut each slice of pork into ½-inch-thick strips.

LIME-GINGER CHICKEN AND RICE
WITH EDAMAME, CARROTS, AND SHIITAKES

SERVES 4 TOTAL TIME: 1 HOUR

WHY THIS RECIPE WORKS We wanted a chicken and rice dish that was packed with vegetables and that had bright, bold flavors, but we didn't want it to be too complicated for a weeknight meal. For a bright flavor profile, we added aromatics like ginger, garlic, and lime zest, which we bloomed in the skillet to deepen their flavors. Carrots, shiitake mushrooms, and frozen shelled edamame gave our dish color, and using frozen edamame meant we didn't have to go through the trouble of shelling the beans ourselves. Cooking the rice at the same time as the chicken infused both with the flavor of the aromatics and the vegetables, but to pump up the flavor before serving, we stirred in a few late additions. Soy sauce, toasted sesame oil, and scallions ensured the whole dish was full-flavored, and peanuts added crunch. Be sure to use chicken breasts that are roughly the same size to ensure even cooking. You will need a 12-inch skillet with a tight-fitting lid for this recipe. The skillet will be fairly full once you add the browned chicken in step 2, so you may want to consider using a straight-sided skillet or sauté pan if you have one. Serve with lime wedges and Sriracha sauce.

WEEKNIGHT FRIENDLY

4 (6- to 8-ounce) boneless, skinless chicken breasts, trimmed
  Salt and pepper
2 tablespoons vegetable oil
1 onion, chopped fine
8 ounces shiitake mushrooms, stemmed and sliced thin
2 tablespoons grated fresh ginger
4 garlic cloves, minced
½ teaspoon grated lime zest plus 2 tablespoons juice
3½ cups chicken broth
1½ cups long-grain white rice
4 carrots, peeled and sliced on bias ½ inch thick
1 cup frozen shelled edamame
⅓ cup unsalted dry-roasted peanuts, chopped
2 tablespoons soy sauce
1 tablespoon toasted sesame oil
2 scallions, sliced thin on bias

1 Pat chicken dry with paper towels and season with salt and pepper. Heat 1 tablespoon vegetable oil in 12-inch skillet over medium-high heat until just smoking. Add chicken and cook until golden brown on 1 side, 4 to 6 minutes; transfer to plate.

2 Add remaining 1 tablespoon vegetable oil to now-empty skillet and heat over medium heat until shimmering. Add onion, mushrooms, and ½ teaspoon salt and cook until vegetables are softened and mushrooms have released their liquid, about 5 minutes. Stir in ginger, garlic, and lime zest and cook until fragrant, about 30 seconds. Stir in broth, rice, and carrots, scraping up any browned bits. Nestle chicken, browned side up, into skillet along with any accumulated juices. Bring to simmer, then reduce heat to medium-low, cover, and simmer gently until chicken registers 160 degrees, about 10 minutes.

3 Transfer chicken to cutting board, tent loosely with aluminum foil, and let rest while finishing rice. Stir edamame into rice mixture in skillet, cover, and cook until liquid is absorbed and rice is tender, 5 to 10 minutes.

4 Off heat, stir peanuts, lime juice, soy sauce, and sesame oil into rice mixture, then season with salt and pepper to taste and gently fluff rice mixture with fork. Slice chicken into ½-inch-thick slices and arrange on top of rice. Sprinkle with scallions and serve.

SWEET-AND-SOUR SALMON WITH BOK CHOY

SERVES 4   TOTAL TIME: 45 MINUTES

WHY THIS RECIPE WORKS Looking for a fresh twist on weeknight salmon and vegetables, we turned to a Vietnamese-inspired sauce that cut through the richness of the fish and every taste bud: salty, sweet, sour, and bitter. We planned to cook all of the components in the same pan, in stages. Cooking the salmon first, a natural instinct, and letting it rest while we cooked the bok choy resulted in fishy-tasting, greasy greens. We reversed the order, browning the bok choy and wilting it with a little water to ensure the ideal tender texture. Using a nonstick skillet allowed us to cut down on oil, helpful with an already oily fish. Cooking the salmon to 125 degrees promised the perfect doneness after the fillets rested on the serving platter. We then used the skillet to cook a bright and tangy lime sauce, which needed to simmer for just a few minutes to reach the perfect consistency for drizzling over our salmon and bok choy. You will need a 12-inch nonstick skillet with a tight-fitting lid for this recipe. Serve with white rice.

⅓ cup packed brown sugar
⅓ cup lime juice (3 limes)
2 tablespoons toasted sesame oil
1 tablespoon fish sauce
2 garlic cloves, minced
1 teaspoon red pepper flakes
3 tablespoons vegetable oil
4 heads baby bok choy (4 ounces each), halved
½ cup water
4 (6-ounce) center-cut, skin-on salmon fillets, 1½ inches thick
   Salt and pepper

1 Whisk sugar, lime juice, sesame oil, fish sauce, garlic, and pepper flakes together in bowl; set aside. Heat 1 tablespoon vegetable oil in 12-inch nonstick skillet over medium-high heat until shimmering. Lay half of bok choy in skillet, cut side down, and cook until lightly browned, 2 to 3 minutes.

2 Turn bok choy over, add ¼ cup water, cover, and cook until lightly browned on second side and stems are crisp-tender, about 2 minutes. Transfer to platter and repeat with 1 tablespoon vegetable oil, remaining bok choy, and remaining water.

3 Pat salmon dry with paper towels and season with salt and pepper. Add remaining 1 tablespoon vegetable oil to now-empty skillet and heat over medium-high heat until just smoking. Carefully lay salmon in skillet, skin side up, and cook until well browned on first side, 4 to 6 minutes.

4 Flip salmon over, reduce heat to medium, and cook until center is still translucent when checked with tip of paring knife and registers 125 degrees (for medium-rare), 3 to 6 minutes; transfer to platter with bok choy.

5 Drain fat from now-empty skillet, add sugar mixture, and cook until slightly thickened and reduced to ½ cup, 3 to 4 minutes. Drizzle sauce over fish and bok choy and serve.

CUTTING YOUR OWN SALMON FILLETS

To ensure uniformly sized fillets, cut 1½-pound center-cut fillet into 4 equal pieces.

THAI CURRY RICE WITH COD

SERVES 4   TOTAL TIME: 45 MINUTES

WHY THIS RECIPE WORKS We wanted to infuse mild cod with the zesty, aromatic flavors of Thai curry and cook up a rice-and-vegetable side that was hearty enough for a satisfying dinner. This dish could easily have involved lots of prep and multiple pans, but we layered the components all in one skillet and timed everything just right for a minimalist but boldly flavored meal. To start, we enhanced our rice with meaty mushrooms and crunchy bamboo shoots; sautéing them all in a gingery scallion oil built lots of flavor quickly. After simmering the rice for 10 minutes, we laid fresh cod fillets on top, ensuring the fish and rice would finish at the same time. We prepared a supersimple red coconut curry sauce in the microwave and drizzled some over the cod to infuse the fish while it cooked. And since cod is a relatively wet fish, its natural juices flavored the rice from above, marrying all the flavors of the dish. Sprinkled with scallions and served with spoonfuls of extra sauce and a bright squeeze of lime, our cod was ready for dinner. You will need a 12-inch nonstick skillet with a tight-fitting lid for this recipe.

WEEKNIGHT FRIENDLY

1 tablespoon vegetable oil

1½ cups long-grain white rice

8 ounces white mushrooms, trimmed and sliced thin

1 (8-ounce) can bamboo shoots, rinsed

2 teaspoons grated fresh ginger

3 scallions, white and green parts separated and sliced thin

2¼ cups water

Salt and pepper

¾ cup canned coconut milk

3 tablespoons red curry paste

4 (6- to 8-ounce) skinless cod fillets, 1 to 1½ inches thick

Lime wedges

1 Heat oil in 12-inch nonstick skillet over medium heat until shimmering. Add rice, mushrooms, bamboo shoots, ginger, and scallion whites. Cook, stirring often, until edges of rice begin to turn translucent, about 2 minutes. Add water and ½ teaspoon salt and bring to boil. Cover, reduce heat to medium-low, and simmer for 10 minutes.

2 Whisk coconut milk and curry paste together in bowl. Pat cod dry with paper towels and season with salt and pepper. Lay fillets, skinned side down, on top of rice mixture and drizzle with one-third of coconut-curry sauce. Cover and cook until liquid is absorbed and cod flakes apart when gently prodded with paring knife and registers 140 degrees, 10 to 12 minutes.

3 Meanwhile, microwave remaining coconut-curry sauce mixture until warm, about 1 minute. Sprinkle scallion greens over fish and rice mixture. Serve with remaining coconut-curry sauce and lime wedges.

GRATING GINGER OR GARLIC

Peel small section of knob of ginger, then grate peeled portion using rasp-style grater. This technique can also be used to grate garlic cloves.

PASTA FRITTATA WITH SAUSAGE AND HOT PEPPERS

SERVES 4 TO 6   TOTAL TIME: 1 HOUR

WHY THIS RECIPE WORKS The best part of most pasta frittatas is the crispy pasta bits at the bottom of the pan, which contrast pleasantly with the creamy eggs. Our version takes this further by developing an entire layer of crisp, golden brown pasta, ensuring great crunch in every bite. Achieving that crust is easy—a happy result of cooking the pasta directly in the skillet. We boiled superthin angel-hair pasta in our skillet, using just 3 cups of water, along with a splash of oil. When the water fully evaporated, the tender pasta began to fry in the oil, yielding lots of crispy strands. We then stirred in eggs that we'd beaten with boldly flavored add-ins: Parmesan, olive oil (which kept the eggs tender), cherry peppers, parsley, and crumbled sausage we'd browned ahead of time. We let the frittata cook, flipping once, until set throughout. To ensure the proper texture, use angel-hair pasta. You will need a 10-inch nonstick skillet with a tight-fitting lid for this recipe. Serve the frittata warm or at room temperature, with a green salad.

8 large eggs

1 ounce Parmesan cheese, grated (½ cup)

3 tablespoons extra-virgin olive oil

3 tablespoons coarsely chopped jarred hot cherry peppers

2 tablespoons minced fresh parsley
Salt and pepper

8 ounces sweet Italian sausage, casings removed, crumbled

2 garlic cloves, sliced thin

3 cups water

6 ounces angel-hair pasta, broken in half

3 tablespoons vegetable oil

1 Whisk eggs, Parmesan, olive oil, cherry peppers, parsley, ½ teaspoon salt, and ½ teaspoon pepper in large bowl until egg is even yellow color.

2 Cook sausage in 10-inch nonstick skillet over medium heat, breaking up sausage with wooden spoon, until fat renders and sausage is about half-cooked, 3 to 5 minutes. Stir in garlic and cook until fragrant, about 30 seconds. Transfer sausage mixture (some sausage will still be raw) to bowl with egg mixture and wipe out skillet.

3 Bring water, pasta, vegetable oil, and ¾ teaspoon salt to boil in now-empty skillet over high heat, stirring occasionally. Cook, stirring occasionally, until pasta is tender, water has evaporated, and pasta starts to sizzle in oil, 8 to 12 minutes. Reduce heat to medium and cook pasta, swirling pan and scraping under edge of pasta with rubber spatula often to prevent sticking (do not stir), until bottom turns golden and starts to crisp, 5 to 7 minutes (lift up edge of pasta to check progress).

4 Using spatula, push some pasta up sides of skillet so entire pan surface is covered with pasta. Pour egg mixture over pasta. Using tongs, lift up loose strands of pasta to allow egg to flow toward pan, being careful not to pull up crisp bottom crust. Cover skillet and cook over medium heat until bottom crust turns golden brown and top of frittata is just set (egg below very top will still be raw), 5 to 8 minutes.

5 Slide frittata onto large plate. Invert frittata onto second large plate and slide it, browned side up, back into skillet. Tuck edges of frittata into skillet with rubber spatula. Continue to cook second side of frittata until light brown, 2 to 4 minutes.

6 Remove skillet from heat and let stand for 5 minutes. Invert frittata onto cutting board, cut into wedges, and serve.

SHAKSHUKA

SERVES 4   TOTAL TIME: 1 HOUR

WHY THIS RECIPE WORKS   Shakshuka is a Tunisian dish of eggs poached in a spiced tomato, onion, and pepper sauce. The key to great shakshuka is balancing the piquancy, acidity, richness, and sweetness of its ingredients. We created a sauce with plenty of flavor by sautéing onion and yellow bell pepper before incorporating some fragrant, contrasting spices, along with tomato paste for an easy umami boost. Canned piquillo peppers instantly added authentic wood fire–smoked flavor. To build a sauce, we added canned diced tomatoes and some water and simmered the mixture until thickened. To finish, we poached eight eggs directly in the sauce, covering the pan to contain the heat for efficient, even cooking, and we served our complex, rich shakshuka with a sprinkling of bright cilantro and salty, creamy feta cheese. Jarred roasted red peppers can be substituted for the piquillo peppers. Serve with pita or crusty bread to mop up the sauce. You will need a 12-inch skillet with a tight-fitting lid for this recipe.

WEEKNIGHT FRIENDLY

3 tablespoons vegetable oil
2 onions, chopped fine
2 yellow bell peppers, stemmed, seeded, and cut into ¼-inch pieces
4 garlic cloves, minced
2 teaspoons tomato paste
1 teaspoon ground cumin
1 teaspoon turmeric
   Salt and pepper
⅛ teaspoon cayenne pepper
1½ cups jarred piquillo peppers, chopped coarse
1 (14.5-ounce) can diced tomatoes
¼ cup water
2 bay leaves
⅓ cup minced fresh cilantro
8 large eggs
2 ounces feta cheese, crumbled (½ cup)

1 Heat oil in 12-inch skillet over medium-high heat until shimmering. Add onions and bell peppers and cook until softened and beginning to brown, 8 to 10 minutes. Stir in garlic, tomato paste, cumin, turmeric, 1½ teaspoons salt, ¼ teaspoon pepper, and cayenne and cook, stirring often, until tomato paste begins to darken, about 3 minutes.

2 Stir in piquillo peppers, tomatoes and their juice, water, and bay leaves and bring to simmer. Reduce heat to medium-low and cook, stirring occasionally, until sauce is slightly thickened, 10 to 15 minutes.

3 Off heat, discard bay leaves and stir in ¼ cup cilantro. Transfer 2 cups sauce to blender and process until smooth, about 1 minute. Return puree to skillet and bring sauce to simmer over medium-low heat.

4 Off heat, make 4 shallow indentations (about 2 inches wide) in surface of sauce using back of spoon. Crack 2 eggs into each indentation and season with salt and pepper. Cover and cook over medium-low heat until egg whites are just set and yolks are still runny, 5 to 10 minutes. Sprinkle with feta and remaining cilantro and serve.

POACHING EGGS FOR SHAKSHUKA

1 Make 4 shallow indentations (about 2 inches wide) in sauce using back of spoon.

2 Crack 2 eggs into each indentation and season with salt and pepper. Cover and cook over medium-low heat until egg whites are just set and yolks are still runny, 5 to 10 minutes.

FIDEOS WITH CHICKPEAS, FENNEL, AND KALE

SERVES 4   TOTAL TIME: 45 MINUTES

WHY THIS RECIPE WORKS   Paella's lesser-known cousin, fideos, boasts small toasted noodles simmered in a smoky tomato sauce. For a weeknight version, we swapped chorizo and shellfish for chickpeas, fennel, and kale. We cooked down diced tomatoes with garlic and smoked paprika to create the sauce, adding white wine for complexity, then simmered the pasta and chickpeas. A run under the broiler created a nice crunchy surface. Serve the fideos with Garlic Aïoli or lemon wedges. You will need a 12-inch broiler-safe skillet for this recipe. The skillet will be quite full once you add the pasta; we recommend using a straight-sided skillet or sauté pan for easier stirring.

8   ounces spaghettini or thin spaghetti, broken into 1- to 2-inch lengths
2   teaspoons plus 2 tablespoons extra-virgin olive oil
12 ounces kale, stemmed and cut into 1-inch pieces
1   fennel bulb, 2 tablespoons fronds minced, stalks discarded, bulb halved, cored, and sliced thin
1   onion, chopped fine
    Salt and pepper
1   (14.5-ounce) can diced tomatoes, drained and chopped fine, juice reserved
3   garlic cloves, minced
1½ teaspoons smoked paprika
2¾ cups water
1   (15-ounce) can chickpeas, rinsed
½   cup dry white wine

1 Toss pasta and 2 teaspoons oil in 12-inch broiler-safe skillet until pasta is evenly coated. Toast pasta over medium-high heat, stirring often, until browned and releases nutty aroma (pasta should be color of peanut butter), 6 to 10 minutes; transfer to bowl.

2 Add remaining 2 tablespoons oil to now-empty skillet and heat over medium heat until shimmering. Add kale, a handful at a time, sliced fennel, onion, and ¼ teaspoon salt and cook until vegetables are softened, about 5 minutes. Stir in tomatoes and cook until mixture is thick, dry, and slightly darkened in color, 4 to 6 minutes. Stir in garlic and paprika and cook until fragrant, about 30 seconds.

3 Stir in toasted pasta until thoroughly combined. Stir in water, chickpeas, wine, reserved tomato juice, ¼ teaspoon salt, and ½ teaspoon pepper. Increase heat to medium-high and simmer, stirring occasionally, until liquid is slightly thickened and pasta is just tender, 8 to 10 minutes. Meanwhile, adjust oven rack 6 inches from broiler element and heat broiler.

4 Transfer skillet to oven and broil until surface of pasta is dry with crisped, browned spots, 5 to 7 minutes. Remove skillet from oven (skillet handle will be hot). Let cool for 5 minutes, then sprinkle with fennel fronds and serve with aïoli.

Garlic Aïoli
MAKES ¾ CUP
Using a mix of vegetable oil and extra-virgin olive oil is crucial to the flavor of the aïoli.

2   large egg yolks
4   teaspoons lemon juice
1   garlic clove, minced
½   teaspoon salt
¼   teaspoon pepper
½   cup vegetable oil
¼   cup extra-virgin olive oil

Process yolks, lemon juice, garlic, salt, and pepper in food processor until combined, about 10 seconds. With processor running, slowly drizzle in vegetable oil, about 1 minute. Transfer mixture to medium bowl and, whisking constantly, slowly drizzle in olive oil. (Aïoli can be refrigerated for up to 4 days.)

PAELLA

SERVES 4 TO 6   TOTAL TIME: 1 HOUR

WHY THIS RECIPE WORKS Paella, Spain's famous rice and seafood dish, can be a big hit at restaurants but an unwieldy and time-consuming production at home. The key to re-creating this recipe was replacing the paella pan with a skillet with a tight-fitting lid and paring down both the prep work and the ingredients while keeping the dish's signature flavors intact. We began by choosing fast-cooking proteins: shrimp, chorizo, and either clams or mussels. Because the shrimp, rice, sausage, and clams all cook at different rates, we cooked them in stages, first sautéing the shrimp, followed by the sausage, and then setting them aside. We used the sausage's fat to cook the aromatics and herbs before toasting the rice, which then soaked up the flavors of clam juice, tomatoes, and saffron. We steamed the clams toward the end, letting them release their liquid into the rice. Now we had a tasty paella recipe that could be cooked in about an hour. If you can't find chorizo, use tasso, andouille, or linguiça. You will need a 12-inch nonstick skillet with a tight-fitting lid for this recipe.

WEEKNIGHT FRIENDLY

1   pound extra-large shrimp (21 to 25 per pound), peeled and deveined
½   teaspoon chili powder
¼   teaspoon pepper
2   tablespoons vegetable oil
8   ounces chorizo sausage, sliced ½ inch thick
1   onion, chopped fine
½   teaspoon minced fresh thyme or ¼ teaspoon dried
3   garlic cloves, minced
1   cup long-grain white rice
2   (8-ounce) bottles clam juice
1   (14.5-ounce) can diced tomatoes, drained
¼   teaspoon saffron threads, crumbled
12   clams or mussels, scrubbed, mussels debearded
½   cup frozen peas
2   tablespoons minced fresh parsley
    Lemon wedges

1 Pat shrimp dry with paper towels and season with chili powder and pepper. Heat 1 tablespoon oil in 12-inch nonstick skillet over medium-high heat until just smoking. Add shrimp and cook until curled and pink on both sides, about 2 minutes. Transfer to bowl and cover with aluminum foil.

2 Add remaining 1 tablespoon oil to skillet and heat until just smoking. Add chorizo and cook until lightly browned, about 3 minutes. Transfer chorizo to bowl with shrimp.

3 Add onion and thyme to fat left in skillet and cook over medium heat until onion is softened, about 5 minutes. Stir in garlic and cook until fragrant, about 30 seconds. Stir in rice and cook until grains are sizzling and lightly toasted, about 1 minute.

4 Stir in clam juice, tomatoes, and saffron, scraping up any browned bits. Bring to boil, then cover, reduce heat to low, and cook until rice is tender and liquid is absorbed, about 15 minutes.

5 Off heat, stir in cooked shrimp and chorizo. Arrange clams over top and sprinkle with peas. Cover and cook over medium heat until shellfish have opened, about 7 minutes, discarding any that don't open.

6 Remove skillet from heat and let stand, covered, for 5 minutes. Sprinkle with parsley. Serve with lemon wedges.

THE SHEET PAN

WEEKNIGHT
FRIENDLY

Chicken Leg Quarters
with Cauliflower and Shallots

The Sheet Pan Room for Plenty

Rimmed baking sheets (also called jelly roll pans, or half sheet pans in restaurant parlance) aren't just for baking or roasting vegetables. Their broad, flat surface proves perfect for preparing a full meal in one fell swoop, complete with side dishes; and the rimmed edges ensure food won't roll off in the oven. Our recipes help to bring this straightforward piece of equipment into regular rotation, turning out everything from fajitas to citrusy, buttery fish on a bed of crisp potatoes. Because they lack the high sides of a skillet or the tight seal of a Dutch oven, sheet pan cooking relies on selecting strong, flavorful ingredients that can stand up to the oven's dry heat. (Don't worry: We've already done that legwork for you.) And not all sheet pans are made equal, so allow us to steer you straight.

Perfect Placement

The oven's steady heat makes the sheet pan's perimeter hotter than the middle, so we quickly noted the importance of arranging hardy ingredients around the edges of the pan, keeping those at risk of overcooking protected in the center. We also used vegetables to prop up proteins, creating a buffer against the pan's heat and helping the dry air circulate and brown the meat more evenly.

Stagger, Don't Settle

The ideal one-pan meal should satisfy on all fronts, and that means coordinating components so they all hit the table hot and perfectly cooked, but we didn't want to limit ourselves to ingredients with similar cooking times. By staggering when ingredients were added to or removed from the pan, we were able to give each component its due time in the oven for an ideal outcome.

Elevate Your Cooking

Even lean cuts of meat render fat and release juices as they cook. While we sometimes take advantage of those juices to moisten our vegetables in the pan, when we have our hearts set on crispness, we turn to our wire rack. Placing a rack snugly in a sheet pan to cook chicken thighs or breaded pork chops kept their surfaces crisp and golden.

Pack It In

Few cooking methods are more hands-off than baking chicken or fish in aluminum foil. These packets create a gentle, steamy environment for food to cook in its own juices. We found that leaving some headroom in the packet encouraged steam to circulate for even cooking, and arranging ingredients to protect the protein from the sheet pan's direct heat helped every element reach ideal doneness at the same time.

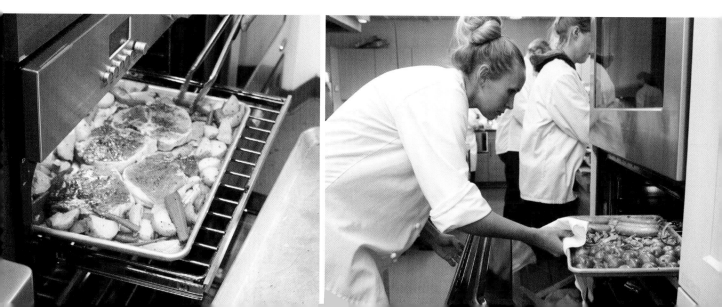

Equipping Your Kitchen

The Sheet Pan
The Unsung Hero

These pans aren't just for baking sheet cakes anymore. We discovered that there is no limit to what these broad, flat pans can do, so long as the pan has a few critical features. After broiling, roasting, and baking with the top-selling pans on the market, we picked our winner. This pan measures in at 18 by 13 inches, boasts a good, sturdy rim, and has a light-colored surface for ideal browning. Solid construction proved more important than the choice of materials: Too-flimsy, too-thin pans warp under high heat and transfer heat too intensely. Our favorite: **Nordic Ware Baker's Half Sheet** ($14.97).

HAVE AN EXTRA ON HAND

You will need only one pan to make these recipes (the only exception is our Huevos Rancheros recipe, which benefits from the insulation a second pan provides), but we recommend owning at least two sheet pans because they have so many uses.

Wire Rack
The All-Important Sidekick

The success of many of our sheet pan recipes depends on a wire rack to elevate the food for ideal crispness. A good rack should be sturdy and able to withstand a hot broiler, it should clean up without warping or damage, and it must fit inside a standard 18 by 13-inch rimmed baking sheet. Our winning model aced every test and features a grid small enough to keep food from falling through. Our favorite: **Libertyware Half Size Sheet Pan Cooling Rack** ($15.99 for a set of two).

SIZZLE WITHOUT A SKILLET

The telltale sign of a great sear is the lively hiss you hear when food hits a hot skillet or grill. When we wanted that sensation in the oven, we preheated our sheet pan to kick-start the browning process the moment our food hit the already-hot pan.

PORK TENDERLOIN WITH GREEN BEANS AND POTATOES

SERVES 4 TOTAL TIME: 1 HOUR

WEEKNIGHT
FRIENDLY

WHY THIS RECIPE WORKS We never tire of tender, mild pork tenderloin. The quick-cooking cut takes well to an array of flavors, and because it is relatively inexpensive, we are happy to serve it any night of the week. To create a satisfying one-pan meal of roasted pork and plenty of vegetables, we seasoned and scattered green beans down the middle of a sheet pan, perching two tenderloins atop the beans to protect the lean meat from drying out while the vegetables roasted and became crisp-tender. As a complement, we chose fingerling potatoes because they cook quickly, and we simply halved them and arranged them cut side down on the sheet pan for some tasty browning. Brushing a layer of hoisin sauce over the meat and roasting it for only 20 minutes produced perfectly cooked pork with balanced sweetness and an appealing caramelized sheen. While the tenderloins rested, we gave the veggies a little extra time in the oven to pick up some color. An easy garlic-chive butter, melted over the resting pork and tossed with the vegetables, made for a rich, flavorful finish. Buy tenderloins that are of equal size and weight so they cook at the same rate. A rasp-style grater makes quick work of turning the garlic into a paste; see page 69.

4 tablespoons unsalted butter, softened
2 tablespoons minced fresh chives
1 garlic clove, minced to paste
  Salt and pepper
1 pound green beans, trimmed
3 tablespoons extra-virgin olive oil
1½ pounds fingerling potatoes, unpeeled, halved lengthwise
2 (12- to 16-ounce) pork tenderloins, trimmed
¼ cup hoisin sauce

1 Adjust oven rack to lower-middle position and heat oven to 450 degrees. Combine butter, chives, garlic, ¼ teaspoon salt, and ¼ teaspoon pepper in bowl; set aside for serving.

2 Toss green beans with 1 tablespoon oil, ¼ teaspoon salt, and ¼ teaspoon pepper in separate bowl. Arrange beans crosswise down center of rimmed baking sheet, leaving room on both sides for potatoes. Toss potatoes with remaining 2 tablespoons oil, ¼ teaspoon salt, and ¼ teaspoon pepper in now-empty bowl. Place potatoes, cut side down, on either side of green beans.

3 Pat pork dry with paper towels, season with pepper, and brush thoroughly with hoisin sauce. Lay tenderloins lengthwise, without touching, on top of green beans. Roast until pork registers 145 degrees, 20 to 25 minutes.

4 Remove sheet from oven and transfer tenderloins to cutting board. Dot each tenderloin with 1 tablespoon chive butter, tent loosely with aluminum foil, and let rest while vegetables finish cooking. Gently stir vegetables on sheet to combine and continue to roast until tender and golden, 5 to 10 minutes longer.

5 Remove sheet from oven, add remaining 2 tablespoons butter to vegetables, and toss to coat. Cut pork into ½-inch-thick slices and serve with vegetables.

ROASTED SALMON, BROCCOLI, AND POTATOES WITH WHOLE-GRAIN MUSTARD SAUCE

SERVES 4   TOTAL TIME: 1 HOUR

WHY THIS RECIPE WORKS Aiming for a balanced, one-pan supper of roast salmon, broccoli, and red potatoes was setting the bar high. These three components require very different cooking times, but we embraced the challenge by using a standard one-pan technique: staggering. We knew the potatoes required the most oven time, but starting them first and adding the broccoli and salmon partway through roasting overcrowded the pan. Instead, we started out with both potatoes and broccoli, roasting them at 500 degrees for just 22 minutes—enough time for the broccoli to take on plenty of color and the spuds to soften. We removed the broccoli from the pan and arranged four salmon fillets in its place. Reducing the oven temperature to 275 degrees let the salmon roast gently while the potatoes finished cooking. In just 11 minutes, the fillets reached a juicy medium-rare and the potatoes boasted tender, creamy interiors beneath their golden-brown crusts. A sharp sauce of chopped chives, whole-grain mustard, and lemon juice gave this simple meal some real pizzazz. Use small red potatoes measuring 1 to 2 inches in diameter.

WEEKNIGHT
FRIENDLY

¼ cup minced fresh chives
5 tablespoons plus 2 teaspoons extra-virgin olive oil
2 tablespoons whole-grain mustard
2 teaspoons lemon juice, plus lemon wedges for serving
1 teaspoon honey
   Salt and pepper
4 (6- to 8-ounce) center-cut, skinless salmon fillets, 1 to 1½ inches thick
1 pound small red potatoes, unpeeled, halved
1 pound broccoli florets, cut into 2-inch pieces

1 Adjust oven rack to lowest position and heat oven to 500 degrees. Combine chives, 2 tablespoons oil, mustard, lemon juice, honey, pinch salt, and pinch pepper in bowl; set aside for serving. Pat salmon dry with paper towels, rub thoroughly with 2 teaspoons oil, and season with salt and pepper; refrigerate until needed.

2 Brush rimmed baking sheet with 1 tablespoon oil. Toss potatoes with 1 tablespoon oil, ½ teaspoon salt, and ½ teaspoon pepper in bowl. Place potatoes, cut side down, on half of sheet. In now-empty bowl, toss broccoli with remaining 1 tablespoon oil, ¼ teaspoon salt, and ¼ teaspoon pepper, then place on empty side of sheet.

3 Roast until potatoes are light golden brown and broccoli is well browned and tender, 22 to 24 minutes, rotating sheet halfway through roasting.

4 Remove sheet from oven and reduce oven temperature to 275 degrees. Transfer broccoli, browned side up, to platter; cover with aluminum foil to keep warm. Place salmon, skinned side down, on now-empty side of sheet and continue to roast until center of salmon is still translucent when checked with tip of paring knife and registers 125 degrees (for medium-rare), 11 to 15 minutes, rotating sheet halfway through roasting.

5 Remove sheet from oven. Transfer potatoes and salmon to platter with broccoli. Serve with lemon wedges and mustard sauce.

ROASTED CHICKEN WITH ROOT VEGETABLES

SERVES 4   TOTAL TIME: 1 HOUR 15 MINUTES

WHY THIS RECIPE WORKS Cooking vegetables and chicken in the same pan has its hazards: From unevenly cooked chicken to greasy, limp vegetables, this seemingly straightforward supper can easily turn out disappointing. To avoid these pitfalls, we opted for chicken parts, which contain less overall fat than a whole bird and can be spaced out so the vegetables can get more direct exposure to the oven's heat. We selected a colorful array of vegetables that take well to roasting—Brussels sprouts, red potatoes, shallots, and carrots—and seasoned them with herbs, salt, pepper, and a bit of sugar to aid in browning. We arranged the more tender sprouts in the cooler center of the pan and scattered the hardier carrots and potatoes around the perimeter. To ensure that the white meat stayed moist while the dark meat cooked through, we placed the breasts (halved to promote even cooking) in the middle of the pan atop the Brussels sprouts for insulation, and arranged the slower-cooking thighs and drumsticks over the other vegetables. A simple thyme-rosemary butter gave the chicken a rich, savory boost. Use Brussels sprouts no bigger than golf balls, as larger ones are often tough and woody.

12 ounces Brussels sprouts, trimmed and halved
12 ounces red potatoes, unpeeled, cut into 1-inch pieces
 8 shallots, peeled and halved lengthwise
 4 carrots, peeled and cut into 2-inch lengths, thick ends halved lengthwise
 6 garlic cloves, peeled
 1 tablespoon vegetable oil
 4 teaspoons minced fresh thyme or 1½ teaspoons dried
 2 teaspoons minced fresh rosemary or ¾ teaspoon dried
 1 teaspoon sugar
    Salt and pepper
 2 tablespoons unsalted butter, melted
3½ pounds bone-in chicken pieces (2 split breasts cut in half crosswise, 2 drumsticks, and 2 thighs), trimmed

1 Adjust oven rack to upper-middle position and heat oven to 475 degrees. Toss Brussels sprouts, potatoes, shallots, carrots, garlic, oil, 2 teaspoons thyme, 1 teaspoon rosemary, sugar, ¾ teaspoon salt, and ¼ teaspoon pepper together in bowl. Combine melted butter, remaining 2 teaspoons thyme, remaining 1 teaspoon rosemary, ¼ teaspoon salt, and ⅛ teaspoon pepper in second bowl. Pat chicken dry with paper towels and season with salt and pepper.

2 Place vegetables in single layer on rimmed baking sheet, arranging Brussels sprouts in center. Place chicken, skin side up, on top of vegetables, arranging breast pieces in center and thighs and drumsticks around perimeter of sheet. Brush chicken with herb butter. Roast until breasts register 160 degrees and drumsticks/thighs register 175 degrees, 35 to 40 minutes, rotating pan halfway through roasting.

3 Remove sheet from oven, tent loosely with aluminum foil, and let rest for 5 minutes. Transfer chicken to platter. Toss vegetables with pan juices, season with salt and pepper to taste, and transfer to platter. Serve.

Variation

ROASTED CHICKEN WITH FENNEL AND PARSNIPS

Substitute 1 fennel bulb, stalks discarded, bulb halved, cored, and sliced into ½-inch wedges, for Brussels sprouts, and ½ pound parsnips, peeled and cut into 2-inch pieces, for carrots.

STEAK WITH SWEET POTATOES AND SCALLIONS

SERVES 4   TOTAL TIME: 1 HOUR 15 MINUTES

WHY THIS RECIPE WORKS When we think steak dinner, some key characteristics spring to mind: tender, juicy meat, a flavorful browned crust, and robust sides like thick-cut potato wedges and a green vegetable. While we usually look to the grill or a ripping-hot skillet to turn out steaks with a strong crust, we saw potential in our sheet pan to prepare the whole meal in one go. Preheating the pan promised the sizzle we love (and the sear that comes with it). A pleasantly bitter coffee rub accentuated the meat's savoriness; chili powder added a touch of heat, and brown sugar guaranteed some appealing caramelization. We decided to use the preheating time to jump-start our sides, so we sliced sweet potatoes into wedges and let them soften in the pan as it heated up. We added the steaks 25 minutes in, scattering some scallions over the potatoes to bring some greenery to the dish. Our steaks reached a juicy medium-rare in just 12 minutes. To give our dish a final, flavorful flourish, we served our steaks with quick-pickled radishes. Don't be afraid to use all of the coffee rub on the steak—it aids in browning as well as adds flavor. The scallions should be left whole; trim off only the small roots.

10 radishes, trimmed and sliced thin
 1 tablespoon lime juice, plus lime wedges for serving
    Salt and pepper
1½ pounds sweet potatoes, unpeeled, cut lengthwise into 1-inch wedges
 2 tablespoons extra-virgin olive oil
16 scallions, trimmed
 2 (1-pound) boneless strip steaks, 1½ to 1¾ inches thick
 2 tablespoons packed dark brown sugar
 1 tablespoon finely ground coffee
 1 tablespoon chili powder

1 Adjust oven rack to lower-middle position and heat oven to 450 degrees. Toss radishes with lime juice and ¼ teaspoon salt in bowl; cover and refrigerate until serving.

2 Toss potatoes with 1½ tablespoons oil, 1 teaspoon salt, and 1 teaspoon pepper in bowl. Place potatoes, skin side down, on half of rimmed baking sheet. Roast until potatoes begin to soften, about 25 minutes.

3 Meanwhile, toss scallions with remaining ½ tablespoon oil, ¼ teaspoon salt, and ¼ teaspoon pepper in bowl. Pat steaks dry with paper towels. Combine sugar, coffee, chili powder, 1½ teaspoons salt, and 1 teaspoon pepper in small bowl, then rub thoroughly over steaks.

4 Lay scallions on top of potatoes. Place steaks on empty side of sheet. Roast until steaks register 120 to 125 degrees (for medium-rare) and potatoes are fully tender, 12 to 15 minutes, rotating sheet halfway through roasting.

5 Remove sheet from oven. Transfer steaks, bottom side up, to cutting board, tent with aluminum foil, and let rest for 5 minutes. Leave vegetables on sheet and tent with foil. Slice steaks thin against grain and serve with vegetables, pickled radishes, and lime wedges.

LEMON-HERB COD FILLETS WITH CRISPY GARLIC POTATOES

SERVES 4   TOTAL TIME: 1 HOUR 15 MINUTES

WHY THIS RECIPE WORKS Easy but elegant, this unconventional take on classic roasted cod and potatoes ensures moist, flaky fish and browned, flavorful potatoes. Seeking to avoid overcooking the fish, we used our russet potatoes as a bed to shield them from the direct heat of the pan. Rather than just pile them onto the pan, we thinly sliced the potatoes; tossed them with melted butter, garlic, and thyme for plenty of flavor; and shingled them in four individual portions for an attractive presentation. After shaping our potato rectangles, we roasted them for 30 minutes, which gave the spuds a crisp, browned exterior and removed excess moisture. We then laid a cod fillet on top of each. To highlight the fish's clean flavor and keep things easy, we topped each fillet with a small pat of butter, a sprig of fresh thyme, and a couple thin slices of lemon (which would add to the appealing look of the dish). We slid our pan back into the oven, where the dry heat melted the butter, basting the fish and drawing the herbal and citrus flavors through the fillets and down over the potatoes. After another 15 minutes, this simple yet striking dish was ready to serve. You can substitute skinless haddock or halibut for the cod.

1½ pounds russet potatoes, unpeeled, sliced into ¼-inch-thick rounds

2 tablespoons unsalted butter, melted, plus 3 tablespoons cut into ¼-inch pieces

3 garlic cloves, minced

4 sprigs fresh thyme, plus 1 teaspoon minced
Salt and pepper

4 (6- to 8-ounce) skinless cod fillets, 1 to 1½ inches thick

1 lemon, thinly sliced

1 Adjust oven rack to lower-middle position and heat oven to 425 degrees. Toss potatoes with melted butter, garlic, minced thyme, ½ teaspoon salt, and ¼ teaspoon pepper in bowl. Shingle potatoes into four 6 by 4-inch rectangular piles on rimmed baking sheet.

2 Roast until spotty brown and just tender, 30 to 35 minutes, rotating sheet halfway through roasting.

3 Pat cod dry with paper towels and season with salt and pepper. Lay 1 cod fillet, skinned side down, on top of each potato pile and top with butter pieces, thyme sprigs, and lemon slices. Bake until cod flakes apart when gently prodded with paring knife and registers 140 degrees, about 15 minutes.

4 Remove sheet from oven. Slide spatula underneath potatoes and cod and gently transfer to individual plates. Serve.

ARRANGING POTATOES

Shingle potato slices in tight rows; the rectangle should measure roughly 4 by 6 inches. Gently push rows together so that potatoes are tidy and cohesive.

HONEY MUSTARD–GLAZED CHICKEN WITH ROASTED SWEET POTATO SALAD

SERVES 4   TOTAL TIME: 1 HOUR

WHY THIS RECIPE WORKS   Honey mustard–glazed chicken is appealing because it's so easy to make, but that's no reason to settle for too-sweet store-bought sauce. We made our own balanced and superflavorful glaze by combining honey, soy sauce, mustard, and cornstarch, which we microwaved to activate the cornstarch's thickening power. Brushing on the glaze both before and after cooking ensured well-seasoned chicken with enough glaze to go around. To turn our chicken into a full meal, we assembled a salad studded with sweet potatoes, which we roasted right alongside our chicken to avoid dirtying another dish. When the potatoes were browned and tender, we tossed them with peppery arugula, thinly sliced fennel, and dried cranberries—a simple salad full of fall flavors and a perfect complement to our zesty chicken.

WEEKNIGHT
FRIENDLY

⅓ cup honey

¼ cup soy sauce

¼ cup yellow mustard

2 teaspoons cornstarch

1 pound sweet potatoes, peeled and cut into ¾-inch pieces

¼ cup extra-virgin olive oil

½ teaspoon smoked paprika
   Salt and pepper

4 (6- to 8-ounce) boneless, skinless chicken breasts, trimmed

5 ounces (5 cups) baby arugula

½ fennel bulb, stalks discarded, bulb halved, cored, and sliced thin

¼ cup dried cranberries

3 tablespoons cider vinegar

1 Adjust oven rack to middle position and heat oven to 450 degrees. Line rimmed baking sheet with aluminum foil and spray with vegetable oil spray. Combine honey, soy sauce, mustard, and cornstarch in bowl and microwave, whisking occasionally, until slightly thickened, 3 to 5 minutes. Let glaze cool slightly, then reserve half in second bowl for serving.

2 Toss sweet potatoes in third bowl with 2 tablespoons oil, paprika, and ¼ teaspoon salt and place on half of prepared sheet. Pat chicken dry with paper towels, season with salt and pepper, and coat thoroughly with remaining glaze. Place chicken on empty side of sheet.

3 Roast until chicken registers 160 degrees and sweet potatoes are tender, about 20 minutes, rotating sheet halfway through roasting.

4 Remove sheet from oven and transfer sweet potatoes to large bowl. Tent chicken loosely with foil and let rest for 5 minutes. Let sweet potatoes cool slightly, then add arugula, fennel, and cranberries. Whisk vinegar, remaining 2 tablespoons oil, ½ teaspoon salt, and ¼ teaspoon pepper together in small bowl, drizzle over salad, and toss gently. Brush chicken with reserved glaze and serve with salad.

SLICING FENNEL

1 Cut off stems and feathery fronds. Trim thin slice from base and remove any tough or blemished outer layers from bulb.

2 Cut bulb in half through base, then use paring knife to remove pyramid-shaped core. Slice each half into thin strips, cutting from base to stem end.

HALIBUT WITH RED POTATOES, CORN, AND ANDOUILLE

SERVES 4   TOTAL TIME: 1 HOUR

WHY THIS RECIPE WORKS Inspired by the summertime flavors of South Carolina's famous shrimp boil, we set out to create a one-dish feast of meaty halibut, smoky andouille sausage, corn, and potatoes, all infused with Old Bay seasoning. But instead of boiling everything in seasoned broth, we roasted our meal on a sheet pan, yearning for the crisp browning this would impart. The trick was keeping the meal mostly hands-off without letting anything overcook. The culinary jigsaw puzzle came together when we roasted the potatoes, corn, and andouille in a very hot oven, then swapped in fish for the corn and dropped the heat. Done this way, the potatoes and sausage crisped, the corn plumped, and the fish reached moist perfection. Mashing up a lemon-spiked Old Bay compound butter, which we slathered over our corn and fish, brought the seasoning's unmistakable flavor to our Lowcountry-style dinner. Note that you need to reduce the oven temperature immediately from 500 to 425 degrees after placing the fish in the oven. Use small red potatoes 1 to 2 inches in diameter.

4 tablespoons unsalted butter, softened
2 teaspoons Old Bay seasoning
1 teaspoon lemon juice
4 (6- to 8-ounce) center-cut, skinless halibut fillets, 1 inch thick
  Salt and pepper
¼ cup vegetable oil
1½ pounds small red potatoes, unpeeled, halved
4 ears corn, husks and silk removed, cut into thirds
12 ounces andouille sausage, sliced 1 inch thick
1 tablespoon minced fresh parsley

1 Adjust oven rack to lowest position and heat oven to 500 degrees. Mash butter, Old Bay, and lemon juice together in bowl; set aside for serving. Pat halibut dry with paper towels and season with salt and pepper; refrigerate until needed.

2 Brush rimmed baking sheet with 1 tablespoon oil. Toss potatoes with 2 tablespoons oil, ¼ teaspoon salt, and ¼ teaspoon pepper in bowl, then place, cut side down, on half of sheet. Toss corn in now-empty bowl with remaining 1 tablespoon oil, ¼ teaspoon salt, and ⅛ teaspoon pepper, then place on empty side of sheet. Nestle andouille onto sheet around corn. Roast until potatoes and andouille are lightly browned and corn kernels are plump, 20 to 25 minutes, rotating sheet halfway through roasting.

3 Remove sheet from oven and reduce oven temperature to 425 degrees. Transfer corn to clean bowl, leaving andouille and potatoes on sheet. Add 2 tablespoons Old Bay butter to corn, toss to coat, and cover bowl tightly with aluminum foil; set aside for serving.

4 Slide andouille to side of sheet with potatoes, then place halibut on now-empty side of sheet. Continue to roast potatoes, andouille, and halibut until fish is just opaque when checked with tip of paring knife and registers 130 degrees, 8 to 10 minutes, rotating sheet halfway through roasting.

5 Remove sheet from oven. Transfer potatoes, andouille, and halibut, browned side up, to platter. Dot remaining Old Bay butter over halibut, cover platter with aluminum foil, and let rest for 5 minutes. Add corn to platter, sprinkle with parsley, and serve.

HALIBUT IN FOIL WITH ZUCCHINI AND TOMATOES

SERVES 4   TOTAL TIME: 1 HOUR

WHY THIS RECIPE WORKS Cooking halibut *en papillote*—baking it in a tightly sealed package to steam in its own juices—is a quick, mess-free way to enhance the fish's mild flavor, and including vegetables in the pouch is a surefire path to an easy and satisfying meal. Using aluminum foil rather than parchment made packet construction simple. For vegetables, we started with zucchini (salted to remove excess moisture), which would cook in the same amount of time as the fish. To give our packets plenty of flavor without overpowering the halibut, we made a tomato "salsa," which added just the right kick. A splash of white wine boosted the flavor even more. The sealed packets needed only 15 to 20 minutes in the oven to steam and baste the fish and soften the vegetables. A final garnish of chopped basil and lemon wedges made the perfect finish. Cod, haddock, red snapper, and sea bass also work well in this recipe as long as the fillets are 1 to 1½ inches thick. Be sure to open each packet promptly after baking to prevent overcooking.

1 pound zucchini, sliced ¼ inch thick
   Salt and pepper
2 plum tomatoes, cored, seeded, and chopped
2 tablespoons extra-virgin olive oil
2 garlic cloves, minced
1 teaspoon minced fresh oregano or ¼ teaspoon dried
⅛ teaspoon red pepper flakes
¼ cup dry white wine
4 (6- to 8-ounce) skinless halibut fillets, 1 to 1½ inches thick
¼ cup chopped fresh basil
   Lemon wedges

1 Toss zucchini with ½ teaspoon salt and let drain in colander for 30 minutes; pat zucchini dry with paper towels, pressing firmly on each slice to remove as much liquid as possible. While zucchini drains, combine tomatoes, oil, garlic, oregano, pepper flakes, ¼ teaspoon salt, and ⅛ teaspoon pepper in bowl.

2 Adjust oven rack to lower-middle position and heat oven to 450 degrees. Cut eight 12-inch sheets of aluminum foil; arrange 4 flat on counter. Shingle zucchini in center of foil sheets and sprinkle with wine. Pat halibut dry with paper towels, season with salt and pepper, and place on top of zucchini. Spread tomato mixture evenly over halibut.

3 Place second square of foil on top of each piece of fish. Press edges of foil together and fold over several times until packet is well sealed and measures about 7 inches square. Place packets on rimmed baking sheet, overlapping as needed. (Packets can be refrigerated for up to 3 hours before cooking.)

4 Bake until halibut registers 140 degrees, 15 to 20 minutes. (To check temperature, poke thermometer through foil of 1 packet and into halibut.)

5 Remove sheet from oven. Transfer halibut packets to individual serving plates, open carefully (steam will escape), and slide contents onto plates. Sprinkle with basil and serve with lemon wedges.

MAKING A FOIL PACKET

1 Lay vegetables in center of foil and top with fish and tomatoes.
2 Place second foil sheet on top and fold edges of foil together to create packet.

CHICKEN PACKETS WITH POTATOES AND CARROTS

SERVES 4   TOTAL TIME: 2 HOURS

WHY THIS RECIPE WORKS Steaming food in aluminum foil gives everyone an individual packet filled with fragrant vegetables and juicy chicken, but the results can be bland and mushy. To ensure full-flavored, perfectly cooked packets, we tossed potatoes, carrots, and onion with lots of garlic browned in the microwave with olive oil, thyme, and red pepper flakes. To assemble the packets, we layered the potatoes under the chicken to protect the lean meat, leaving space for steam to circulate to ensure even cooking. Be sure to use chicken breasts that are roughly the same size to ensure even cooking. Note that this recipe calls for kosher salt, not table salt; if using table salt, cut all salt amounts by half. Be sure to refrigerate the pouches for at least 1 hour before cooking.

5 tablespoons extra-virgin olive oil

6 garlic cloves, sliced thin

1 teaspoon minced fresh thyme or ¼ teaspoon dried

¼ teaspoon red pepper flakes

12 ounces Yukon Gold potatoes, unpeeled, sliced ¼ inch thick

2 carrots, peeled, quartered lengthwise, and cut into 2-inch lengths

½ large red onion, sliced ½ inch thick, layers separated
    Kosher salt and pepper

4 (6- to 8-ounce) boneless, skinless chicken breasts, trimmed

2 tablespoons lemon juice

2 tablespoons minced fresh chives

1 Spray centers of four 20 by 12-inch sheets of heavy-duty aluminum foil with vegetable oil spray. Combine oil, garlic, thyme, and pepper flakes in large bowl and microwave until garlic begins to brown, 1 to 1½ minutes. Add potatoes, carrots, onion, and 1 teaspoon salt to garlic oil and toss to coat.

2 Pat chicken dry with paper towels. Sprinkle ⅛ teaspoon salt evenly on each side of each chicken breast, then season with pepper. Position 1 piece of prepared foil with long side parallel to edge of counter. In center of foil, arrange one-quarter of potato slices in 2 rows perpendicular to edge of counter. Lay chicken breasts on top of potato slices. Place vegetables around chicken. Drizzle any remaining garlic oil left in bowl over chicken.

3 Bring short sides of foil together and crimp to seal tightly. Crimp remaining open ends of packets, leaving as much headroom as possible inside packets. Place packets on large plate and refrigerate for at least 1 hour or up to 24 hours.

4 Adjust oven rack to lowest position and heat oven to 475 degrees. Place packets on rimmed baking sheet and bake until chicken registers 160 degrees, 18 to 23 minutes. (To check temperature, poke thermometer through foil of 1 packet and into chicken.) Remove sheet from oven and let chicken rest in packets for 3 minutes.

5 Transfer chicken packets to individual serving plates, open carefully (steam will escape), and slide contents onto plates. Drizzle lemon juice over chicken and vegetables, sprinkle with chives, and serve.

Variation

CHICKEN PACKETS WITH SWEET POTATOES AND RADISHES

Substitute 1 tablespoon grated fresh ginger for thyme, sweet potatoes for Yukon Gold potatoes, celery ribs for carrots, rice vinegar for lemon juice, and minced fresh cilantro for chives. Add 4 radishes, trimmed and quartered, to vegetables in step 1.

MEATLOAF WITH SOUR CREAM AND CHIVE SMASHED POTATOES

SERVES 4 TO 6   TOTAL TIME: 1 HOUR 45 MINUTES

WHY THIS RECIPE WORKS Meatloaf and mashed potatoes have been a staple on American tables for decades; we thought it was time to bring them together in the same sheet pan as well, rethinking elements of both to avoid a lot of hassle. Retooling our classic free-form meatloaf was straightforward: To avoid sautéing onions and aromatics in a skillet, we replaced them with garlic powder and fresh chives (the latter would also go nicely with our potatoes). Our plan for the potatoes was to skip peeling and boiling and simply roast them alongside the meatloaf until tender, then smash them. We considered starchy russets for their smooth texture, but we were after more boldly flavored smashed potatoes. Red potatoes lent great color, and their thin skin didn't require peeling, so we roasted 2 pounds of similar-size potatoes (so they'd cook evenly) and smashed them with sour cream, milk, chives, and a little vinegar for brightness. If you cannot find meatloaf mix, substitute 12 ounces each 90 percent lean ground beef and ground pork. Place the saltines in a zipper-lock bag and use a rolling pin to crush them. Use red potatoes measuring 1 to 3 inches in diameter.

½ cup ketchup
¼ cup packed light brown sugar
7 teaspoons cider vinegar
1¼ cups milk
½ cup minced fresh chives
1 large egg
2 teaspoons Dijon mustard
2 teaspoons Worcestershire sauce
½ teaspoon garlic powder
½ teaspoon dried thyme
Salt and pepper
14 square saltines, crushed (⅔ cup)
1½ pounds meatloaf mix
2 pounds medium red potatoes, unpeeled, halved
1 cup sour cream

1 Adjust oven rack to middle position and heat oven to 350 degrees. Set wire rack in rimmed baking sheet lined with aluminum foil. Fold piece of heavy-duty foil into 10 by 6-inch rectangle, lay on half of rack, then poke holes in foil with skewer about every ½ inch. Spray rack and foil with vegetable oil spray.

2 Combine ketchup, sugar, and 4 teaspoons vinegar in bowl. In large bowl, mix together ½ cup milk, ¼ cup chives, egg, mustard, Worcestershire, garlic powder,

thyme, 1 teaspoon salt, and ½ teaspoon pepper. Stir in crushed saltines. Add meatloaf mix and knead with hands until evenly blended.

3 Transfer meat mixture to foil rectangle on prepared sheet and shape into 9 by 5-inch meatloaf. Brush with half of ketchup mixture. Place potatoes in single layer on empty side of rack. Bake for 45 minutes.

4 Brush meatloaf with remaining ketchup mixture and continue to bake until meatloaf registers 160 degrees and potatoes are tender, 15 to 25 minutes. Remove sheet from oven and heat broiler. Broil meatloaf and potatoes until well browned, about 5 minutes.

5 Remove sheet from oven. Transfer meatloaf to cutting board and let rest for 10 minutes. Meanwhile, transfer potatoes to large bowl and mash coarsely with potato masher, leaving some larger chunks. Combine sour cream and remaining ¾ cup milk in bowl and microwave until warmed, about 1 minute. Fold warm sour cream mixture, remaining ¼ cup chives, remaining 1 tablespoon vinegar, ½ teaspoon salt, and ¼ teaspoon pepper into mashed potatoes. Slice meatloaf and serve with potatoes.

CHICKEN PIZZAIOLA WITH ROASTED BROCCOLI AND GARLIC BREAD

SERVES 4   TOTAL TIME: 1 HOUR

WHY THIS RECIPE WORKS Pizza-flavored chicken? We were intrigued by the idea of translating the family-friendly flavors of pizza night into a chicken dinner, complete with vegetable side and garlic bread, and preparing it using just one sheet pan. Instead of dough, we used boneless, skinless chicken breasts as our base, topping them with tomato sauce, a sprinkle of mozzarella and Parmesan cheeses, and a layer of pepperoni. While the flavors were spot-on, the pepperoni slid right off the chicken during baking. Chopping it smaller, adding it halfway through cooking—nothing could get it to adhere. A simpler fix—microwaving the pepperoni until crisp and sprinkling it on the chicken after cooking—provided the solution. All around the chicken we scattered simply seasoned broccoli, letting it roast until browned and tender. Both elements finished together, delicious and perfectly cooked. As for our garlic bread, our pan was already full, so we wrapped the bread in aluminum foil and set it directly on the rack below to warm up, which worked like a charm. We found that canned tomato sauce works well here. Depending on the size of the loaf of bread, you may need to trim it. A rasp-style grater makes quick work of turning the garlic into a paste; see page 69.

3 tablespoons extra-virgin olive oil

3 garlic cloves, minced to paste
  Salt and pepper

1 (7 by 5-inch) loaf Italian bread, halved horizontally

1 pound broccoli florets, cut into 1-inch pieces

4 (6- to 8-ounce) boneless, skinless chicken breasts, trimmed

¼ cup tomato sauce

2 ounces mozzarella cheese, shredded (½ cup)

1 ounce Parmesan cheese, grated (½ cup)

1 ounce sliced pepperoni, quartered

1 tablespoon chopped fresh basil

1 Adjust oven racks to upper-middle and lower-middle positions and heat oven to 450 degrees. Combine oil, garlic, ¼ teaspoon salt, and ¼ teaspoon pepper in bowl. Brush cut sides of bread with two-thirds of garlic oil, press bread halves back together, and wrap in aluminum foil. Toss broccoli with remaining garlic mixture.

2 Pat chicken dry with paper towels and season with salt and pepper. Place chicken in center of rimmed baking sheet and top evenly with tomato sauce. Combine mozzarella and Parmesan in separate bowl, then sprinkle over chicken. Scatter broccoli on sheet around chicken.

3 Place foil-wrapped bread on lower rack, and place sheet with chicken and broccoli on upper rack. Bake until chicken registers 160 degrees and broccoli is tender, 20 to 25 minutes, rotating sheet halfway through baking.

4 Meanwhile, microwave pepperoni on paper towel–lined plate to render fat, about 30 seconds.

5 Remove sheet from oven. Sprinkle pepperoni over chicken, tent loosely with foil, and let rest for 5 minutes. Slice garlic bread. Before serving, sprinkle basil over chicken.

BEEF FAJITAS

SERVES 4   TOTAL TIME: 45 MINUTES

WHY THIS RECIPE WORKS We love a good fajita dinner, but the thought of heating the grill and preparing all the components can relegate it to strictly restaurant fare. We took another look and decided that this seemed like a perfect opportunity to create a hands-off version using a sheet pan to cook the steak and peppers simultaneously. Without a grill's deep char, we sought other means to achieve great flavor. We started by mixing a simple spice rub, rubbing it on both our flank steak and a combination of poblano chiles and red bell peppers. We placed them all on a baking sheet pre-heated to encourage browning, and set it under the broiler. While the steak tasted great, we thought we could achieve better browning. Sugar can encourage browning, but it made the steak too sweet. So we turned to baking soda, which increases browning in baked goods. Sure enough, just ½ teaspoon helped to jump-start browning without leaving any flavor behind. To warm the tortillas, we simply wrapped them in aluminum foil and placed them directly on the lower rack while the fajitas cooked. To top the fajitas, we prepared some quick-pickled radishes with shallot and lime juice, marinating the mixture while we cooked our meal. The lime juice's acid took the harsh edge off the raw shallot and radishes and brought a welcome bite to each fajita. Serve the fajitas as is or with salsa, shredded cheese, and sour cream.

WEEKNIGHT FRIENDLY

12 (6-inch) flour tortillas

5 radishes, trimmed and sliced thin

1 shallot, sliced thin

¼ cup lime juice (2 limes), plus lime wedges for serving

1 teaspoon sugar

   Salt and pepper

2 red bell peppers, stemmed, seeded, and sliced thin

2 poblano chiles, stemmed, seeded, and sliced thin

2 tablespoons vegetable oil

1 tablespoon chili powder

1½ teaspoons ground cumin

1 (1½-pound) flank steak, trimmed

½ teaspoon baking soda

1 Adjust oven racks to middle and lowest positions, place rimmed baking sheet on upper rack, and heat oven to 450 degrees. Wrap tortillas in aluminum foil and place on lower rack. Combine radishes, shallot, lime juice, sugar, and ⅛ teaspoon salt in bowl; cover and refrigerate until serving.

2 Toss bell peppers and poblanos with 1 tablespoon oil, 1 teaspoon chili powder, ½ teaspoon cumin, and ½ teaspoon salt in bowl. Pat steak dry with paper towels. Combine remaining 2 teaspoons chili powder, remaining 1 teaspoon cumin, 1½ teaspoons salt, 1 teaspoon pepper, and baking soda together in small bowl, then rub thoroughly over steak.

3 Brush remaining 1 tablespoon oil evenly over hot sheet, lay steak in center of sheet, then scatter bell peppers and poblanos around steak. Heat broiler and broil on middle rack until steak and peppers are lightly browned and steak registers 120 to 125 degrees (for medium-rare), 6 to 10 minutes, flipping steak halfway through broiling.

4 Remove sheet from oven. Transfer steak to cutting board, tent loosely with foil, and let rest for 5 minutes. Leave vegetables on sheet, season with salt and pepper to taste, and tent with foil. Turn oven off but leave tortillas in oven until serving.

5 Slice steak against grain into ¼-inch-thick slices and transfer, along with vegetables, to platter. Serve with warmed tortillas, pickled radish mixture, and lime wedges.

TERIYAKI CHICKEN THIGHS WITH SESAME VEGETABLES

SERVES 4   TOTAL TIME: 1 HOUR 15 MINUTES

WHY THIS RECIPE WORKS We wanted an fresh take on teriyaki that would yield crispy chicken in a sweet-sticky sauce. Sheet-pan roasting proved ideal: We could crisp the chicken before applying a glaze all while preparing a vegetable "stir-fry" in the same pan. We browned chicken thighs in the oven, slashing the skin and placing them on a wire rack to render and drain away the fat. We tossed sliced bell pepper and mushrooms with garlic and ginger and spread them alongside the chicken to roast. Snap peas went in 10 minutes later so they wouldn't overcook. Briefly broiling everything crisped the thighs' skin further. As for the teriyaki sauce, a few pantry items did the trick; we thickened it in the microwave before brushing it on our chicken. Serve with white rice. Be sure to use bone-in chicken thighs for this recipe; do not substitute chicken breasts. You can substitute 5 tablespoons white wine or sake mixed with 5 teaspoons sugar for the mirin. Depending on your wire rack, you may need to place parchment paper underneath the vegetables to prevent them from falling through.

8 (5- to 7-ounce) bone-in chicken thighs, trimmed
2 tablespoons vegetable oil
1 red bell pepper, stemmed, seeded, and cut into ¼-inch-wide strips
8 ounces shiitake mushrooms, stemmed and sliced thin
3 garlic cloves, minced
1 tablespoon grated fresh ginger
8 ounces snap peas, strings removed
5 tablespoons mirin
5 tablespoons soy sauce
¼ cup water
3 tablespoons sugar
2 teaspoons cornstarch
⅛ teaspoon red pepper flakes
1 tablespoon toasted sesame oil
1 tablespoon toasted sesame seeds
½ teaspoon salt

1 Adjust oven rack to middle position and heat oven to 450 degrees. Set wire rack in rimmed baking sheet lined with aluminum foil. Make 3 diagonal slashes through skin of each thigh with sharp knife (do not cut into meat). Brush chicken with 1 tablespoon vegetable oil. Lay chicken, skin side up, on half of prepared rack and roast for 20 minutes.

2 Toss bell pepper and mushrooms in bowl with remaining 1 tablespoon vegetable oil, half of garlic, and half of ginger. Spread vegetables over empty side of rack and continue to roast for 10 minutes. Sprinkle snap peas over vegetables and continue to roast until chicken registers 165 degrees and vegetables start to brown, about 10 minutes.

3 Remove sheet from oven. Adjust oven rack 8 inches from broiler element and heat broiler. Broil chicken and vegetables until well browned and registers 175 degrees, 3 to 5 minutes.

4 While chicken and vegetables broil, combine mirin, soy sauce, water, sugar, cornstarch, pepper flakes, remaining garlic, and remaining ginger in bowl and microwave, whisking occasionally, until thickened, 3 to 5 minutes.

5 Remove sheet from oven, brush chicken with 3 tablespoons of sauce, and let rest for 5 minutes. Transfer vegetables to clean bowl, toss with sesame oil, sesame seeds, and salt. Serve vegetables and chicken with remaining sauce.

CHICKEN LEG QUARTERS WITH CAULIFLOWER AND SHALLOTS

SERVES 4 TOTAL TIME: 1 HOUR

WHY THIS RECIPE WORKS A sadly underutilized cut, chicken leg quarters take to roasting like a duck to water, growing tender as they cook while the skin crisps up beautifully. For our one-pan supper, we paired them with cauliflower, which also shines when roasted. Deeply slashing the chicken helped the seasonings (garlic, lemon zest, sage) to penetrate the meat and the fat to render for crispier skin. Arranging the chicken around the pan's edges exposed it to the oven's heat and protected the cauliflower from drying out; the chicken's juices helped soften the cauliflower. Toward the end of cooking, we scattered grape tomatoes over the cauliflower for color and juicy bursts of acidity, then used the broiler to impart pleasant charring. Note that this recipe calls for kosher salt, not table salt; if using table salt, cut all salt amounts by half. Some leg quarters are sold with the backbone attached; removing it (with a heavy chef's knife) before cooking makes the chicken easier to serve. If you substitute cherry tomatoes for grape tomatoes, halve them before adding to the pan.

WEEKNIGHT FRIENDLY

1 head cauliflower (2 pounds), cored and cut into 8 wedges through stem
6 shallots, peeled and halved
¼ cup extra-virgin olive oil
2 tablespoons chopped fresh sage or 2 teaspoons dried
Kosher salt and pepper
4 (10-ounce) chicken leg quarters, trimmed
2 garlic cloves, minced
1 teaspoon grated lemon zest, plus lemon wedges for serving
7½ ounces grape tomatoes
1 tablespoon chopped fresh parsley

1 Adjust 1 oven rack to lower-middle position and second rack 6 inches from broiler element, and heat oven to 475 degrees. Gently toss cauliflower, shallots, 2 tablespoons oil, 1 tablespoon sage, 1 teaspoon salt, and ½ teaspoon pepper together on rimmed baking sheet. Place cauliflower pieces, cut side down, in single layer in center of sheet.

2 Pat chicken dry with paper towels. Make 4 diagonal slashes through skin and meat of each leg quarter with sharp knife (each slash should reach bone). Season chicken with salt and pepper. Place each piece of chicken, skin side up, in 1 corner of sheet; rest chicken directly on sheet, not on vegetables.

3 Whisk garlic, lemon zest, remaining 2 tablespoons oil, and remaining 1 tablespoon sage together in bowl. Brush skin side of chicken with seasoned oil mixture. Transfer sheet to lower rack and roast until chicken registers 175 degrees, cauliflower is browned, and shallots are tender, 25 to 30 minutes, rotating sheet halfway through roasting.

4 Remove sheet from oven and heat broiler. Scatter tomatoes over vegetables. Place sheet on upper rack and broil until chicken skin is browned and crisp and tomatoes have begun to wilt, 3 to 5 minutes.

5 Remove sheet from oven and let rest for 5 minutes. Sprinkle with parsley and serve with lemon wedges.

SLASHING LEG QUARTERS

Using sharp knife, make 4 diagonal slashes through skin and meat of each leg quarter (each slash should reach bone).

ROASTED PORK CHOPS AND VEGETABLES WITH PARSLEY VINAIGRETTE

SERVES 4   TOTAL TIME: 1 HOUR

WHY THIS RECIPE WORKS Thick-cut bone-in pork chops deliver the succulence of a larger roast but cook in just 10 to 15 minutes, making them perfect weeknight treats. They stand up to high heat and bold flavors, so it was natural to pair them with roasted root vegetables and to season everything well for a memorably flavor-packed one-pan meal. We partially roasted the vegetables—a rustic mix of thick-sliced Yukon Gold potatoes, carrot spears, and fennel wedges—to give them a good head start. To add base notes of flavor, we tossed them with minced fresh rosemary and peeled whole garlic cloves, which turn deliciously creamy when roasted. Once the vegetables had softened and had taken on some color, we added our pork chops, which we'd seasoned with a bold rub of pepper, salt, paprika, and coriander for a deeply flavored crust. We whisked up a simple parsley vinaigrette to drizzle over the pork, ensuring our meal would end on a high note. Note that this recipe calls for kosher salt, not table salt; if using table salt, cut all salt amounts by half. Be sure to use pork chops that measure between 1 and 1½ inches thick for this recipe.

1 pound Yukon Gold potatoes, unpeeled, halved lengthwise, and cut crosswise into ½-inch-thick slices

1 pound carrots, peeled and cut into 3-inch lengths, thick ends quartered lengthwise

1 fennel bulb, stalks discarded, bulb halved, cored, and cut into ½-inch-thick wedges

10 garlic cloves, peeled

2 teaspoons minced fresh rosemary or ¾ teaspoon dried

⅓ cup extra-virgin olive oil
   Kosher salt and pepper

1 teaspoon paprika

1 teaspoon ground coriander

4 (12-ounce) bone-in center-cut pork chops, 1 to 1½ inches thick, trimmed

4 teaspoons red wine vinegar

2 tablespoons minced fresh parsley

1 small shallot, minced

⅛ teaspoon sugar

1 Adjust oven rack to upper-middle position and heat oven to 450 degrees. Toss potatoes, carrots, fennel, garlic, rosemary, 1 tablespoon oil, 1½ teaspoons salt, and ¼ teaspoon pepper together in bowl. Spread vegetables in single layer on rimmed baking sheet. Roast until beginning to soften, about 25 minutes.

2 While vegetables roast, combine 2 teaspoons salt, 1 teaspoon pepper, paprika, and coriander in bowl. Pat pork dry with paper towels and cut 2 slits, about 2 inches apart, through fat on edges of each chop. Rub chops with 1 teaspoon oil, then season thoroughly with spice mixture.

3 Lay chops on top of vegetables and continue to roast until chops register 145 degrees and vegetables are tender, 10 to 15 minutes, rotating sheet halfway through roasting.

4 Remove sheet from oven, tent loosely with aluminum foil, and let rest for 5 minutes. Whisk remaining ¼ cup oil, vinegar, parsley, shallot, sugar, ½ teaspoon salt, and ¼ teaspoon pepper together in bowl. Drizzle vinaigrette over pork before serving.

LEMON-THYME ROASTED CHICKEN WITH RATATOUILLE

SERVES 4   TOTAL TIME: 45 MINUTES

WHY THIS RECIPE WORKS Roasted chicken and ratatouille is simplicity on a plate: the flavors of summer in perfect balance. Yet despite its simple nature, the preparation can be onerous, requiring multiple pans and cooking stages for the ratatouille alone. Seeking an easier method, we turned to a sheet pan. Not only would its large surface area accommodate both the chicken and the vegetables, but exposing the food to dry heat would prevent the vegetables from becoming soggy—a hallmark of bad ratatouille. We selected bone-in chicken breasts, which gave us juicy, tender meat without being too fussy or producing too much grease. To get nicely golden skin, we preheated the baking sheet, oiled it to prevent sticking, and placed the chicken, skin side down, on the pan to sear them. We chopped eggplant and zucchini into bite-size pieces and tossed them with canned tomatoes (ideal for year-round cooking), seasoning them with garlic and plenty of thyme to drive home the authentic flavor. We scattered the vegetables opposite the chicken. Halfway through roasting, we flipped the chicken, stirred the vegetables, and added lemon wedges to roast for a flavor boost. Peeking in 5 minutes later, we stirred the vegetables again—they were really beginning to soften—and then once more to ensure that every piece was cooked and all the excess liquid could evaporate. Minutes later, our chicken was ready, the ratatouille was tender and moist but not wet, and we even had juicy roasted lemon wedges to squeeze over everything. All that was missing was some crusty bread.

WEEKNIGHT FRIENDLY

1 (14.5-ounce) can diced tomatoes, drained
12 ounces eggplant, cut into ½-inch pieces
2 zucchini (6 ounces each), cut into ½-inch pieces
3 tablespoons extra-virgin olive oil
1 tablespoon minced fresh thyme or 1½ teaspoons dried
2 garlic cloves, minced
  Salt and pepper
4 (10- to 12-ounce) bone-in split chicken breasts, trimmed
1 lemon, quartered
2 tablespoons minced fresh parsley

1 Adjust oven rack to upper-middle position, place rimmed baking sheet on rack, and heat oven to 450 degrees. Toss tomatoes, eggplant, zucchini, 2 tablespoons oil, 1 teaspoon thyme, garlic, ½ teaspoon salt, and ¼ teaspoon pepper together in bowl. Pat chicken dry with paper towels and season with salt, pepper, and remaining 2 teaspoons thyme.

2 Brush remaining 1 tablespoon oil evenly over hot sheet. Place chicken, skin side down, on 1 side of sheet and spread vegetables in single layer on other side. Roast until chicken releases from sheet and vegetables begin to wilt, about 10 minutes.

3 Flip chicken, skin side up, and stir vegetables. Place lemon quarters, cut side down, on sheet. Continue to roast, stirring vegetables occasionally, until chicken registers 160 degrees and vegetables are tender, 10 to 15 minutes.

4 Remove sheet from oven, tent loosely with aluminum foil, and let rest for 5 minutes. Transfer chicken to platter. Toss vegetables with pan juices, season with salt and pepper to taste, and transfer to platter. Sprinkle parsley over vegetables and serve with roasted lemon wedges.

CRUNCHY PARMESAN-CRUSTED PORK CHOPS WITH WINTER SQUASH AND CRANBERRY SAUCE

SERVES 4 TOTAL TIME: 1 HOUR

WHY THIS RECIPE WORKS Our goal was a menu of fall flavors—but with little work. We wanted pork chops that stayed crunchy, succulent roasted squash, and a cranberry sauce to boot. To achieve this, we found an unlikely sidekick in the microwave, which helped us prepare each element with ease. For pork chops with maximum crunch, we wanted a coating of Parmesan-seasoned panko, but it didn't brown sufficiently in the oven. Pretoasting the panko in the microwave with some oil proved the key to a perfectly browned crust on our juicy chops. Elevating the pork on a wire rack ensured our crust stayed crunchy. As for our side, we sliced acorn squash into rings for a beautiful scalloped shape, then softened them in the microwave so they would finish roasting at the same time as the pork. A sweet-tart cranberry sauce rounded out our menu. The microwave helped again here; it easily cooked our cranberries, producing the perfect sauce for our hearty roasted dinner. For more instructions on toasting panko, see page 194.

¼ cup all-purpose flour

2 large eggs

3 tablespoons Dijon mustard

2 cups panko bread crumbs, toasted

2 ounces Parmesan cheese, grated (1 cup)

¼ cup minced fresh parsley

3 tablespoons extra-virgin olive oil
    Salt and pepper

4 (6- to 8-ounce) boneless pork chops, ¾ to 1 inch thick, trimmed

1 large acorn squash (2 pounds), sliced into ½-inch-thick rings and seeded

1 cup plus 1 tablespoon sugar

12 ounces (3 cups) fresh or thawed frozen cranberries

¼ cup water

¼ teaspoon five-spice powder

1 Adjust oven rack to middle position and heat oven to 425 degrees. Spread flour into shallow dish. Whisk eggs and mustard together in second shallow dish. Toss toasted panko, Parmesan, parsley, and 2 tablespoons oil together in third shallow dish and season with salt and pepper.

2 Spray wire rack with vegetable oil spray, then set in rimmed baking sheet lined with aluminum foil. Pat pork dry with paper towels, cut 2 slits, about 2 inches apart, through fat on edges of each pork chop, and season with salt and pepper. Working with 1 chop at a time, dredge in flour, dip in egg mixture, then coat with toasted panko mixture, pressing gently to adhere. Lay breaded chops on 1 side of prepared wire rack, spaced at least ¼ inch apart.

3 Meanwhile, place squash on large plate, brush with remaining 1 tablespoon oil, and season with salt and pepper. Microwave squash until it begins to soften but still holds its shape, 8 to 10 minutes.

4 Place squash on prepared wire rack opposite pork, slightly overlapping if needed, and sprinkle with 1 tablespoon sugar. Bake pork chops and squash until chops register 145 degrees and squash is lightly tender, 20 to 30 minutes. Remove sheet from oven and let rest for 5 minutes.

5 While chops bake, combine cranberries, remaining 1 cup sugar, water, five-spice powder, and ¼ teaspoon salt in bowl and microwave, stirring occasionally, until cranberries are broken down and juicy, about 10 minutes. Coarsely mash cranberries with fork and serve with pork chops and squash.

HERBED SALMON CAKES WITH ASPARAGUS AND LEMON-HERB SAUCE

SERVES 4   TOTAL TIME: 45 MINUTES

WHY THIS RECIPE WORKS A good salmon cake delivers rich flavor and tender texture; the best veers away from flavor-muting binders at all costs. We used a food processor to chop salmon into a mix of both fine and larger pieces for a varied and not overly dense texture. A single slice of bread provided just enough binding, and a combination of shallot, parsley, mustard, and capers complemented the salmon; a bit of mayonnaise ensured our patties would stay moist. Broiling the patties made them easy to flip and kept them from overcooking. We arranged them on one end of a baking sheet, leaving plenty of room for a broiler-friendly vegetable—asparagus—to cook simultaneously. A quick lemon and parsley sauce added a touch of class. Be sure to use raw salmon here; do not substitute cooked or canned salmon. Don't overprocess the salmon in step 2, or the cakes will have a pasty texture. Lay the salmon cakes close together on the baking sheet so that the asparagus has a little extra space for browning.

WEEKNIGHT FRIENDLY

Lemon-Herb Sauce
- ¼ cup mayonnaise
- 1 tablespoon lemon juice
- 1 scallion, minced
- 2 teaspoons minced fresh parsley
  Salt and pepper

Salmon Cakes and Asparagus
- 1 slice hearty white sandwich bread, torn into 1-inch pieces
- 1 pound skinless salmon, cut into 1-inch pieces
- 1 shallot, minced
- 2 tablespoons mayonnaise
- 2 tablespoons minced fresh parsley
- 1 tablespoon Dijon mustard
- 2 teaspoons capers, rinsed and minced
  Salt and pepper
- 1 pound asparagus, trimmed
- 1 teaspoon extra-virgin olive oil

1 **For the lemon-herb sauce** Combine all ingredients in bowl and season with salt and pepper to taste. Cover and refrigerate until serving.

2 **For the salmon cakes and asparagus** Adjust oven rack 3 inches from broiler element and heat broiler. Pulse bread in food processor to coarse crumbs, about 4 pulses, then transfer to large bowl; you should have about ¾ cup crumbs. Working in 2 batches, pulse salmon in food processor until coarsely ground, about 4 pulses; transfer to bowl with bread crumbs and toss to combine.

3 Whisk shallot, mayonnaise, parsley, mustard, capers, ½ teaspoon salt, and ⅛ teaspoon pepper together in small bowl, then gently fold into salmon mixture until well combined. Divide salmon mixture into 4 equal portions and gently pack into 1-inch-thick patties.

4 Place salmon cakes on 1 side of rimmed baking sheet. Toss asparagus with oil, ½ teaspoon salt, and ¼ teaspoon pepper and spread in single layer on empty side of sheet. Broil until cakes are lightly browned on both sides, barely translucent at center, and register 120 to 125 degrees (for medium-rare), and asparagus is lightly browned and tender, 8 to 12 minutes, flipping cakes and turning asparagus halfway through broiling.

5 Remove sheet from oven, transfer salmon and asparagus to platter, and let rest for 5 minutes. Serve with lemon-herb sauce.

CHORIZO, CORN, AND TOMATO TOSTADAS WITH LIME CREMA

SERVES 4   TOTAL TIME: 45 MINUTES

WHY THIS RECIPE WORKS Tostadas are flat, crisped tortillas that serve as a crunchy base for rich, flavorful toppings. While they are often eaten as snacks, we wanted a meal-size version, so we piled on plenty of toppings. All these components could easily become laborious, so to simplify things we used a sheet pan to brown chorizo and corn, then smartly deployed our other ingredients. While the chorizo and corn cooked, we warmed tostadas—spread with a flavorful black bean-jalapeño mixture—directly on the oven rack below. In addition to using the chiles, we tossed some of their brine with the beans for added flavor, and tossed more of it with coleslaw mix for a quick-pickled cabbage topping. Fresh cherry tomatoes and lime juice added tang; more lime juice went into an easy crema that brought richness. Sprinkled with queso fresco and cilantro, our tostadas were hefty enough for a meal and hit all of our taste buds. Look for tostadas next to the taco kits at most supermarkets; our favorite brand of tostadas is Mission Tostadas Estilo Casero.

1 (14-ounce) bag green coleslaw mix
1 tablespoon finely chopped jarred jalapeños, plus ¼ cup brine
 Salt and pepper
½ cup sour cream
3 tablespoons lime juice
8 ounces Spanish-style chorizo sausage, halved lengthwise and sliced ¼ inch thick
4 ears corn, kernels cut from cobs
1 tablespoon vegetable oil
1 (15-ounce) can black beans, rinsed
¼ cup vegetable broth
12 (6-inch) corn tostadas
6 ounces cherry tomatoes, quartered
4 ounces queso fresco or feta cheese, crumbled (1 cup)
¼ cup fresh cilantro leaves

1 Adjust oven racks to upper-middle and lower-middle positions, place rimmed baking sheet on upper rack, and heat oven to 450 degrees. Toss coleslaw mix with 3 tablespoons jalapeño brine in bowl and season with salt and pepper to taste; set aside for serving. In second bowl, whisk sour cream and 2 tablespoons lime juice together; set aside for serving.

2 Combine chorizo, corn, and oil together in third bowl and spread in single layer on hot sheet. Cook until browned, about 15 minutes.

3 While the chorizo and corn are roasting, combine beans, broth, jalapeños, and remaining 1 tablespoon brine in clean bowl and microwave until warm, about 2 minutes. Mash beans with potato masher until spreadable, season with salt and pepper to taste, and spread evenly over tostadas. During final 5 minutes of roasting chorizo, place tostadas directly on lower oven rack to warm through.

4 Remove sheet from oven, transfer chorizo-corn mixture to large bowl, and stir in tomatoes and remaining 1 tablespoon lime juice. Divide mixture evenly among tostadas. Top tostadas with slaw, lime crema, queso fresco, and cilantro. Serve.

BRATWURST SANDWICHES WITH RED POTATO AND KALE SALAD

SERVES 4   TOTAL TIME: 45 MINUTES

WHY THIS RECIPE WORKS To elevate bratwurst sandwiches, typically reserved for game day, into a complete meal perfect for any day, we highlighted their meaty flavor with a mustardy potato and baby kale salad, using a sheet pan to make the cooking easy. We started by roasting brats, potatoes, and onions all together on the sheet pan. By selecting small red potatoes and cutting them in half, we could roast everything for the same amount of time, keeping the process supersimple. While the sausage and vegetables were cooking, we quickly whisked together a flavorful vinaigrette of whole-grain mustard, red wine vinegar, and olive oil. We spread the same whole-grain mustard into the toasty buns to match our vinaigrette's flavor profile. As soon as they hit the salad bowl, the warm potatoes absorbed plenty of our zippy vinaigrette and, with the addition of baby kale and sliced radishes, gave us a the perfect side to serve with our brats. Toasting the buns on the rack saved us the use of a pan and mimicked the feel of grilled buns. Use small red potatoes measuring 1 to 2 inches in diameter.

WEEKNIGHT FRIENDLY

1 pound small red potatoes, unpeeled, halved
7 tablespoons extra-virgin olive oil
  Salt and pepper
2 red onions, halved and sliced ¼ inch thick
1 pound bratwurst (4 sausages)
2 tablespoons red wine vinegar
¼ cup whole-grain mustard
4 hot dog buns
5 ounces (5 cups) baby kale
4 radishes, trimmed and sliced thin

1 Adjust oven rack to middle position, place rimmed baking sheet on rack, and heat oven to 425 degrees. Toss potatoes with 2 tablespoons oil, ½ teaspoon salt, and ¼ teaspoon pepper in bowl. In separate bowl, toss onions with 1 tablespoon oil.

2 Place bratwurst on 1 side of hot sheet and spread potatoes, cut side down, on other side. Scatter onions around bratwurst on sheet. Roast until sausages register 160 degrees and potatoes are tender, 25 to 30 minutes, flipping bratwurst halfway through roasting.

3 While the bratwurst and vegetables are roasting, whisk remaining ¼ cup oil, vinegar, 2 tablespoons mustard, ½ teaspoon salt, and ¼ teaspoon pepper together in large bowl.

4 Remove sheet from oven. Add potatoes to dressing in large bowl and toss to coat; cover to keep warm. Tent onions and bratwurst, still on sheet, with aluminum foil to keep warm. Place hot dog buns directly on rack and toast until lightly browned, about 5 minutes.

5 Remove rolls from oven. Spread remaining 2 tablespoons mustard evenly into rolls, then top with bratwurst and onions. Add kale and radishes to potatoes and toss gently to combine. Serve immediately with sandwiches.

ITALIAN SAUSAGE WITH PEPPERS, ONIONS, TOMATOES, AND POLENTA

SERVES 4   TOTAL TIME: 1 HOUR

WEEKNIGHT
FRIENDLY

WHY THIS RECIPE WORKS Dinner doesn't get more comforting than roasted sausage served with a tomatoey sauce of peppers and onions and cheesy polenta. To streamline this classic combo, avoiding multiple bubbling pots, we cooked everything together on a sheet pan. A hot pan meant we could not only brown our sausages nicely but also give our onions and peppers the slightly charred edge that we love. To get our vegetables saucy quickly, we used grape tomatoes, which broke down easily, giving the onions and peppers a bright, acidic finish to complement the sausages. To adapt polenta to our sheet pan and keep things simple, we started with a cooked log, sliced it in half, and roasted the pieces alongside everything else. Since it didn't brown up much by the time everything else was cooked, we flipped it over, sprinkled it with some Parmesan, and broiled the whole sheet to achieve good caramelization, not only on the polenta but on the sausages, onions, and peppers too—a satisfying finish to our rustic dinner.

¼ cup extra-virgin olive oil

12 ounces grape tomatoes

1 onion, halved and sliced thin

1 red bell pepper, stemmed, seeded, and cut into ¼-inch-wide strips

1 garlic clove, minced

1 teaspoon minced fresh rosemary
 Salt and pepper

1 pound sweet or hot Italian sausage

1 (18-ounce) tube cooked polenta, sliced in half lengthwise

1 ounce Parmesan cheese, grated (½ cup)

2 tablespoons chopped fresh basil

1 Adjust oven rack to upper-middle position and heat oven to 450 degrees. Brush rimmed baking sheet with 1 tablespoon oil.

2 Toss tomatoes, onion, bell pepper, remaining 3 tablespoons oil, garlic, rosemary, ½ teaspoon salt, and ¼ teaspoon pepper together in large bowl. Scatter tomato mixture evenly over half of prepared sheet. Place sausages and polenta, cut side down, on empty side of sheet.

3 Roast until sausages are browned and reach 160 degrees, 25 to 30 minutes, flipping halfway through roasting. Remove sheet from oven and heat broiler.

4 Turn polenta over and sprinkle with Parmesan. Broil polenta and sausages until Parmesan is bubbly and beginning to brown, 3 to 5 minutes. Remove sheet from oven, transfer polenta to cutting board, and slice into 1-inch-thick pieces. Sprinkle basil over polenta and serve with sausages and tomato mixture.

PORK AND BROCCOLI RABE CHEESESTEAK SANDWICHES

SERVES 4   TOTAL TIME: 1 HOUR

WHY THIS RECIPE WORKS The underdog rival for the title of Philly's best sandwich loads up a hoagie (aka Italian sub) roll with juicy pork, garlicky broccoli rabe, provolone, and vinegary hot peppers: a feast in a bun. Sandwich shops prepare each component separately hours in advance, but for a streamlined home version, we roasted the meat, greens, and peppers side by side on a sheet pan. For our meat, we skipped the standard roasted pork shoulder (too big, too slow) in favor of quick-cooking pork tenderloin. To ensure it was flavorful and juicy, we seasoned it heavily with rosemary and fennel seeds, and then roasted it until just cooked through, keeping the center slightly pink. We then shaved it as thinly as possible to mimic the usual shreds of long-cooked pork shoulder. Finally, we tossed it with some oil and vinegar to punch up the flavor and keep it moist. Alongside the tenderloin, we roasted our vegetables: broccoli rabe, tossed with lots of garlic and some pepper flakes for added dimensions of flavor; and sweet red bell pepper, which complemented the bitter greens. While the meat rested, we used our pan to toast the rolls; slices of provolone melted over the buns gave us the extra richness we needed to make these sandwiches perfect.

WEEKNIGHT FRIENDLY

1 (16-ounce) pork tenderloin, trimmed
6 tablespoons extra-virgin olive oil
  Salt and pepper
1 tablespoon minced fresh rosemary
1 tablespoon fennel seeds
1 pound broccoli rabe, trimmed and cut into 1-inch pieces
4 garlic cloves, minced
1 teaspoon red pepper flakes
2 red bell peppers, stemmed, seeded, and sliced thin
4 (6-inch) Italian sub rolls, split lengthwise
6 ounces sliced provolone cheese
2 tablespoons red wine vinegar

1 Adjust oven rack to middle position and heat oven to 450 degrees. Rub tenderloin with 2 tablespoons oil, season with salt and pepper, and sprinkle with rosemary and fennel seeds. Place on 1 side of rimmed baking sheet and roast for 10 minutes.

2 Toss broccoli rabe with 2 tablespoons oil, garlic, and pepper flakes in bowl. In separate bowl, toss bell peppers with 1 tablespoon oil and season with salt and pepper. Remove sheet from oven and flip pork. Spread broccoli rabe and bell peppers on hot sheet next to pork. Continue to roast until pork reaches 145 degrees and broccoli rabe and bell peppers are browned, about 20 minutes.

3 Remove sheet from oven. Transfer pork to cutting board, tent loosely with aluminum foil, and let rest for 5 minutes. Transfer vegetables to bowl and cover with foil to keep warm. Wipe sheet clean with paper towels, lay split rolls open on sheet, and top with cheese. Bake rolls until bread is lightly toasted and cheese is melted, about 5 minutes.

4 Slice pork as thinly as possible, transfer to clean bowl, and toss with remaining 1 tablespoon oil and vinegar. Nestle pork, broccoli, and bell peppers into warm rolls and serve.

BREAKFAST PIZZA

SERVES 6   TOTAL TIME: 1 HOUR 15 MINUTES

WHY THIS RECIPE WORKS Putting egg on pizza creates an easy, unexpected upgrade to Sunday brunch. The trick is achieving a crisp, golden-brown crust without overcooking the eggs. To do that, we parbaked the crust for 5 minutes before adding the toppings. The remaining baking time cooked the eggs perfectly, with golden just-set yolks. To ensure all the eggs cooked at the same rate, we formed little wells in our shredded cheese topping to contain the eggs so they wouldn't run all over the pizza. A bonus layer of cottage cheese seasoned with spices and rendered bacon fat under the eggs tethered the elements together with a silky creaminess. A sprinkle of crispy bacon, precooked in the sheet pan, added smoky flavor, and baking the crust in some of the bacon's fat ensured maximum crispiness. Small-curd cottage cheese is sometimes labeled "country style." Room-temperature dough is much easier than cold to shape, so pull the dough from the fridge about 1 hour before you start cooking.

6 slices bacon

8 ounces mozzarella cheese, shredded (2 cups)

1 ounce Parmesan cheese, grated (½ cup)

4 ounces (½ cup) small-curd cottage cheese

¼ teaspoon dried oregano

Salt and pepper

Pinch cayenne pepper

1 pound store-bought pizza dough, room temperature

1 tablespoon extra-virgin olive oil

6 large eggs

2 scallions, sliced thin

1 Adjust oven racks to middle and lowest positions and heat oven to 400 degrees. Place bacon in single layer on rimmed baking sheet and cook on upper rack until crisp, about 15 minutes, rotating sheet halfway through baking. Transfer bacon to paper towel–lined plate, let cool slightly, then crumble. Transfer rendered bacon fat to small bowl and reserve. Let sheet cool to room temperature, about 10 minutes.

2 Increase oven temperature to 500 degrees. Combine mozzarella and Parmesan in bowl. In separate bowl, combine cottage cheese, oregano, ¼ teaspoon pepper, cayenne, and 1 tablespoon reserved bacon fat. Brush 1 tablespoon bacon fat over cooled, now-empty sheet.

3 Press and roll dough into 15 by 11-inch rectangle on lightly floured counter, then transfer to prepared sheet and push to edges of pan. Brush edges of dough with oil. Bake on lower rack until top of crust appears dry and bottom is just beginning to brown, about 5 minutes.

4 Remove sheet from oven and press on air bubbles with spatula to flatten. Spread cottage cheese mixture evenly over crust, leaving 1-inch border around edge, then sprinkle with crumbled bacon and cheese mixture. Using back of spoon, hollow out six 3-inch-wide holes in cheese. Crack 1 egg into each hole and season each with salt and pepper.

5 Continue to bake pizza until crust is light golden around edges and eggs are just set, 9 to 10 minutes for slightly runny yolks or 11 to 12 minutes for soft-cooked yolks, rotating sheet halfway through baking.

6 Remove sheet from oven. Transfer pizza to cutting board and let cool for 5 minutes. Sprinkle with scallions, slice, and serve.

HUEVOS RANCHEROS

SERVES 4   TOTAL TIME: 1 HOUR 15 MINUTES

WHY THIS RECIPE WORKS To make huevos rancheros more manageable, we prepared them on a sheet pan. We built a strong tomato sauce by roasting diced tomatoes, onion, and chiles on the pan for concentrated flavors and nice char. Stirring in the tomato juice created a saucy bed for our eggs. After sprinkling on pepper Jack cheese, we created eight wells with a spoon, then cracked in our eggs. We soon discovered that the key to oven-poached eggs was adding a second baking sheet for insulation, but was it still a one-pan meal? The second pan didn't need washing, so we think so. We like our eggs slightly runny; if you prefer well-done eggs, cook them to the end of the time range in step 4. Use heavyweight rimmed baking sheets; flimsy sheets will warp. Serve with hot sauce.

2   (28-ounce) cans diced tomatoes
1   tablespoon packed brown sugar
1   tablespoon lime juice
1   onion, chopped
½   cup canned chopped green chiles
¼   cup extra-virgin olive oil
3   tablespoons chili powder
4   garlic cloves, sliced thin
    Salt and pepper
8   (6-inch) corn tortillas
4   ounces pepper Jack cheese, shredded (1 cup)
8   large eggs
1   avocado, halved, pitted, and diced
2   scallions, sliced thin
¼   cup minced fresh cilantro

1 Adjust oven racks to lowest and middle positions and heat oven to 500 degrees. Drain tomatoes in fine-mesh strainer set over bowl, pressing with rubber spatula to extract as much juice as possible. Combine 1¾ cups drained tomato juice, sugar, and lime juice in bowl and set aside; discard extra drained juice.

2 Combine tomatoes, onion, chiles, oil, chili powder, garlic, and ½ teaspoon salt in bowl, then spread mixture out evenly on rimmed baking sheet. Wrap tortillas in aluminum foil and place on lower rack. Place sheet with tomato mixture on upper rack and roast until charred in spots, 35 to 40 minutes, stirring and redistributing into even layer halfway through roasting.

3 Remove sheet from oven and place inside second rimmed baking sheet. Carefully stir reserved tomato juice mixture into roasted vegetables, season with salt and pepper to taste, and spread into even layer. Sprinkle cheese over top and, using back of spoon, hollow out eight 3-inch-wide holes in mixture. Crack 1 egg into each hole and season with salt and pepper.

4 Bake until whites are just beginning to set but still have some movement when sheet is shaken, 7 to 8 minutes for slightly runny yolks or 9 to 10 minutes for soft-cooked yolks, rotating sheet halfway through baking.

5 Remove sheet from oven and top with avocado, scallions, and cilantro. To serve, slide spatula underneath eggs and sauce and gently transfer to warm tortillas.

MAKING HUEVOS RANCHEROS

1 Using back of spoon, hollow out eight 3-inch wells.
2 Crack 1 egg into each hole.

THE DUTCH OVEN

WEEKNIGHT FRIENDLY

Italian Sausage with White Beans and Kale.

The Dutch Oven The Original Low-and-Slow Vessel

The pride of every kitchen, the Dutch oven is on every gift registry and in every well-stocked cabinet (if it ever sees a day when it's not in use). A good Dutch oven is a kitchen essential, heavy and thick enough to conduct and retain heat and deep enough to handle large cuts of meat and quarts of cooking liquid. While this vessel is ideal for braises, stews, and chilis (all of which we feature in this chapter), we asked this pot to do much more.

Cook Pasta in the Sauce

Dutch ovens are perfect for serving up a pasta feast, but to keep our recipes truly one-pan we needed to eliminate the pot of boiling water. The key to cooking pasta through without all that water is to use an intensely flavored, moisture-heavy cooking liquid that can easily work as a sauce. We like using combinations of water, wine, the liquid from canned tomatoes, and broth, depending on the flavor profile of the dish. This trick saved time and turned out a pot of fully loaded pasta.

Steam the Sides

When we wanted sides that didn't disappear into the dish, we looked to our steamer basket to hold vegetables above the fray. Placing our steamer basket above the protein and cooking liquid allowed vegetables like broccoli and asparagus to steam through under the Dutch oven's tight seal without turning soggy, a trick that made it easy to serve up a distinct side right from the same pot containing even the sauciest entrée.

Natural Body Builders

Great stews are defined by their thick, rich texture. Rather than lengthen our ingredient lists with added thickening agents, we used the low-and-slow cooking technique to our stews' advantage, allowing starchy ingredients to break down and add body naturally. From cooking sweet potatoes until they started to disintegrate to simmering quinoa until it sloughed off its starch, our best thickeners were right there all along.

ENAMEL CLEANUP

Dutch ovens are prone to staining, and while we're not concerned with keeping ours pristine, staining is problematic when the bottom of the pot darkens so much that we can't monitor browning. The best way to deep-clean a stained pot is to let it soak overnight in a solution of one part bleach and three parts water, and then wash thoroughly with soap and water.

Equipping Your Kitchen

Dutch Oven
The King of the Home Kitchen

A heavyweight Dutch oven is a piece you'll have for years, and during our extensive tests, our preferences were clear: Look for a heavy enameled cast-iron pot with a tight-fitting lid. Too-narrow pots make browning a chore, so we prefer Dutch ovens that are at least 8 inches wide and can hold 6 quarts or more. Light-colored interiors lead to uneven browning, so we stick to pots with creamy-colored enamel. In this category we have two winners: The first is the gold standard of Dutch ovens, built to last a lifetime, while its mate is a more affordable, slightly heavier option we also love. Our favorites: **Le Creuset 7¼-Quart Round French Oven** ($349.95) and **Cuisinart 7 Qt. Round Covered Casserole** ($121.94).

Steamer Basket
The Unexpected Accessory

We didn't expect to be reaching for our steamer basket for these recipes, but this piece made it possible to pair steamed vegetables with slow-cooking (and saucy) main dishes like Smothered Pork Chops with Broccoli (page 141) and Braised Blade Steaks with Mushrooms, Vidalias, and Steamed Asparagus (page 142). The legs were just high enough to lift spears of asparagus or broccoli florets above a bubbling braise, and the perforated basket allowed escaping steam to cook the vegetables to perfection. Despite a host of new baskets on the market, the classic collapsible stainless steel models still won us over every time. Our favorite: **OXO Good Grips Pop-Up Steamer** ($16.99).

PREFER A LIGHTER POT?

Sometimes hauling out a 13-pound Dutch oven for a simple meal can seem excessive. Lacking the enameled surface, lighter stainless-steel models tend to run a little hot, but these pots can still produce a gorgeous fond and will work just as well with all of our recipes. Our favorite: **All-Clad Stainless 8-Quart Stockpot** ($279.95).

CHICKEN IN A POT WITH RED POTATOES, CARROTS, AND SHALLOTS

SERVES 4   TOTAL TIME: 2 HOURS

WHY THIS RECIPE WORKS   It sounded so simple: Add root vegetables to classic *poulet en cocotte*, where a chicken bakes in a covered pot, yielding unbelievably tender meat (albeit with soft skin) and a sauce of the chicken's own concentrated juices. But after an hour of baking, the vegetables were underdone. Adding jus-weakening liquid was a faux pas, yet we forged ahead, adding chicken broth and wine for acidity and mild sweetness. Now we had tender vegetables, but the jus had lost intensity. To counter that, we browned the chicken to build fond, which deepened the jus, and sautéed our potatoes, carrots, and shallots. With some browning on our bird, we were reluctant to put on the lid, but was that still critical? The increased liquid in the Dutch oven's confined space meant an uncovered roasting might intensify the sauce without evaporating too much, while bathing our vegetables in flavor. The domino effect we'd started by adding vegetables paid off, and we were left with succulent meat, crisped skin, superflavorful vegetables, and a killer sauce.

1 (3½- to 4-pound) whole chicken, giblets discarded
   Salt and pepper
1 tablespoon vegetable oil
1½ pounds red potatoes, unpeeled, cut into 1-inch pieces
1 pound carrots, peeled and cut into 1-inch pieces
4 shallots, peeled and halved
3 garlic cloves, minced
1 teaspoon minced fresh thyme or ¼ teaspoon dried
½ cup dry white wine
½ cup chicken broth, plus extra as needed
1 bay leaf
2 tablespoons unsalted butter
1 tablespoon lemon juice
1 tablespoon minced fresh parsley

1 Adjust oven rack to lower-middle position and heat oven to 350 degrees. Pat chicken dry with paper towels, tuck wingtips behind back, and season with salt and pepper. Heat oil in Dutch oven over medium-high heat until just smoking. Add chicken, breast side down, and brown lightly, about 5 minutes. Carefully flip chicken breast side up and cook until back is well browned, 6 to 8 minutes; transfer to large plate.

2 Pour off all but 1 tablespoon fat left in pot. Add potatoes, carrots, shallots, and ½ teaspoon salt and cook over medium heat until vegetables are just beginning to brown, 5 to 7 minutes. Stir in garlic and thyme and cook until fragrant, about 30 seconds. Stir in wine, broth, and bay leaf, scraping up any browned bits.

3 Off heat, return chicken, breast side up, and any accumulated juices to pot, on top of vegetables. Transfer pot to oven and cook, uncovered, until breast registers 160 degrees and thighs register 175 degrees, 55 to 65 minutes.

4 Remove pot from oven. Transfer chicken to carving board and let rest for 20 minutes. Using slotted spoon, transfer vegetables to platter, and cover with aluminum foil to keep warm.

5 Discard bay leaf. Pour liquid left in pot into fat separator and let settle for 5 minutes. (You should have ¾ cup defatted liquid; add extra broth as needed to equal ¾ cup.) Return defatted liquid to now-empty pot and simmer until it measures ½ cup, 5 to 7 minutes. Off heat, whisk in butter and lemon juice and season with salt and pepper to taste. Sprinkle vegetables with parsley, carve chicken, and serve with sauce.

BAKED ZITI WITH SPINACH AND SAUSAGE

SERVES 4 TO 6   TOTAL TIME: 1 HOUR

WHY THIS RECIPE WORKS A pan of baked ziti is always an appealing thought but something of a chore in practice, and often more work than one wants to put into a simple dinner. Streamlining this multipot affair into just one Dutch oven was the first step toward simplification, and we started with a quick-to-make but meaty sauce. First we browned sweet Italian sausage and garlic. The addition of canned tomato sauce was convenient, and following that with canned diced tomatoes provided instant brightness. Oregano and red pepper flakes contributed complexity and some heat, while just ½ teaspoon of sugar tempered the tomatoes' acidity. To round out the flavor of our sauce with a lively note, we stirred in ¼ cup basil along with the noodles. We cooked the pasta directly in our sauce, adding 2 cups of water to ensure there was enough liquid to adequately cook the ziti. Simmering the pasta until it was only partially cooked kept the noodles from turning mushy when we placed our ziti under the broiler. And since no baked ziti is complete without plenty of oozy, gooey cheese, we stirred in grated Parmesan and cubed mozzarella before moving the pot to the oven. We then dolloped the surface with ricotta and gave it a final topping of more mozzarella and Parmesan, which melted and browned into a crust. To make this a true one-pot meal, we also stirred in a pile of baby spinach with the cheese. Part-skim ricotta and part-skim mozzarella cheese can be substituted here if desired. Do not use preshredded cheese, as it does not melt well.

8 ounces sweet Italian sausage, casings removed
3 garlic cloves, minced
1 (28-ounce) can tomato sauce
1 (14.5-ounce) can diced tomatoes
1½ teaspoons minced fresh oregano or ½ teaspoon dried
¾ teaspoon salt
½ teaspoon sugar
⅛ teaspoon red pepper flakes
2 cups water
12 ounces (3¾ cups) ziti
6 tablespoons chopped fresh basil
7 ounces (7 cups) baby spinach, chopped coarse
6 ounces whole-milk mozzarella cheese,
   cut into ¼-inch pieces (1½ cups)
2 ounces Parmesan cheese, grated (1 cup)
8 ounces (1 cup) whole-milk ricotta cheese

1 Cook sausage in Dutch oven over medium-high heat, breaking meat into ½-inch pieces, until lightly browned, about 5 minutes. Stir in garlic and cook until fragrant, about 30 seconds. Stir in tomato sauce, tomatoes and their juice, oregano, salt, sugar, and pepper flakes and bring mixture to boil. Reduce heat to medium-low and simmer until thickened, about 10 minutes.

2 Stir in water, pasta, and ¼ cup basil, increase heat to high, and bring to boil. Reduce heat to medium and simmer vigorously, stirring often, until pasta is still very firm but just starting to soften, 6 to 8 minutes. Meanwhile, adjust oven rack 8 inches from broiler element and heat broiler.

3 Off heat, stir in spinach, ¾ cup mozzarella, and ½ cup Parmesan. Dollop surface of pasta evenly with ricotta. Top with remaining ¾ cup mozzarella and remaining ½ cup Parmesan.

4 Broil ziti until cheese is bubbling and beginning to brown, 5 to 7 minutes. Transfer pot to wire rack and let cool for 10 minutes. Sprinkle with remaining 2 tablespoons basil and serve.

MILK-CAN SUPPER

SERVES 6 TO 8   TOTAL TIME: 1 HOUR 15 MINUTES

WHY THIS RECIPE WORKS Invented to feed a crowd of cowboys, a milk-can supper is a hearty mix of vegetables and sausage traditionally layered into a large milk can and cooked over an open fire. We swapped out the milk can for a Dutch oven but left the basic technique untouched. We put sturdy potatoes on the bottom closest to the heat, followed by cabbage, then the comparatively delicate onions, carrots, and corn. Rather than risk overcooking the bell peppers, we added them partway through. Browning bratwurst developed its meaty flavor and created a fond that lent a savory backbone to the cooking liquid. Beer gave the dish a complex toasty flavor, and garlic, bay leaves, and thyme rounded out the seasonings. You will need an 8-quart Dutch oven for this recipe. If your Dutch oven is slightly smaller than 8 quarts, the lid may not close all the way when you start cooking, but as the contents of the pot cook, they will decrease in volume, so you'll soon be able to clamp on the lid. Use small red potatoes measuring 1 to 2 inches in diameter. Light-bodied American lagers, such as Budweiser, work best in this recipe.

1 tablespoon vegetable oil

2½ pounds bratwurst

2 pounds small red potatoes, unpeeled

1 head green cabbage (2 pounds), cored and cut into 8 wedges

3 ears corn, husks and silk removed, ears cut into thirds

6 carrots, peeled and cut into 2-inch pieces

1 onion, halved and cut through root end into 8 wedges

4 garlic cloves, peeled and smashed

10 sprigs fresh thyme

2 bay leaves

1 teaspoon salt

½ teaspoon pepper

1½ cups beer

2 green bell peppers, stemmed, seeded, and cut into 1-inch-wide strips

1 Heat oil in Dutch oven over medium heat until shimmering. Add bratwurst and brown on all sides, 6 to 8 minutes. Transfer sausages to cutting board and cut each in half crosswise.

2 Arrange potatoes in single layer in now-empty pot. Arrange cabbage wedges in single layer on top of potatoes. Layer corn, carrots, onion, garlic, thyme sprigs, bay leaves, salt, and pepper over cabbage. Pour beer over vegetables and lay browned bratwurst on top.

3 Bring to boil over medium-high heat (wisps of steam will be visible). Cover, reduce heat to medium, and simmer for 15 minutes. Add bell peppers and continue to simmer, covered, until potatoes are tender, about 15 minutes. (Use long skewer to test potatoes for doneness.)

4 Transfer bratwurst and vegetables to large platter, discarding thyme sprigs and bay leaves. Sprinkle 1 cup cooking liquid over bratwurst and vegetables. Serve, passing remaining cooking liquid separately.

SMOTHERED PORK CHOPS WITH BROCCOLI

SERVES 4   TOTAL TIME: 1 HOUR 30 MINUTES

WHY THIS RECIPE WORKS Our take on this Southern staple yields fork-tender pork chops in a rich, oniony gravy. Browning blade-cut chops in bacon fat (reserving crisped bacon for garnish) created a savory foundation for the gravy. We sautéed onion, garlic, and aromatics in the fat before adding a little flour and some chicken broth. Finally, we nestled in our browned chops and transferred the pot to the oven, where the tough cut of pork rendered its fat slowly, becoming tender and juicy in the braising liquid during the 1-hour simmer. For a vegetable side, we followed the clever advice of one test cook who suggested placing a steamer basket of broccoli over the chops when they were nearly done cooking. Nicking the edges of the pork chops ensured that they didn't curl during browning. Serve with egg noodles, rice, or mashed potatoes.

3 slices bacon, chopped fine
4 (8- to 10-ounce) bone-in blade-cut pork chops, ¾ inch thick, trimmed
  Salt and pepper
¼ cup extra-virgin olive oil
1 onion, halved and sliced thin
4 garlic cloves, minced
1 teaspoon minced fresh thyme or ¼ teaspoon dried
½ teaspoon red pepper flakes
2 tablespoons water
2 tablespoons all-purpose flour
1¾ cups chicken broth
2 bay leaves
1 pound broccoli florets, cut into 1-inch pieces
2 tablespoons minced fresh parsley

1 Adjust oven rack to lower-middle position and heat oven to 300 degrees. Cook bacon in Dutch oven over medium heat until crisp, 5 to 7 minutes; transfer to paper towel–lined plate. Pour off all but 2 tablespoons fat left in pot.

2 Cut 2 slits, about 2 inches apart, through fat on edges of each pork chop. Pat chops dry with paper towels and season with salt and pepper. Heat fat left in pot over medium-high heat until just smoking. Add chops (they will overlap slightly) and brown on both sides, 7 to 10 minutes; transfer to separate plate.

3 Add 2 tablespoon oil, onion, and ¼ teaspoon salt to now-empty pot and cook over medium heat, stirring often, until onion is lightly browned, 8 to 10 minutes. Stir in garlic, thyme, and pepper flakes and cook until fragrant, about 30 seconds. Stir in water, scraping up any browned bits. Reduce heat to medium-low, add flour, and cook, stirring often, until well browned, about 5 minutes.

4 Slowly whisk in broth, scraping up any browned bits and smoothing out any lumps. Add bay leaves. Nestle browned chops and any accumulated juices into onion mixture. Cover, transfer pot to oven, and cook until chops are almost fork-tender, about 1 hour.

5 Remove pot from oven, uncover, and place steamer basket on top of chops. Add broccoli to steamer, cover pot, and continue to cook in oven until broccoli is tender, about 20 minutes

6 Remove pot from oven and remove basket of broccoli from pot. Toss broccoli in bowl with remaining 2 tablespoons oil and season with salt and pepper to taste. Transfer chops to platter, tent loosely with aluminum foil, and let rest while finishing sauce. Using large spoon, skim any fat from surface of stew. Bring stew to simmer over medium heat and cook until thickened, about 5 minutes. Discard bay leaves and season with salt and pepper to taste. Spoon sauce over chops, sprinkle with bacon and parsley, and serve with broccoli.

BRAISED BLADE STEAKS WITH MUSHROOMS, VIDALIAS, AND STEAMED ASPARAGUS

SERVES 4   TOTAL TIME: 3 HOURS 15 MINUTES

WHY THIS RECIPE WORKS We don't typically think of braising steaks, but tough blade steaks turn meltingly tender when simmered, producing a sauce full of beefy flavor. Along with them we braised classic partners: earthy mushrooms (two kinds for textural contrast) and sweet Vidalia onions. Dry sherry added complexity. To avoid using another pot, we steamed a side of asparagus in a basket right over the meat and tossed it with a lemon-chive compound butter, then used more lemon and chives to balance our rich sauce. Make sure to use asparagus spears between ¼ and ½ inch in diameter. Any sweet onion, such as Walla Walla, can be substituted for the Vidalia onion. Serve with buttered egg noodles or white rice.

4 (6- to 8-ounce) beef blade steaks, ¾ to 1 inch thick, trimmed
   Salt and pepper
3 tablespoons vegetable oil
12 ounces cremini mushrooms, trimmed and sliced thin
12 ounces portobello mushroom caps, halved and sliced thin
2 Vidalia onions, halved and sliced thin
1 tablespoon minced fresh thyme or 1 teaspoon dried
1½ teaspoons paprika
2 tablespoons all-purpose flour
¾ cup dry sherry
¾ cup chicken broth
1 pound thin asparagus, trimmed
1 tablespoon unsalted butter, softened
1 tablespoon grated lemon zest plus 2 tablespoons juice
3 tablespoons minced fresh chives

1 Adjust oven rack to lower-middle position and heat oven to 325 degrees. Pat steaks dry with paper towels and season with salt and pepper. Heat 1 tablespoon oil in Dutch oven over medium-high heat until just smoking. Add steaks and brown on both sides, 7 to 10 minutes; transfer to plate.

2 Add 1 tablespoon oil and cremini and portobello mushrooms to now-empty pot, cover, and cook over medium heat until mushrooms begin to release their liquid, about 5 minutes. Uncover and cook, stirring often, until mushrooms begin to brown, 10 to 12 minutes; transfer to bowl.

3 Add remaining 1 tablespoon oil, onions, thyme, paprika, and ½ teaspoon salt to now-empty pot and cook over medium heat, stirring often, until onions are softened, 8 to 10 minutes. Stir in flour and cook for 30 seconds. Stir in sherry, scraping up any browned bits and smoothing out any lumps. Stir in broth and mushroom mixture and bring to simmer.

4 Nestle browned steaks and any accumulated juices into pot and bring to simmer. Cover, transfer pot to oven, and cook until steaks are very tender, about 2 hours.

5 Remove pot from oven, uncover, and place steamer basket on top of steaks. Add asparagus to steamer, cover pot, and continue to cook in oven until asparagus is tender, 10 to 15 minutes. Meanwhile, mash softened butter, lemon zest, and 1 tablespoon chives together with fork in large bowl.

6 Remove pot from oven and remove basket of asparagus from pot. Transfer asparagus to bowl with butter mixture and toss until butter is melted. Transfer steaks to platter, tent loosely with aluminum foil, and let rest while finishing sauce. Strain braising liquid through fine-mesh strainer into fat separator; spoon strained vegetables over steaks. Defat braising liquid, stir in lemon juice and remaining 2 tablespoons chives, and season with salt and pepper to taste. Serve steaks and asparagus, passing sauce separately.

ISRAELI COUSCOUS WITH CLAMS, LEEKS, AND TOMATOES

SERVES 4 TOTAL TIME: 1 HOUR

WHY THIS RECIPE WORKS A brothy bowl of shellfish and tiny pasta is traditional seaside comfort food in parts of Italy. We set out to create a one-pot version, using clams for their clean flavor and opting for easy-to-prepare Israeli couscous, which has an appealing, pearl-like shape. We kept our ingredients list simple; we wanted to ensure the briny clam flavor was showcased and not overpowered by too many other elements. To start, we built a base of sweet leeks, garlic, fragrant tarragon, and plenty of white wine—all classic pairings with seafood. As a next step, we cooked our couscous, then finally, we steamed the clams on top. But by the time the shells opened, the couscous had turned to mush and we couldn't access the little pearls of pasta to fluff before serving. Our solution was to reverse the cooking order, first steaming the clams in the aromatic broth until they just opened, and then setting them aside so they wouldn't become rubbery. This freed up the pot to cook the couscous in our liquid—now flavored with the clam's juices—which we stretched with chicken broth. The couscous pearls came out perfectly, and their starch helped subtly thicken the broth. Fresh tomatoes and bright lemon zest enhanced the briny flavor. We returned the clams to the pot, along with their juices, to let everything warm through before serving. A sprinkling of lightly licorice-flavored tarragon was the perfect finish to the dish. Serve with crusty bread.

WEEKNIGHT FRIENDLY

2 tablespoons unsalted butter

1½ pounds leeks, white and light green parts only, halved lengthwise, sliced thin, and washed thoroughly

3 garlic cloves, minced

2 tablespoons minced fresh tarragon

1 cup dry white wine

4 pounds littleneck clams, scrubbed

2½ cups chicken broth

2 cups Israeli couscous

3 tomatoes, cored, seeded, and chopped

1 teaspoon grated lemon zest

Salt and pepper

1 Melt butter in Dutch oven over medium heat. Add leeks and cook until softened, about 4 minutes. Stir in garlic and 1 tablespoon tarragon and cook until fragrant, about 30 seconds. Stir in wine, increase heat to high, and bring to boil. Add clams, cover, and cook, stirring occasionally, until clams have opened, 5 to 7 minutes.

2 Using slotted spoon, transfer clams to large bowl and tent loosely with aluminum foil; discard any clams that refuse to open. Reduce heat to medium, add chicken broth and couscous to pot, and bring to simmer. Cover and cook until couscous is nearly tender and some broth remains, 8 to 10 minutes.

3 Off heat, stir in tomatoes and lemon zest and season with salt and pepper to taste. Nestle clams and any accumulated juices into couscous mixture. Cover and let sit until heated through, about 5 minutes. Sprinkle with remaining 1 tablespoon tarragon before serving.

BRAISED CHICKEN THIGHS WITH CHARD AND MUSTARD

SERVES 4 TOTAL TIME: 2 HOURS 15 MINUTES

WHY THIS RECIPE WORKS Hearty and rustic, braised bone-in chicken thighs become juicy and tender as they simmer and lend their rich flavor to the surrounding sauce. The only question is what to do about the skin: Browning it brings rich flavor, but we weren't excited about eating flabby skin—inevitable after a long simmer. So, after browning skin-on thighs to develop lots of flavorful fond, we discarded the skin. Then we built our braise with bold ingredients: sturdy chard; garlic, thyme, and an umami-packed anchovy fillet for flavor; lemon zest for brightness; and bay leaves for depth. Cooking the chicken thighs for a full hour (to 200 degrees rather than the standard 175 for doneness) allowed the collagen to melt into rich gelatin, adding body and depth to the sauce. A dollop of mustard added sharp contrast to the sauce's richness. We like to use green or white Swiss chard here; if using red chard, note that the sauce will take on a reddish hue. Serve with rice or egg noodles.

8 (6-ounce) bone-in chicken thighs, trimmed
   Salt and pepper
1 tablespoon extra-virgin olive oil
1 pound Swiss chard, stems chopped fine, leaves sliced thin
1 onion, chopped fine
6 garlic cloves, minced
1 tablespoon minced fresh thyme or 2 teaspoons dried
1 anchovy fillet, rinsed and minced
2 tablespoons all-purpose flour
1½ cups chicken broth
½ cup dry white wine
2 bay leaves
1 teaspoon grated lemon zest
1 tablespoon whole-grain mustard

1 Adjust oven rack to lower-middle position and heat oven to 300 degrees. Pat chicken dry with paper towels and season with salt and pepper. Heat oil in Dutch oven over medium-high heat until just smoking. Add half of chicken and brown on both sides, 7 to 10 minutes; transfer to plate and remove skin. Repeat with remaining chicken.

2 Pour off all but 2 tablespoons fat left in pot and heat over medium-high heat until shimmering. Add chard stems and onion and cook until softened and lightly browned, 5 to 7 minutes. Stir in garlic, thyme, and anchovy and cook until fragrant, about 30 seconds. Stir in flour and cook for 30 seconds. Whisk in broth and wine, scraping up any browned bits and smoothing out any lumps.

3 Add bay leaves and browned chicken and any accumulated juices. Bring to simmer, cover, and transfer pot to oven. Cook until chicken is very tender and almost falling off bone, about 1 hour.

4 Remove pot from oven. Transfer chicken to platter, tent loosely with aluminum foil, and let rest while finishing sauce. Let liquid in pot settle for 5 minutes, then skim any fat from surface using large spoon. Stir in chard leaves and lemon zest, bring to simmer, and cook until sauce is thickened, about 10 minutes.

5 Off heat, discard bay leaves, stir in mustard, and season with salt and pepper to taste. Pour sauce over chicken and serve. (Chicken and sauce can be refrigerated for up to 2 days; add additional broth as needed to loosen sauce when reheating.)

Variation

BRAISED CHICKEN THIGHS WITH SPINACH WITH GARLIC
Omit chard and mustard. Add 10 ounces chopped curly-leaf spinach and 2 additional minced garlic cloves to pot with lemon zest.

KOREAN-STYLE BEEF SHORT RIBS WITH BOK CHOY

SERVES 6   TOTAL TIME: 3 HOURS

WHY THIS RECIPE WORKS Tender braised short ribs make for a warm, hearty dinner on a cold day. For a new take on this classic, we turned to a distinctly Korean flavor profile that would combine sweet and savory ingredients for a hands-off meal. To eliminate an all-day wait for dinner, we used boneless short ribs, which cook faster than bone-in; this trick also helped reduce the amount of fat rendered from the meat. After browning the meat first, we deglazed the pan with sake, enhancing the dish's flavor profile. We knew that pear is often used in Korean beef marinades as a tenderizer, so we tried it here. The pear also balanced the acidity of the rice vinegar, adding sweetness and subtle fruit flavor. Pairing them with soy sauce, sugar, and sesame oil yielded an intense sauce with lots of umami. To round out our dinner, we steamed some baby bok choy atop the beef until just tender, and then drizzled both with the cornstarch-thickened sauce. Serve with white rice.

1   pear, peeled, halved, cored, and chopped coarse
½   cup soy sauce
6   tablespoons sugar
2   tablespoons toasted sesame oil
1   tablespoon rice vinegar
3½ pounds boneless English-style short ribs, trimmed
    Salt and pepper
1   tablespoon vegetable oil
1   onion, chopped fine
6   garlic cloves, minced
4   teaspoons grated fresh ginger
1   cup sake
4   heads baby bok choy (2 to 3 ounces each), halved
1   tablespoon cornstarch

1 Adjust oven rack to lower-middle position and heat oven to 300 degrees. Process pear, soy sauce, sugar, sesame oil, and rice vinegar in food processor until smooth, about 30 seconds.

2 Pat beef dry with paper towels and season with salt and pepper. Heat vegetable oil in Dutch oven over medium-high heat until just smoking. Add half of beef and brown on all sides, 7 to 10 minutes; transfer to large plate. Repeat with remaining beef.

3 Add onion to fat left in pot and cook over medium heat, stirring occasionally, until softened, 5 to 7 minutes. Stir in garlic and ginger and cook until fragrant, about 30 seconds. Stir in sake and simmer, scraping up any browned bits, until reduced by half, about 2 minutes. Stir in pear mixture and browned beef and any accumulated juices and bring to simmer. Cover, transfer pot to oven, and cook until tender, 2 to 2½ hours.

4 Remove pot from oven, uncover, and place steamer basket on top of meat. Add bok choy to steamer, cover pot, and continue to cook in oven until bok choy is tender, 5 to 10 minutes.

5 Remove pot from oven. Remove basket of bok choy from pot and transfer bok choy to platter. Transfer beef to platter and tent with aluminum foil. Strain braising liquid through fine-mesh strainer into fat separator, discarding solids, then defat liquid.

6 Combine ¼ cup defatted liquid with cornstarch in bowl. Return remaining liquid to simmer in now-empty pot over medium heat. Whisk cornstarch mixture to combine, then whisk into simmering liquid in pot and cook until slightly thickened, about 2 minutes. Remove from heat and season with salt and pepper to taste. Serve short ribs and bok choy, passing sauce separately.

SIMPLE POT ROAST WITH ROOT VEGETABLES

SERVES 6 TOTAL TIME: 4 HOURS

WHY THIS RECIPE WORKS When it comes to pot roast, keeping it simple is best. We started with a chuck-eye roast, a well-marbled cut that is great for braising. Opening the roast along its natural seam to make two separate lobes and then trimming excess fat eliminated greasiness and promised a quicker cooking time and more thorough seasoning. A stovetop sear created a well-caramelized exterior, but because it's difficult to keep the stove at a steady temperature for a lengthy braise, we moved to the oven after browning the aromatics, adding in both chicken and beef broths (for a balanced but meaty flavor) and returning the roasts to the pot. A good pot roast should always be tender. Slowly increasing the cooking time during our testing to 3 to 3½ hours produced a roast so tender that a fork poked into the meat met with no resistance. When we sliced into the roast we found that the fat and connective tissue had dissolved into the meat, giving each bite a silky texture and rich flavor. Use a good-quality, medium-bodied wine, such as a Côtes du Rhône or a Pinot Noir, for this dish.

1 (3½- to 4-pound) boneless beef chuck-eye roast, pulled into 2 pieces at natural seam, trimmed, and tied at 1-inch intervals
Salt and pepper
3 tablespoons vegetable oil
1 onion, chopped
1 celery rib, chopped
4 garlic cloves, minced
2 teaspoons sugar
1 teaspoon fresh minced thyme or ¼ teaspoon dried
1 cup chicken broth
1 cup beef broth
1 cup water
1½ pounds carrots, peeled and cut into 3-inch pieces
1½ pounds red potatoes, unpeeled, cut into 1½-inch pieces
1½ pounds parsnips, peeled and cut into 3-inch pieces
⅓ cup red wine

1 Adjust oven rack to lower-middle position and heat oven to 300 degrees. Pat beef dry with paper towels and season with salt and pepper. Heat 2 tablespoons oil in Dutch oven over medium-high heat until just smoking. Add both beef roasts and brown on all sides, 7 to 10 minutes; transfer to large plate.

2 Add remaining 1 tablespoon oil, onion, and celery to now-empty pot and cook over medium heat until vegetables are softened, 5 to 7 minutes. Stir in garlic, sugar, and thyme and cook until fragrant, about 30 seconds. Stir in broths and water, scraping up any browned bits.

3 Add browned roasts and any accumulated juices to pot and bring to simmer. Cover, transfer pot to oven, and cook for 2 hours, flipping roasts halfway through cooking.

4 Remove pot from oven. Nestle carrots into pot around meat and sprinkle potatoes and parsnips over top. Return covered pot to oven and cook until meat and vegetables are very tender, 1 to 1½ hours.

5 Remove pot from oven. Transfer roasts to carving board, tent loosely with aluminum foil, and let rest while finishing sauce. Transfer vegetables to large bowl, season with salt and pepper to taste, and cover to keep warm.

6 Using large spoon, skim any fat from surface of braising liquid. Stir in wine and simmer until sauce measures 2 cups, about 15 minutes. Season with salt and pepper to taste. Remove twine from roasts, slice meat against grain into ¼-inch-thick slices, and serve with vegetables and sauce.

PORK LOIN EN COCOTTE WITH KALE, SHALLOTS, AND MUSTARD

SERVES 4 TO 6   TOTAL TIME: 1 HOUR 45 MINUTES

WHY THIS RECIPE WORKS The process for cooking *en cocotte* is simple: Place a browned roast, along with a few aromatics, in a Dutch oven, cover, and bake in a low oven, where the meat essentially steams in that contained, moist-heat environment. Never ones to mess with simplicity, we decided to give this basic pork loin roast just a touch of modern flair. Introducing kale to the pot seemed like a good start—the pork's juices would flavor the greens as they cooked. Seasoning the pork with herbes de Provence delivered a heady dose of flavors and fragrances all at once. After browning the roast and softening some shallots, we built up our cooking liquid, boosting the rendered juices and residual fond with chicken broth. We gave the hearty kale a head start, allowing it to wilt before adding in the browned roast. We removed the pork when it had reached 140 degrees, letting it come to temperature while resting on the cutting board. We used that time to finish the kale, letting the cooking liquid evaporate and infuse the greens with flavor. The addition of butter and mustard finished off this saucy, rich accompaniment to the juicy herbed pork. This recipe works best with a pork roast that is about 7 to 8 inches long and 4 to 5 inches wide; we prefer a blade-end roast. We like to leave a ¼-inch-thick layer of fat on top of the roast; if your roast has a thicker fat cap, trim it back to be about ¼ inch thick. You can substitute 1 teaspoon each dried thyme, dried rosemary, and dried marjoram for the herbes de Provence in this recipe. You will need a Dutch oven with a tight-fitting lid for this recipe.

1 (2½- to 3-pound) boneless center-cut pork loin roast, trimmed and tied at 1½-inch intervals
1 tablespoon herbes de Provence
  Salt and pepper
3 tablespoons vegetable oil
1 pound shallots, peeled and quartered
1 cup chicken broth
1 pound kale, stemmed and cut into 1-inch pieces
1 tablespoon unsalted butter
1 tablespoon whole-grain mustard

1 Adjust oven rack to lowest position and heat oven to 250 degrees. Pat pork dry with paper towels and season with herbes de Provence, salt, and pepper. Heat 2 tablespoons oil in Dutch oven over medium-high heat until just smoking. Add pork and brown on all sides, 7 to 10 minutes; transfer to large plate.

2 Add remaining 1 tablespoon oil and shallots to pot and cook over medium heat until shallots are softened and lightly browned, 5 to 7 minutes. Stir in broth, scraping up any browned bits, and bring to simmer. Stir in kale, cover, and cook, stirring occasionally, until bright green and wilted, about 5 minutes.

3 Off heat, nestle browned pork and any accumulated juices into pot. Place large sheet of aluminum foil over pot and press to seal, then cover tightly with lid. Transfer pot to oven and cook until pork registers 140 degrees, 35 to 55 minutes.

4 Remove pot from oven. Transfer pork to cutting board, tent loosely with foil, and let rest 20 minutes. Meanwhile, continue to simmer kale over medium-high heat until tender and liquid has nearly evaporated, 3 to 5 minutes. Stir in butter and mustard, season with salt and pepper to taste, and cover to keep warm.

5 Remove twine from pork and slice against grain into ¼-inch-thick slices. Serve with kale.

BEEF EN COCOTTE WITH CREAMY MUSHROOM BARLEY AND SALSA VERDE

SERVES 6 TOTAL TIME: 1 HOUR 30 MINUTES

WHY THIS RECIPE WORKS Succulent beef cooked in a sealed Dutch oven was the basis for this recipe, but we wanted a creamy mushroom and barley side out of the same pot. While a beef roast would typically reach medium-rare in far less time than that needed to cook barley, the barley provided insulation that brought the beef's cooking time into closer alignment with its own. This dish warranted luxurious flavors, so we incorporated porcini mushrooms, cognac for deglazing, and Parmesan to enrich the creamy barley. To cut the richness, we made a bright sauce inspired by chimichurri, the perfect accent to our elegant one-pot supper. To keep the barley from becoming greasy, trim the beef well. You will need a Dutch oven with a tight-fitting lid for this recipe.

Beef

- 1 (3- to 4-pound) boneless top sirloin roast, trimmed and tied once around middle
  Salt and pepper
- 3 tablespoons vegetable oil
- 8 ounces white mushrooms, trimmed and sliced thin
- 1¼ cups pearl barley, rinsed
- 1 onion, chopped
- ½ ounce dried porcini mushrooms, rinsed and minced
- 3 garlic cloves, minced
- 1 tablespoon tomato paste
- 1 teaspoon minced fresh thyme or ¼ teaspoon dried
- 3 tablespoons cognac
- 2 cups beef broth
- 1 cup chicken broth
- 1 cup water
- 1 ounce Parmesan cheese, grated (½ cup)

Salsa Verde

- 5 tablespoons extra-virgin olive oil
- ¼ cup minced fresh parsley
- 2 teaspoons sherry vinegar
- 1 garlic clove, minced
  Salt and pepper

1 For the beef Adjust oven rack to lowest position and heat oven to 250 degrees. Pat beef dry with paper towels and season with salt and pepper. Heat 2 tablespoons oil in Dutch oven over medium-high heat until just smoking. Add beef and brown on all sides, 7 to 10 minutes; transfer to plate.

2 Add remaining 1 tablespoon oil, white mushrooms, barley, onion, and porcini mushrooms to now-empty pot and cook over medium heat until onion is softened, 5 to 7 minutes. Stir in garlic, tomato paste, and thyme and cook until fragrant, about 30 seconds. Stir in cognac, scraping up any browned bits, and cook until almost completely evaporated, about 30 seconds. Stir in broths and water and bring to simmer.

3 Off heat, add browned beef and any accumulated juices. Place large sheet of aluminum foil over pot and press to seal, then cover tightly with lid. Transfer pot to oven and cook until roast registers 120 degrees (for medium-rare), 60 to 80 minutes.

4 Remove pot from oven. Transfer beef to carving board, tent loosely with foil, and let rest 20 minutes. (If barley is underdone, continue to cook over medium heat, adding additional water as needed, until tender.) Stir Parmesan into barley mixture and cook over medium heat until creamy, 1 to 2 minutes. Season with salt and pepper to taste, and cover to keep warm.

5 For the salsa verde Whisk all ingredients together in bowl and season with salt and pepper to taste. Remove twine from beef and slice against grain into ¼-inch-thick slices. Serve beef with barley and sauce.

CHICKEN STEW WITH CHEDDAR BISCUITS

SERVES 8   TOTAL TIME: 2 HOURS

WHY THIS RECIPE WORKS The aha! moment for preparing tender chicken stew and perfectly flaky biscuits together in one pot came when we inverted the Dutch oven lid and baked the biscuits on it, above the stew. Sogginess averted. Swiss chard, sweet potatoes, and turnips put a modern spin on this soul-satisfying Sunday supper.

Biscuits

  2 cups (10 ounces) all-purpose flour
  2 ounces sharp cheddar cheese, shredded (½ cup)
  2 teaspoons sugar
  2 teaspoons baking powder
  ½ teaspoon salt
1½ cups heavy cream

Filling

  4 (10- to 12-ounce) bone-in split chicken breasts, trimmed
     Salt and pepper
  2 tablespoons vegetable oil
  1 onion, chopped fine
 10 ounces Swiss chard, stems chopped, leaves cut into 1-inch pieces
  3 garlic cloves, minced
  ¼ cup all-purpose flour
  2 cups chicken broth
 12 ounces sweet potatoes, peeled and cut into ½-inch pieces
  8 ounces turnips, peeled and cut into ½-inch pieces
  ½ cup heavy cream
  ¼ cup minced fresh parsley
  2 tablespoons dry sherry

1 For the biscuits Adjust oven rack to lowest position and heat oven to 425 degrees. Whisk flour, cheddar, sugar, baking powder, and salt together in bowl. Stir in cream and mix until dough forms, about 30 seconds. Turn dough out onto lightly floured counter and knead dough briefly until smooth, about 30 seconds. Flatten dough into 7-inch circle and cut into 8 wedges. Cover with plastic wrap and set aside.

2 For the filling Pat chicken dry with paper towels and season with salt and pepper. Heat 1 tablespoon oil in

Dutch oven over medium-high heat until just smoking. Add chicken, skin side down, and brown on 1 side, 6 to 8 minutes; transfer to plate.

3 Add remaining 1 tablespoon oil, onion, chard stems, and ½ teaspoon salt to now-empty pot and cook over medium heat until onion is softened, about 5 minutes. Stir in garlic and cook until fragrant, about 30 seconds. Stir in flour and cook for 30 seconds. Slowly whisk in broth, scraping up any browned bits and smoothing out any lumps.

4 Stir in sweet potatoes and turnips. Nestle chicken, browned side up, and any accumulated juices into pot. Place lid upside down on pot and cover with trimmed piece of parchment paper. Lay biscuits on lid with wide ends flush to edge of lid. Bake until biscuits are golden brown and chicken registers 160 degrees, 25 to 30 minutes, rotating pot halfway through baking.

5 Remove pot from oven and reduce oven temperature to 300 degrees. Transfer biscuits to wire rack and let cool. Transfer chicken to cutting board, let cool slightly, and shred into bite-size pieces using 2 forks, discarding skin and bones.

6 Meanwhile, stir chard leaves into pot and continue to cook in oven, uncovered and stirring occasionally, until filling is thickened and vegetables are tender, 10 to 15 minutes.

7 Remove pot from oven and stir in shredded chicken, cream, parsley, and sherry. Season with salt and pepper to taste. Cover and let chicken heat through for 10 minutes. Arrange biscuits on top of filling before serving.

CLASSIC CHICKEN STEW WITH WINTER VEGETABLES

SERVES 6 TO 8 TOTAL TIME: 2 HOURS

WHY THIS RECIPE WORKS When we think of chicken stew, we imagine tender, moist chunks of chicken paired with potatoes and vegetables, all enveloped in a glossy, thick sauce. We wanted to serve ourselves a bowl of this comforting stew without spending all day in the kitchen. Working with rich, meaty boneless thighs (rather than a whole bird) seemed like a surefire way to streamline this dish without sacrificing flavor. Browning the thighs on the stovetop added a dose of richness, and the rendered fat aided in browning and melding the flavors of the aromatics: onions, garlic, and fresh thyme. Some flour ensured a smooth, thick texture as we poured in white wine and chicken broth. To make this chicken stew hearty, we introduced a rustic mix of winter vegetables: red potatoes, celery root, parsnips, and carrots, all cut into rough chunks and added to the broth. Chicken stew is at its best when it's gently simmered, so after adding the browned chicken we transferred the pot to a 300-degree oven to cook undisturbed for an hour. The work was now done: All that our stew needed was a sprinkling of parsley to freshen it up before serving. Do not substitute boneless, skinless chicken breasts for the thighs in this recipe. Turnips, rutabagas, or parsley root can be substituted for the carrots, celery root, or parsnips if desired.

3 pounds boneless, skinless chicken thighs, trimmed and cut into 1-inch pieces
  Salt and pepper
3 tablespoons vegetable oil
2 onions, chopped fine
4 garlic cloves, minced
1 teaspoon minced fresh thyme or ¼ teaspoon dried
¼ cup all-purpose flour
3½ cups chicken broth
½ cup dry white wine
8 ounces red potatoes, unpeeled, cut into ¾-inch pieces
8 ounces celery root, peeled and cut into ¾-inch pieces
8 ounces parsnips, peeled and sliced ½ inch thick
3 carrots, peeled and sliced ½ inch thick
2 bay leaves
¼ cup minced fresh parsley

1 Adjust oven rack to lower-middle position and heat oven to 300 degrees. Pat chicken dry with paper towels and season with salt and pepper. Heat 1 table-spoon oil in Dutch oven over medium-high heat until just smoking. Add half of chicken and brown on both sides, 7 to 10 minutes; transfer to large bowl. Repeat with 1 tablespoon oil and remaining chicken.

2 Heat remaining 1 tablespoon oil in now-empty pot over medium heat until shimmering. Add onions and ¼ teaspoon salt and cook until onions are softened, about 5 minutes. Stir in garlic and thyme and cook until fragrant, about 30 seconds. Stir in flour and cook for 30 seconds. Whisk in broth and wine, scraping up any browned bits and smoothing out any lumps.

3 Stir in potatoes, celery root, parsnips, carrots, bay leaves, and browned chicken and any accumulated juices, and bring to simmer. Cover, transfer pot to oven, and cook until chicken is very tender, 50 to 60 minutes.

4 Remove pot from oven and discard bay leaves. (Stew can be refrigerated for up to 2 days; add additional broth as needed to loosen sauce when reheating.) Stir in parsley and season with salt and pepper to taste before serving.

BEST BEEF STEW

SERVES 6 TO 8   TOTAL TIME: 3 HOURS 45 MINUTES

WHY THIS RECIPE WORKS Beef stew is rarely as complex as its aroma would suggest, but we wanted meaty flavor that surpassed all expectations. We seared pieces of chuck-eye in batches to avoid any steaming, then caramelized our vegetables. Along with garlic, wine, and chicken broth, we added umami-boosting tomato paste and anchovies, and salt pork for extra savory character. To mimic the mouth-coating texture of stews made with collagen-rich homemade stock, we added gelatin and flour for a glossy sheen and wonderfully rich taste. Look for salt pork that is roughly 75 percent lean; rinse the salt pork before cooking or the stew will taste overly salty. Use a good-quality, medium-bodied wine, such as Côtes du Rhône or Pinot Noir, for this stew.

2 garlic cloves, minced
4 anchovy fillets, rinsed and minced
1 tablespoon tomato paste
4 pounds boneless beef chuck-eye roast, pulled apart at seams, trimmed, and cut into 1½-inch pieces
2 tablespoons vegetable oil
1 large onion, sliced thin
4 carrots, peeled and cut into 1-inch pieces
¼ cup all-purpose flour
2 cups red wine
2 cups chicken broth
2 bay leaves
4 sprigs fresh thyme
4 ounces salt pork, rinsed
1 pound Yukon Gold potatoes, unpeeled, cut into 1-inch pieces
1½ cups frozen pearl onions, thawed
2 teaspoons unflavored gelatin
½ cup water
1 cup frozen peas, thawed
   Salt and pepper

1 Adjust oven rack to lower-middle position and heat oven to 300 degrees. Mash garlic and anchovies together in bowl into paste, then stir in tomato paste.

2 Pat beef dry with paper towels. Heat 1 tablespoon oil in Dutch oven over medium-high heat until just smoking. Add half of beef and brown on all sides, 7 to 10 minutes; transfer to bowl. Repeat with remaining 1 tablespoon oil and remaining beef, then return first batch of beef to pot.

3 Reduce heat to medium and stir in onion and carrots. Cook, scraping up any browned bits, until onion is softened, 1 to 2 minutes. Stir in garlic mixture and cook until fragrant, about 30 seconds. Stir in flour and cook for 30 seconds.

4 Slowly stir in wine, scraping up any browned bits and smoothing out any lumps. Increase heat to high and simmer until thickened and reduced slightly, about 2 minutes. Stir in broth, bay leaves, thyme sprigs, and salt pork and bring to simmer. Cover, transfer pot to oven, and cook for 1½ hours.

5 Remove pot from oven. Discard salt pork and bay leaves and stir in potatoes. Return covered pot to oven and cook until potatoes are nearly tender, about 45 minutes.

6 Using large spoon, skim any fat from surface of stew and remove thyme sprigs. Stir in pearl onions and cook over medium heat until potatoes and onions are tender and meat offers little resistance when poked with fork, about 15 minutes. Meanwhile, sprinkle gelatin over water in bowl and let sit until gelatin softens, about 5 minutes.

7 Increase heat to high, stir in softened gelatin mixture and peas, and simmer until gelatin is fully dissolved and stew is thickened, about 3 minutes. Season with salt and pepper to taste and serve. (Stew can be refrigerated for up to 2 days; add additional broth as needed to loosen sauce when reheating.)

FRENCH-STYLE PORK STEW

SERVES 8   TOTAL TIME: 2 HOURS 30 MINUTES

WHY THIS RECIPE WORKS In the realm of stews, pork is either overlooked in favor of other proteins or overpowered by more assertive ingredients. We wanted a robust and satisfying (but not heavy) stew that put pork in the forefront. We took inspiration from a classic French dish, *potée*, a stew that uses multiple parts of the pig, at least one of which is always smoked, to yield a deep, meaty flavor. For our version, we chose a mix of pork butt for a base of tasty, succulent meat; collagen-rich smoked ham hocks, which would impart a silky consistency and smokiness; and kielbasa for a firm bite and additional smoky flavor. For our vegetables, the traditional potatoes, carrots, and cabbage were perfect. We started to build a flavorful backbone by cooking onion, garlic, and herbs de Provence. We then added our liquid (mostly water, to keep the stew from becoming heavy, plus chicken broth to prevent the flavors from becoming washed out), and added the pork and ham hocks. Because the pork would take 2 hours to become perfectly tender, we added our other ingredients in stages to prevent them from becoming mushy. About halfway through, we removed the ham hocks to shred the meat, which we added back to the stew. A final sprinkle of fresh parsley rounded out our flavors and added freshness. Pork butt roast is often labeled Boston butt in the supermarket. Serve with crusty bread.

2 tablespoons vegetable oil

1 onion, chopped

Salt and pepper

3 garlic cloves, minced

2 teaspoons herbes de Provence

3 pounds boneless pork butt roast, pulled apart at seams, trimmed, and cut into 1½-inch pieces

1¼ pounds smoked ham hocks

5 cups water

4 cups chicken broth

1 pound Yukon Gold potatoes, unpeeled, cut into ¾-inch pieces

4 carrots, peeled and cut into ½-inch pieces

12 ounces kielbasa sausage, halved lengthwise and sliced ½ inch thick

½ head savoy cabbage, cored and shredded (8 cups)

¼ cup minced fresh parsley

1 Adjust oven rack to middle position and heat oven to 325 degrees. Heat oil in Dutch oven over medium heat until shimmering. Add onion, ½ teaspoon salt, and ¼ teaspoon pepper and cook until onion is softened and lightly browned, 5 to 7 minutes. Stir in garlic and herbes de Provence and cook until fragrant, about 30 seconds. Add pork, ham hocks, water, and broth, and bring to simmer. Cover, transfer pot to oven, and cook until pork is tender, 1¼ to 1½ hours.

2 Remove pot from oven. Transfer ham hocks to cutting board, let cool slightly, then shred into bite-size pieces using 2 forks, discarding skin and bones. While ham hocks cool, stir potatoes and carrots into stew, return covered pot to oven, and cook until vegetables are almost tender, 20 to 25 minutes.

3 Remove pot from oven and stir in shredded ham, kielbasa, and cabbage. Return covered pot to oven and cook until kielbasa is heated through and cabbage is wilted and tender, 15 to 20 minutes. (Stew can be refrigerated for up to 2 days; add additional broth as needed to loosen sauce when reheating.) Stir in parsley and season with salt and pepper to taste before serving.

ITALIAN-STYLE LAMB STEW WITH GREEN BEANS, TOMATOES, AND BASIL

SERVES 6 TO 8   TOTAL TIME: 3 HOURS

WHY THIS RECIPE WORKS For a lamb stew with deep flavor, selecting the right cut of meat was half the battle. We found that using boneless lamb shoulder gave us the same bold flavor as lamb leg, but for less money. It also was perfect for braising, turning meltingly tender as it cooked. To start, we browned the meat before building our stewing liquid. Onions, garlic, tomatoes, and rosemary gave us a flavor backbone, while a little flour ensured the stew would have the spoon-clinging consistency we desired. Chicken broth was too strong and took over the stew, but a combination of water and white wine was flavorful and kept clean lamb flavor in the foreground. To keep the potatoes and green beans from breaking down completely, we added them halfway through cooking. A final sprinkling of basil just before serving added pleasant freshness. If you can't find boneless lamb shoulder, substitute 4½ pounds bone-in lamb shoulder chops, 1 to 1½ inches thick, trimmed and cut off the bone into 1½-inch cubes.

3 pounds boneless lamb shoulder, pulled apart at seams, trimmed, and cut into 1½-inch pieces
  Salt and pepper
3 tablespoons vegetable oil
3 onions, chopped
3 garlic cloves, minced
¼ cup all-purpose flour
½ cup dry white wine
1¾ cups water
1 (14.5-ounce) can diced tomatoes
1 tablespoon minced fresh rosemary
  or 1 teaspoon dried
2 pounds Yukon Gold potatoes, peeled and cut into ½-inch pieces
12 ounces green beans, trimmed and halved
¼ cup chopped fresh basil

1 Adjust oven rack to lower-middle position and heat oven to 300 degrees. Pat lamb dry with paper towels and season with salt and pepper. Heat 1 tablespoon oil in Dutch oven over medium-high heat until just smoking. Add half of lamb and brown on all sides, 6 to 8 minutes; transfer to large bowl. Repeat with 1 tablespoon oil and remaining lamb.

2 Add remaining 1 tablespoon oil, onions, and ¼ teaspoon salt to now-empty pot and cook over medium heat, stirring often, until onions are softened, about 5 minutes. Add garlic and cook until fragrant, about 30 seconds. Stir in flour and cook for 30 seconds.

3 Whisk in wine and 1 cup water, scraping up any browned bits and smoothing out any lumps. Slowly add remaining ¾ cup water. Add tomatoes and their juice, rosemary, ½ teaspoon salt, and browned lamb and any accumulated juices, and bring to simmer. Cover, transfer pot to oven, and cook for 1 hour.

4 Remove pot from oven. Stir in potatoes and sprinkle beans over top. Return covered pot to oven and cook until meat and vegetables are tender, 50 to 60 minutes. (Stew can be refrigerated for up to 2 days; add additional broth as needed to loosen sauce when reheating.) Stir in basil and season with salt and pepper to taste before serving.

QUINOA AND VEGETABLE STEW

SERVES 6 TO 8   TOTAL TIME: 1 HOUR

WHY THIS RECIPE WORKS Quinoa stews are one-pot meals beloved in several South American regions, but many authentic recipes call for obscure ingredients, such as annatto powder or Peruvian varieties of potatoes and corn. We set out to make a simple stew with traditional flavors but an easy-to-navigate ingredient list. We found that paprika has a similar flavor profile to annatto powder; we rounded it out with cumin and coriander. Red bell pepper, tomatoes, red potatoes, sweet corn, and frozen peas provided a colorful mix of vegetables. We added the quinoa after the potatoes had softened, cooking it until it released starch to help give the stew body. Finally, we added the traditional garnishes: queso fresco, avocado, and cilantro. We like the convenience of prewashed quinoa. If you buy unwashed quinoa (or if you are unsure whether it's washed), be sure to rinse it before cooking to remove its bitter protective coating. This stew tends to thicken as it sits; add additional warm vegetable broth as needed before serving to loosen. Do not omit the garnishes, as they are important to the flavor of the stew.

2 tablespoons vegetable oil

1 onion, chopped

1 red bell pepper, stemmed, seeded, and cut into ½-inch pieces

5 garlic cloves, minced

1 tablespoon paprika

2 teaspoons ground coriander

1½ teaspoons ground cumin

6 cups vegetable broth

1 pound red potatoes, unpeeled, cut into ½-inch pieces

1 cup prewashed white quinoa

1 cup fresh or frozen corn

2 tomatoes, cored and chopped coarse

1 cup frozen peas
  Salt and pepper

8 ounces queso fresco or feta cheese, crumbled (2 cups)

1 avocado, halved, pitted, and diced

½ cup minced fresh cilantro

1 Heat oil in Dutch oven over medium heat until shimmering. Add onion and bell pepper and cook until softened, 5 to 7 minutes. Stir in garlic, paprika, coriander, and cumin and cook until fragrant, about 30 seconds. Stir in broth and potatoes and bring to boil over high heat. Reduce heat to medium-low and simmer gently for 10 minutes.

2 Stir in quinoa and simmer for 8 minutes. Stir in corn and simmer until potatoes and quinoa are just tender, 5 to 7 minutes. Stir in tomatoes and peas and cook until heated through, about 2 minutes.

3 Off heat, season with salt and pepper to taste. (Stew can be refrigerated for up to 2 days; add additional broth as needed to loosen sauce when reheating.) Sprinkle individual portions with queso fresco, avocado, and cilantro before serving.

BRAZILIAN BLACK BEAN AND PORK STEW

SERVES 6 TO 8   TOTAL TIME: 3 HOURS

WHY THIS RECIPE WORKS The Brazilian black bean and pork stew known as *feijoada* espouses humble, old-world frugality, traditionally using up every last bit of the pig. For a less daunting path to complex flavor, we went with boneless pork butt roast, some bacon, and smoky linguiça, all cuts requiring minimal prep. A little baking soda gave the stew a more appealing color because it helped the black beans preserve their dark hue; without it, the beans will turn grayish. Pork butt roast is often labeled Boston butt in the supermarket. Be sure to serve this stew with the accompanying salsa-like hot sauce; it is traditional and adds important flavor. For more spice, reserve, mince, and add the ribs and seeds from the jalapeño chile.

Stew

- 1 (3½- to 4-pound) boneless pork butt roast, pulled apart at seams, trimmed, and cut into 1½-inch pieces
  Salt and pepper
- 3 tablespoons vegetable oil
- 4 slices bacon, chopped fine
- 1 onion, chopped fine
- 4 garlic cloves, minced
- 1 tablespoon chili powder
- 1 teaspoon ground cumin
- 1 teaspoon ground coriander
- 7 cups water
- 1 pound (2 ½ cups) dried black beans, picked over and rinsed
- 2 bay leaves
- ⅛ teaspoon baking soda
- 1 pound linguiça sausage, cut into ½-inch pieces

Hot Sauce

- 2 tomatoes, cored, seeded, and chopped fine
- 1 onion, chopped fine
- 1 small green bell pepper, stemmed, seeded, and chopped fine
- 1 jalapeño chile, stemmed, seeded, and minced
- ⅓ cup white wine vinegar
- 3 tablespoons extra-virgin olive oil
- 1 tablespoon minced fresh cilantro
- ½ teaspoon salt

1 For the stew Adjust oven rack to lower-middle position and heat oven to 325 degrees. Pat pork dry with paper towels and season with salt and pepper. Heat 1 tablespoon oil in Dutch oven over medium-high heat until just smoking. Add half of pork and brown well on all sides, 7 to 10 minutes; transfer to large bowl. Repeat with 1 tablespoon oil and remaining pork.

2 Add bacon to fat left in pot and cook over medium heat until crisp, 5 to 7 minutes. Stir in remaining 1 tablespoon oil, onion, and ¼ teaspoon salt and cook until onion is softened, about 5 minutes. Stir in garlic, chili powder, cumin, and coriander and cook until fragrant, about 30 seconds.

3 Stir in water, beans, bay leaves, baking soda, ¼ teaspoon salt, and browned pork and any accumulated juices, and bring to simmer. Cover, transfer pot to oven, and cook for 1½ hours.

4 Remove pot from oven and stir in linguiça. Return covered pot to oven and cook until meat and beans are fully tender, about 30 minutes.

5 For the hot sauce While the stew cooks, combine all ingredients in bowl and let sit at room temperature until flavors meld, about 30 minutes. (Sauce can be refrigerated for up to 2 days.)

6 Remove stew from oven and discard bay leaves. (Stew can be refrigerated for up to 2 days; add additional water as needed to loosen sauce when reheating.) Season with salt and pepper to taste and serve with hot sauce.

HEARTY BEEF AND VEGETABLE CHILI

SERVES 6 TO 8   TOTAL TIME: 3 HOURS 15 MINUTES

WHY THIS RECIPE WORKS For a beef and vegetable chili that was greater than the sum of its parts, we examined the use of each ingredient carefully. We started with well-marbled, inexpensive beef chuck-eye for its ability to become meltingly tender. We browned it for rich flavor and then stewed it long enough to make it fork-tender. An aromatic base of garlic, cumin, chipotle, and chili powder gave our stew real depth of flavor and some heat. The heat balanced out the sweetness of our sweet potatoes and bell pepper, and mild beer added further complexity. We added a quarter of the potatoes in the beginning, knowing that they would break down to thicken our stew, and we stirred in the beans with the tomatoes so that they cooked enough to absorb flavor but not so much that they fell apart. Once our meat was tender, we added the rest of our potatoes and bell pepper, cooking them just long enough to have toothsome chunks in our stew. Light-bodied American lagers, such as Budweiser, work best in this recipe. Serve with lime wedges, sliced avocado, cilantro leaves, sour cream, and shredded Monterey Jack or cheddar cheese.

3½ pounds boneless beef chuck-eye roast, pulled apart at seams, trimmed, and cut into 1-inch pieces
    Salt and pepper
3   tablespoons vegetable oil
1   onion, chopped
1½ pounds sweet potatoes, peeled and cut into ½-inch pieces (3½ cups)
3   garlic cloves, minced
1   tablespoon ground cumin
1   tablespoon minced canned chipotle chile in adobo sauce
2   teaspoons chili powder
1   (28-ounce) can diced tomatoes
1½ cups beer
2   (15-ounce) cans black beans, rinsed
1   red bell pepper, stemmed, seeded, and cut into ½-inch pieces
4   scallions, sliced thin

1 Adjust oven rack to middle position and heat oven to 300 degrees. Pat beef dry with paper towels and season with salt and pepper. Heat 1 tablespoon oil in Dutch oven over medium heat until shimmering. Add half of beef and brown on all sides, 6 to 8 minutes; transfer to large bowl. Repeat with 1 tablespoon oil and remaining beef.

2 Add remaining 1 tablespoon oil to now-empty pot and heat until shimmering. Add onion and ¾ cup sweet potatoes and cook until just beginning to brown, 5 to 7 minutes. Stir in garlic, cumin, chipotle, chili powder, and 1 teaspoon salt and cook until fragrant, about 30 seconds. Add tomatoes and their juice, beer, beans, and browned beef and any accumulated juices, scraping up any browned bits.

3 Bring chili to simmer. Cover, transfer pot to oven, and cook, stirring occasionally, until sweet potatoes are broken down and beef is just tender, about 1 hour 40 minutes.

4 Stir in remaining sweet potatoes and bell pepper and continue to cook until meat and sweet potatoes are tender, about 20 minutes.

5 Remove pot from oven, uncover, and let chili stand until thickened slightly, about 15 minutes. (Chili can be refrigerated for up to 2 days; add additional broth as needed to loosen sauce when reheating.) Season with salt and pepper to taste and sprinkle with scallions before serving.

INDIAN-STYLE CHICKEN CURRY

SERVES 4 TO 6   TOTAL TIME: 1 HOUR 45 MINUTES

WHY THIS RECIPE WORKS We wanted to serve up a bold, authentic-tasting curry using supermarket staples. Working with bone-in, skin-on chicken parts meant we could count on some flavorful renderings to enrich the curry sauce. After browning the meat in our Dutch oven, we softened chopped onion and bloomed curry powder and garam masala right in the juices for a complex base without much effort. Garlic, a minced jalapeño, fresh ginger, and tomato paste brought in tons of extra flavor. The result: a superfragrant, richly spiced base. Adding a bit of water produced an intense braising liquid for our chicken parts. Once the meat was fully cooked, we finished off the curry sauce. Canned coconut milk and butter added richness and body to the curry, while chopped tomatoes and frozen peas offered convenient color and freshness. This sauce was plenty thick, so we cooked it just enough to warm the vegetables before spooning it over the tender chicken. For more spice, reserve, mince, and add the ribs and seeds from the jalapeño chile. We prefer the richer flavor of regular coconut milk here; however, light coconut milk can be substituted. Serve with rice.

4 pounds bone-in chicken pieces (split breasts cut in half, drumsticks, and/or thighs), trimmed
Salt and pepper
2 tablespoons vegetable oil
2 onions, chopped fine
2 tablespoons curry powder
6 garlic cloves, minced
1 jalapeño chile, stemmed, seeded, and minced
1 tablespoon grated fresh ginger
1 tablespoon tomato paste
1 teaspoon garam masala
1 cup water
2 plum tomatoes, cored, seeded, and chopped fine
½ cup frozen peas
½ cup canned coconut milk
2 tablespoons unsalted butter
¼ cup minced fresh cilantro

1 Pat chicken dry with paper towels and season with salt and pepper. Heat 1 tablespoon oil in Dutch oven over medium-high heat until just smoking. Add half of chicken and brown on both sides, 7 to 10 minutes; transfer to large bowl. Repeat with remaining 1 tablespoon oil and remaining chicken.

2 Add onions and ½ teaspoon salt to fat left in pot and cook until onions are softened, about 5 minutes. Stir in curry powder, garlic, jalapeño, ginger, tomato paste, and garam masala, and cook until fragrant, about 30 seconds. Gradually stir in water, scraping up any browned bits.

3 Nestle browned thighs and drumsticks (not breast pieces) and any accumulated juices into pot and bring to simmer. Cover, reduce heat to medium-low, and simmer for 30 minutes.

4 Add breast pieces and any accumulated juices to pot and continue to simmer, covered, until breasts register 160 degrees and drumsticks/thighs register 175 degrees, about 20 minutes, flipping chicken halfway through cooking.

5 Stir tomatoes, peas, coconut milk, and butter into pot and simmer gently until peas are heated through, 1 to 2 minutes. Stir in cilantro and season with salt and pepper to taste. Serve.

EGGPLANT AND SWEET POTATO CURRY

SERVES 4 TO 6   TOTAL TIME: 1 HOUR 15 MINUTES

WHY THIS RECIPE WORKS For a vegetarian take on curry, we sought out robust spices and a balanced sauce. Garlic, serrano chile, ginger, and tomato paste, cooked in curry powder and garam masala, created a bold base. Following an Indian cooking method called *bhuna*, we sautéed green beans and eggplant in the aromatics before adding pureed diced tomatoes for an assertive sauce. Coconut milk unified this simple dish. We prefer the richer flavor of regular coconut milk here; however, light coconut milk can be substituted. For more spice, reserve, mince, and add the ribs and seeds from the serrano chile. Serve with rice and Cilantro-Mint Chutney.

1 (14.5-ounce) can diced tomatoes
3 tablespoons vegetable oil
4 teaspoons curry powder
1½ teaspoons garam masala
2 onions, chopped fine
12 ounces sweet potatoes, peeled and cut into 1-inch pieces
Salt and pepper
3 garlic cloves, minced
1 serrano chile, stemmed, seeded, and minced
1 tablespoon grated fresh ginger
1 tablespoon tomato paste
1 pound eggplant, cut into ½-inch pieces
8 ounces green beans, trimmed and cut into 1-inch lengths
1½ cups water
1 (15-ounce) can chickpeas, rinsed
½ cup canned coconut milk
¼ cup minced fresh cilantro

1 Pulse diced tomatoes and their juice in food processor until nearly smooth, with ¼-inch pieces visible, about 3 pulses.

2 Heat oil in Dutch oven over medium-high heat until shimmering. Add curry powder and garam masala and cook until fragrant, about 10 seconds. Stir in onions, potatoes, and ¼ teaspoon salt and cook, stirring occasionally, until onions are browned and potatoes are golden brown at edges, about 10 minutes.

3 Reduce heat to medium. Stir in garlic, serrano, ginger, and tomato paste and cook until fragrant, about 30 seconds. Add eggplant and green beans and cook, stirring constantly, until vegetables are coated with spices, about 2 minutes.

4 Gradually stir in water, scraping up any browned bits. Stir in chickpeas and processed tomatoes and bring to simmer. Cover, reduce heat to medium-low, and simmer gently until vegetables are tender, 20 to 25 minutes.

5 Uncover, stir in coconut milk, and continue to cook until warmed through, 1 to 2 minutes. Off heat, stir in cilantro, season with salt and pepper to taste, and serve.

Cilantro-Mint Chutney

MAKES ABOUT 1 CUP

We prefer the richer flavor of whole-milk yogurt here; however, low-fat yogurt or nonfat yogurt can be substituted.

2 cups fresh cilantro leaves
1 cup fresh mint leaves
⅓ cup plain whole-milk yogurt
¼ cup finely chopped onion
1 tablespoon lime juice
1½ teaspoons sugar
½ teaspoon ground cumin
¼ teaspoon salt

Process all ingredients in food processor until smooth, about 20 seconds, scraping down sides of bowl as needed. (Chutney can be refrigerated for up to 1 day.)

CLASSIC ARROZ CON POLLO

SERVES 6   TOTAL TIME: 2 HOURS

WHY THIS RECIPE WORKS For a streamlined Mexican arroz con pollo full of classic flavors, we briefly marinated bone-in chicken thighs in a mixture of vinegar, salt, pepper, and oregano. Next we stewed the meat with tomato sauce, olives, capers, and rice until it became fall-off-the-bone tender while the rice cooked evenly. We started the chicken skin-on to maximize the flavorful renderings but then removed it after cooking. Using spoons rather than forks to pull the cooked meat apart gave us appealing chunks instead of shreds. To keep the dish from becoming greasy, it is important to remove excess fat and most of the skin from the chicken thighs, leaving just enough skin to protect the meat. Long-grain rice can be substituted for the medium-grain rice; however, you will need to increase the amount of water to ¾ cup.

6 garlic cloves, minced

5 teaspoons distilled white vinegar

1½ teaspoons minced fresh oregano or ½ teaspoon dried
   Salt and pepper

4 pounds bone-in chicken thighs, trimmed

2 tablespoons extra-virgin olive oil

1 onion, chopped fine

1 small green bell pepper, stemmed, seeded, and chopped fine

¼ teaspoon red pepper flakes

¼ cup minced fresh cilantro

1¾ cups chicken broth

1 (8-ounce) can tomato sauce

¼ cup water, plus extra as needed

3 cups medium-grain white rice

½ cup pitted green Manzanilla olives, halved

1 tablespoon capers, rinsed

½ cup jarred whole pimentos, cut into 2 by ¼-inch strips
   Lemon wedges

1 Adjust oven rack to middle position and heat oven to 350 degrees. Combine garlic, 1 tablespoon vinegar, oregano, 1 teaspoon salt, and ½ teaspoon pepper in large bowl. Add chicken, toss to coat, and cover; let sit at room temperature for 15 minutes.

2 While chicken marinates, heat 1 tablespoon oil in Dutch oven over medium heat until shimmering. Add onion and bell pepper and cook until softened, 5 to 7 minutes. Stir in pepper flakes and cook until fragrant, about 30 seconds. Stir in 2 tablespoons cilantro.

3 Push vegetables to side of pot and increase heat to medium-high. Add chicken, skin side down, to cleared area of pot and cook lightly on both sides, 2 to 4 minutes per side, reducing heat if chicken begins to brown. Stir in broth, tomato sauce, and water and bring to simmer. Cover, reduce heat to medium-low, and simmer for 20 minutes.

4 Stir in rice, olives, capers, and ¾ teaspoon salt and bring to simmer. Cover, transfer pot to oven, and cook, stirring often, until chicken registers 175 degrees, rice is tender, and liquid has been absorbed, about 30 minutes. (If pot appears dry and begins to scorch after 20 minutes, stir in additional ¼ cup water.)

5 Remove pot from oven and transfer chicken to cutting board; cover pot and set aside. Let chicken cool slightly, then shred into bite-size pieces using 2 soup-spoons, discarding skin and bones. Toss chicken chunks, pimentos, remaining 2 teaspoons vinegar, remaining 1 tablespoon oil, and remaining 2 table-spoons cilantro in clean bowl and season with salt and pepper to taste.

6 Place chicken on top of rice, cover, and let stand until warmed through, about 5 minutes. Serve with lemon wedges.

BIRYANI-STYLE CHICKEN AND RICE WITH CARAMELIZED ONIONS, CARDAMOM, AND RAISINS

SERVES 6   TOTAL TIME: 2 HOURS

WHY THIS RECIPE WORKS Inspired by the warming, complex spices used in traditional chicken biryani, we set out to reinvent chicken and rice with Indian flair. After browning chicken thighs to boost their flavor, we created a darkly sweet base by caramelizing sliced onions with brown sugar. To that we added a bold, colorful array of spices—fresh ginger, cardamom, cumin, and saffron—and bloomed their flavors before adding in our cooking liquid: chicken broth. We simmered the browned chicken in this richly flavored liquid before adding in the rice and moving the whole production to the oven to finish cooking in its gentle, even heat. After about 20 minutes and a few periodic stirs, the grains had taken on a golden hue and tender texture. We shredded the chicken for easier eating and stirred in some raisins and minced cilantro for bursts of sweetness and freshness. To keep the dish from becoming greasy, it is important to remove excess fat from the chicken thighs and most of the skin from the chicken thighs, leaving just enough skin to protect the meat. Be sure to stir the rice gently when cooking in step 3; aggressive stirring will make it gluey.

2½ pounds bone-in chicken thighs, trimmed
    Salt and pepper
1 tablespoon extra-virgin olive oil
3 onions, sliced thin
1 teaspoon packed brown sugar
4 garlic cloves, minced
2 teaspoons grated fresh ginger
½ teaspoon ground cardamom
½ teaspoon ground cumin
⅛ teaspoon saffron threads, crumbled
1 teaspoon minced fresh thyme or ¼ teaspoon dried
2½ cups chicken broth
2 cups long-grain white rice, rinsed
⅓ cup raisins
3 tablespoons minced fresh cilantro
½ teaspoon grated lemon zest plus 4 teaspoons juice

1 Adjust oven rack to middle position and heat oven to 350 degrees. Pat chicken dry with paper towels and season with salt and pepper. Heat oil in Dutch oven over medium-high heat until just smoking. Add half of chicken, skin side down, and brown on 1 side, 6 to 8 minutes; transfer to large plate. Repeat with remaining chicken.

2 Pour off all but 2 tablespoons fat left in pot. Add onions, sugar, and ½ teaspoon salt and cook over medium heat, stirring often, until onions are deep golden brown, 25 to 35 minutes. Stir in garlic, ginger, cardamom, cumin, saffron, and thyme and cook until fragrant, about 30 seconds. Stir in broth, scraping up any browned bits. Add chicken, browned side up, and any accumulated juices and bring to simmer. Cover and simmer gently for 20 minutes.

3 Stir in rice. Cover, transfer pot to oven, and cook, stirring occasionally, until chicken registers 175 degrees, rice is tender, and liquid has been absorbed, 20 to 30 minutes.

4 Remove pot from oven and transfer chicken to cutting board; cover pot and set aside. Let chicken cool slightly, then shred into bite-size pieces using 2 forks, discarding skin and bones. Gently stir shredded chicken, raisins, cilantro, and lemon zest and juice into rice, and season with salt and pepper to taste. Cover and let stand until chicken is warmed through, about 5 minutes. Serve.

LENTILS AND RICE WITH YOGURT SAUCE AND CRUNCHY TOASTED ALMONDS

SERVES 4 TO 6   TOTAL TIME: 1 HOUR 30 MINUTES

WHY THIS RECIPE WORKS Vegetarian comfort food at its best, this dish is a textbook example of how a few humble ingredients can add up to something satisfying and complex. We used a pilaf method to cook the rice and lentils, blooming warm spices and toasting the rice in shallot-infused oil to deepen the flavor and enhance the rice's nuttiness. Giving the lentils a 15-minute head start ensured that they finished cooking along with the rice. Soaking the rice in hot water gave it a fluffy, not sticky, texture. To make our hearty dish more of a complete meal, we added baby spinach, which wilted as the mixture sat covered for 10 minutes. A sprinkle of toasted almonds provided much-needed textural contrast, and a bracing garlicky yogurt sauce made the perfect finishing touch. We prefer the richer flavor of whole-milk yogurt here; however, low-fat or nonfat yogurt can be substituted. Either large green or brown lentils works well in this recipe; do not substitute French green lentils, or *lentilles du Puy*.

Yogurt Sauce

- 1 cup plain whole-milk yogurt
- 2 tablespoons lemon juice
- ½ teaspoon minced garlic
- ½ teaspoon salt

Lentils and Rice

- 8½ ounces (1¼ cups) large green or brown lentils, picked over and rinsed
- Salt and pepper
- 1¼ cups basmati rice
- 3 tablespoons vegetable oil
- 2 shallots, minced
- 3 garlic cloves, minced
- 1½ teaspoons ground coriander
- 1½ teaspoons ground cumin
- ¾ teaspoon ground cinnamon
- 6 ounces (6 cups) baby spinach
- ¼ cup sliced almonds, toasted

1 For the yogurt sauce Whisk all ingredients together in bowl; cover and refrigerate until serving.

2 For the lentils and rice Bring lentils, 4 cups water, and 1 teaspoon salt to boil in Dutch oven over high heat. Reduce heat to low and cook until lentils are tender, 15 to 17 minutes. Drain lentils and transfer to large bowl.

3 While lentils cook, place rice in medium bowl, add hot tap water to cover by 2 inches, and let stand 15 minutes. Using hands, gently swish rice to release excess starch, then carefully pour off water. Continue to add cold tap water to bowl of rice, swish gently, and pour off starchy water 4 to 5 more times until water runs almost clear. Drain rice in fine-mesh strainer.

4 Add oil and shallots to now-empty pot and cook over medium heat until shallots are softened, 3 to 5 minutes. Stir in garlic, coriander, cumin, cinnamon, and ¼ teaspoon pepper and cook until fragrant, about 30 seconds. Stir in drained rice and cook, stirring occasionally, until edges of rice begin to turn translucent, about 3 minutes. Stir in 2½ cups water and 1 teaspoon salt and bring to boil. Stir in lentils, reduce heat to low, cover, and cook until rice is tender and liquid has been absorbed, about 12 minutes.

5 Remove pot from heat and place spinach on top of lentils and rice. Lay clean dish towel over pot, cover with lid, and let sit for 10 minutes. Using fork, fluff lentils and rice and incorporate wilted spinach. Season with salt and pepper to taste, sprinkle with almonds, and serve with yogurt sauce.

SPICY PORK TINGA AND RICE

SERVES 4 TO 6   TOTAL TIME: 2 HOURS 30 MINUTES

WHY THIS RECIPE WORKS Spiced with chipotle chiles and bathed in a tomatoey sauce, pork tinga is a rich stew-like dish from Mexico. Rather than spooning it onto crispy tostadas, we used rice to absorb the sauce's flavors in this simple one-pot meal. The challenge lay in maintaining the dish's bold essence while achieving perfectly tender pork and well-cooked rice, all in the same pot. Early attempts were lackluster in flavor, so we browned the pork in batches to develop a golden brown crust. The technique worked, imparting a meaty richness to the rice as it simmered away. We built upon our rich fond by adding onions, garlic, herbs, and chipotle chile in adobe sauce. The chipotles lent a subtle heat, as well as smokiness and depth. To provide a more substantial, meaty bite with the rice, we again veered away from many recipes that shred the pork and instead chose to leave the tender, cooked pork in chunks. Finally, we finished our dish with a sprinkling of fresh chopped scallions and cilantro, along with a splash of lime juice. You can vary the spice level of this dish by adjusting the amount of chipotle chiles. Pork butt roast is often labeled Boston butt in the supermarket.

1 (2-pound) boneless pork butt roast, pulled apart at
  seams, trimmed, and cut into 1-inch pieces
  Salt and pepper
2 tablespoons extra-virgin olive oil
2 onions, chopped fine
5 garlic cloves, minced
1–2 tablespoons minced canned chipotle chile in
  adobo sauce
2 teaspoons minced fresh oregano or
  ½ teaspoon dried
1 teaspoon minced fresh thyme or ¼ teaspoon dried
2 cups chicken broth
1 (8-ounce) can tomato sauce
1½ cups long-grain white rice, rinsed
½ cup minced fresh cilantro
3 scallions, sliced thin
1 tablespoon lime juice

1 Adjust oven rack to lower-middle position and heat to 300 degrees. Pat pork dry with paper towels and season with salt and pepper. Heat 1 tablespoon oil in Dutch oven over medium-high heat until just smoking. Add half of pork and brown on all sides, 7 to 10 minutes; transfer to large bowl. Repeat with remaining 1 tablespoon oil and remaining pork.

2 Add onions and ½ teaspoon salt to fat left in pot and cook over medium heat until onions are softened, about 5 minutes. Stir in garlic, chipotle, oregano, and thyme and cook until fragrant, about 30 seconds. Stir in broth and tomato sauce, scraping up any browned bits.

3 Add browned pork and any accumulated juices and bring to simmer. Cover, transfer pot to oven, and cook until pork is tender, 75 to 90 minutes.

4 Remove pot from oven and increase oven temperature to 350 degrees. Using large spoon, skim any fat from surface of broth. Stir in rice, return covered pot to oven, and cook, gently stirring every 10 minutes, until rice is tender and liquid has been absorbed, 20 to 30 minutes.

5 Remove pot from oven and stir in cilantro, scallions, and lime juice. Season with salt and pepper to taste. Cover and let stand 5 minutes before serving.

MEDITERRANEAN BAKED CHICKEN AND BULGUR

SERVES 4 TOTAL TIME: 1 HOUR

WHY THIS RECIPE WORKS For a Mediterranean spin on a classic weeknight meal—chicken with vegetables and a grain—we chose bulgur, which we could cook in the microwave, and paired it with bold spices, juicy chicken breasts, and savory, stewed eggplant for a complete meal that was ready in no time. We seared boneless, skinless chicken breasts on just one side, an unfussy way to create flavorful browning. Removing them from the pot, we then cooked eggplant with some aromatics—onion, garlic, coriander, and fenugreek—which built layers of flavor. Next, we stirred in diced tomatoes and placed our chicken on top. In about 15 minutes, everything was perfectly cooked. While the chicken simmered, we made quick work of our side dish, microwaving the bulgur with broth and curry powder for a quick, flavor-packed accompaniment. As soon as the chicken was fully cooked, we removed it from the pot and stirred quick-wilting baby spinach into the warm vegetables. Adding cilantro to the bulgur and sprinkling more over the chicken and vegetables added freshness, and a squeeze of lime delivered instant brightness. When shopping, do not confuse bulgur with cracked wheat, which has a much longer cooking time and will not work in this recipe.

WEEKNIGHT
FRIENDLY

4 (6- to 8-ounce) boneless, skinless chicken breasts, trimmed
Salt and pepper
2 tablespoons extra-virgin olive oil
1 pound eggplant, cut into ½-inch pieces
1 onion, chopped
3 garlic cloves, minced
2 teaspoons ground coriander
1 teaspoon ground fenugreek
1 (14.5-ounce) can diced tomatoes, drained
1½ cups chicken broth
1 cup fine-grind bulgur
2 teaspoons curry powder
¼ cup minced fresh cilantro
4 ounces (4 cups) baby spinach
Lime wedges

1 Pat chicken dry with paper towels and season with salt and pepper. Heat 1 tablespoon oil in Dutch oven over medium-high heat until just smoking. Add chicken and brown on 1 side, about 5 minutes; transfer to large plate.

2 Add remaining 1 tablespoon oil, eggplant, onion, ½ teaspoon salt, and ½ teaspoon pepper to now-empty pot and cook over medium heat until vegetables are softened and beginning to brown, 5 to 7 minutes. Stir in garlic, coriander, and fenugreek and cook until fragrant, about 30 seconds. Stir in tomatoes. Nestle chicken, browned side up, and any accumulated juices into pot. Reduce heat to low, cover, and simmer gently until chicken registers 160 degrees, 12 to 15 minutes.

3 While chicken cooks, whisk broth, bulgur, curry powder, and ½ teaspoon salt together in large bowl. Microwave, covered, until bulgur is tender and has absorbed all liquid, about 5 minutes. Fluff bulgur with fork, stir in 2 tablespoons cilantro, and cover with aluminum foil to keep warm.

4 Transfer chicken to platter and cover with foil to keep warm. Stir spinach into eggplant mixture left in pot and cook over medium heat, stirring occasionally, until spinach is wilted and tender, about 3 minutes. Season with salt and pepper to taste and sprinkle with remaining 2 tablespoons cilantro. Serve with lime wedges.

ITALIAN SAUSAGE WITH WHITE BEANS AND KALE

SERVES 4   TOTAL TIME: 1 HOUR

WHY THIS RECIPE WORKS Nothing is more comforting on a cool night than a flavorful bowl of hearty beans and sausage. For a new take on this simple dish, we paired creamy, tender white beans and robust kale with meaty Italian sausage. Since we aimed to cook down a lot of kale, the Dutch oven was the ideal vessel. We wanted the sausages to be napped in a velvety sauce, so we started by pureeing cannellini beans with canned diced tomatoes. The canned tomatoes' juices and some chicken broth thinned out and deepened the flavor of the thick puree. Next, we ensured the sausages held their shape by pricking the casings with a fork before cooking. After browning them to build some fond, we removed the sausages, softened chopped onion in their meaty renderings, and added garlic and the bean-tomato puree to the pot. Adding in extra diced tomatoes created some textural contrast, and wilting a whole pound of kale was as easy as stirring it into the pot, covering it, and letting it simmer away. We returned the browned sausages to the pot along with more cannellinis during the last 10 minutes of cooking, allowing the sausages to cook through and the beans to absorb some of the flavorful broth before serving. Serve with crusty bread.

2 (15-ounce) cans cannellini beans, rinsed
1 (28-ounce) can diced tomatoes, drained with juice reserved
1 cup chicken broth
2 tablespoons extra-virgin olive oil
1 pound sweet or hot Italian sausage, pricked all over with fork
1 onion, chopped fine
3 garlic cloves, minced
1 pound kale, stemmed and chopped
  Salt and pepper

1 Puree ½ cup beans, ½ cup tomatoes, reserved tomato juice, and chicken broth in food processor until smooth, about 30 seconds.

2 Heat oil in Dutch oven over medium heat until shimmering. Add sausages and brown on all sides, about 5 minutes; transfer to plate.

3 Add onion to fat left in pot and cook until softened, 5 to 7 minutes. Stir in garlic and cook until fragrant, about 30 seconds. Stir in tomato puree mixture, kale, remaining drained tomatoes, and ¼ teaspoon salt, scraping up any browned bits. Cover and simmer, stirring occasionally, until kale is wilted and tender, about 15 minutes.

4 Stir in remaining beans, then nestle browned sausages and any accumulated juices into pot. Cover and simmer until sausages register 160 degrees and sauce is thickened slightly, about 10 minutes. Season with salt and pepper to taste and serve.

PASTA WITH SAUSAGE, KALE, AND WHITE BEANS

SERVES 4   TOTAL TIME: 1 HOUR

WHY THIS RECIPE WORKS We had our hearts set on a stick-to-your-ribs one-pot pasta loaded with tender bites of browned sausage, hearty kale, and creamy cannellini beans. To streamline this classic combination, rather than boiling the pasta separately or removing the sausage from the pot once it had browned, we built flavor in layers, allowing the addition of each component to build a creamy sauce that tied the dish together. After browning the sausage, we added chopped onion and a can of cannellini beans and cooked them right alongside the meat. Some of the beans broke down, creating an effortlessly creamy sauce, and those that held their shape absorbed lots of meaty flavor along the way. To boost the sausage's robust seasoning, we stirred in minced garlic, fennel seeds, oregano, and red pepper flakes, blooming their fragrances in the hearty base. When it came to the pasta, orecchiette's earlike shape promised to trap the hearty sauce without getting too entwined with the kale. We added the orecchiette along with both water and chicken broth and brought the mixture to a simmer. Incorporating the chopped kale in stages worked best, as adding it all at once caused the pasta to cook unevenly by forming an unwanted insulating barrier around the orecchiette. Plus, the longer-cooked kale blended into the sauce while the kale added later contributed nice texture to the dish. Our finished dish boasted perfectly al dente pasta with plenty of flavor—an ideal weeknight dinner. You can substitute 8 ounces of other pasta shapes for the orecchiette; however, the cup amounts will vary as follows: 2½ cups for ziti, penne, and campanelle; 3 cups for medium shells; and 3¼ cups for farfalle.

WEEKNIGHT FRIENDLY

2 tablespoons extra-virgin olive oil
1 pound hot Italian sausage, casings removed
1 onion, chopped fine
1 (15-ounce) can cannellini beans, rinsed
6 garlic cloves, minced
1½ teaspoons minced fresh oregano or ½ teaspoon dried
½ teaspoon fennel seeds
⅛ teaspoon red pepper flakes
3 cups chicken broth
1 cup water
8 ounces (2¼ cups) orecchiette
12 ounces kale, stemmed and chopped
1 ounce Pecorino Romano cheese, grated (½ cup), plus extra for serving
Salt and pepper

1 Heat 1 tablespoon oil in Dutch oven over medium-high heat until just smoking. Add sausage and cook, breaking meat into ½-inch pieces, until lightly browned, 5 to 7 minutes. Stir in onion and beans and cook until onion is softened, 5 to 7 minutes. Stir in garlic, oregano, fennel seeds, and pepper flakes and cook until fragrant, about 30 seconds.

2 Stir in broth and water, increase heat to high, and bring to boil. Stir in pasta and half of kale. Cover, reduce heat to medium, and simmer vigorously for 4 minutes. Place remaining kale in pot without stirring, cover, and continue to cook until kale is just tender, about 4 minutes.

3 Stir to incorporate kale and simmer, uncovered and stirring occasionally, until most of liquid is absorbed and orecchiette is tender, 3 to 6 minutes. Off heat, stir in Pecorino and remaining 1 tablespoon oil. Season with salt and pepper to taste and serve with extra Pecorino.

PENNE WITH CHICKEN, ARTICHOKES, CHERRY TOMATOES, AND OLIVES

SERVES 4 TOTAL TIME: 1 HOUR

WHY THIS RECIPE WORKS Pasta with chicken and vegetables makes for a convenient and satisfying weeknight meal—so long as it doesn't turn out bland. We set out to create a Mediterranean-style pasta that was lightly sauced and full of character. Boneless chicken breasts were an obvious starting point; we sliced and cooked them quickly then focused on the sauce. Penne pairs well with brothy sauces because the liquid binds to the tubes, inside and out. With this in mind, we browned minced onion with garlic, oregano, and red pepper flakes, then deglazing with wine for a slightly acidic base. Pouring in chicken broth and water, we simmered our penne in this flavorful liquid. Halfway through cooking, we started to introduce our Mediterranean flavors by adding frozen artichokes. Once the pasta was nearly cooked and the liquid had reduced to a tasty sauce, we stirred in quartered cherry tomatoes for a hit of bright acidity, kalamata olives for briny contrast, and grated Parmesan for a subtle creaminess. You can substitute 8 ounces of other pasta shapes for the penne; however, the cup amounts will vary as follows: 2¼ cups for orecchiette, 2½ cups for ziti and campanelle; 3 cups for medium shells; and 3¼ cups for farfalle. If necessary, add hot water, 1 tablespoon at a time, to adjust the consistency of the sauce before serving.

1 pound boneless, skinless chicken breasts, trimmed and sliced thin crosswise
Salt and pepper
3 tablespoons extra-virgin olive oil
1 onion, chopped fine
6 garlic cloves, minced
1 teaspoon minced fresh oregano or ¼ teaspoon dried
⅛ teaspoon red pepper flakes
½ cup dry white wine
2 cups chicken broth
1¾ cups water
8 ounces (2½ cups) penne
9 ounces frozen artichoke hearts, thawed
12 ounces cherry tomatoes, quartered
½ cup pitted kalamata olives
2 ounces Parmesan cheese, grated (1 cup), plus extra for serving
2 tablespoons minced fresh parsley

1 Pat chicken dry with paper towels and season with salt and pepper. Heat 2 tablespoons oil in Dutch oven over medium-high heat until just smoking. Add chicken, breaking up any clumps, and cook without stirring until lightly browned and just cooked through, 2 to 3 minutes; transfer to bowl and cover to keep warm.

2 Add remaining 1 tablespoon oil and onion to pot and cook over medium heat until onion is softened, about 5 minutes. Stir in garlic, oregano, and pepper flakes and cook until fragrant, about 30 seconds. Stir in wine, scraping up any browned bits, and cook until nearly evaporated, about 1 minute.

3 Stir in broth, water, pasta, and ½ teaspoon salt, increase heat to high, and bring to boil. Reduce heat to medium and simmer vigorously, stirring often, for 10 minutes. Stir in artichokes and continue to cook until pasta is tender and sauce is thickened, 5 to 8 minutes.

4 Reduce heat to low and stir in tomatoes, olives, cooked chicken and any accumulated juices, and Parmesan. Cook, tossing pasta gently, until well coated, 1 to 2 minutes. Season with salt and pepper to taste, sprinkle with parsley, and serve with additional Parmesan.

CREAMY PASTA WITH MUSHROOMS, BUTTERNUT SQUASH, AND PINE NUTS

SERVES 4 TO 6   TOTAL TIME: 1 HOUR 15 MINUTES

WHY THIS RECIPE WORKS We wanted to create a pasta dish that brought out the delicate, earthy flavor hiding in supermarket mushrooms. We selected cremini mushrooms, which have a meatier texture and a more intense, woodsy flavor than button mushrooms but are still readily available. Butternut squash heightened the dish's wintertime appeal and gave it heft and a subtle sweetness that perfectly complemented the mushrooms. To start, we sautéed the mushrooms with shallots, garlic, thyme, and a small amount of salt to help them release their liquid, then added the squash. The liquid released by the mushrooms was just enough to steam the squash, and cooking both together gave the smaller mushroom pieces time to brown and create fond. We removed the vegetables, and then poured in chicken broth and water to cook our pasta. Tubular *mezzi* ("shortened") rigatoni mimicked the shape of the squash, and their ridged edges held the sauce well. Adding heavy cream toward the end of cooking, and then stirring vigorously while mixing in Parmesan cheese, drew out the pasta's starches and created a thick, creamy sauce, into which we folded our meaty cooked vegetables. A splash of lemon juice, a sprinkling of fresh chives, and some toasted pine nuts were the perfect finishes to the dish. You can substitute 1 pound of rigatoni, ziti, penne, medium shells, farfalle, or campanelle for the mezzi rigatoni if desired.

1   tablespoon extra-virgin olive oil
2   large shallots, minced
3   garlic cloves, minced
4   teaspoons minced fresh thyme or 1½ teaspoons dried
12 ounces cremini mushrooms, trimmed and sliced thin
    Salt and pepper
1½ pounds butternut squash, peeled, seeded, and cut into ½-inch pieces (4 cups)
2½ cups water
2   cups chicken broth
1   pound mezzi rigatoni
½   cup heavy cream
2   ounces Parmesan cheese, grated (1 cup)
1   tablespoon lemon juice
2   tablespoons minced fresh chives
¼   cup pine nuts, toasted

1 Heat oil in Dutch oven over medium heat until shimmering. Add shallots and cook until softened, about 3 minutes. Stir in garlic and thyme and cook until fragrant, about 30 seconds. Stir in mushrooms and ½ teaspoon salt and cook until mushrooms begin to release their liquid, about 4 minutes. Stir in squash, cover, and cook, stirring occasionally, until squash is tender and lightly browned, about 12 minutes. Transfer vegetables to bowl and cover to keep warm.

2 Add water, broth, and ¼ teaspoon salt to now-empty Dutch oven, scraping up any browned bits. Increase heat to high and bring to boil. Stir in pasta, reduce heat to medium, and simmer vigorously, stirring often, until pasta is nearly tender, about 10 minutes.

3 Stir in cream and continue to simmer until pasta is tender and has absorbed most of liquid, about 4 minutes.

4 Add Parmesan and stir vigorously until sauce is creamy and pasta is well coated, about 30 seconds. Stir in reserved vegetables and lemon juice and cook until heated through, about 1 minute. Off heat, stir in chives and season with salt and pepper to taste. Sprinkle with pine nuts and serve.

BUCATINI WITH PEAS, KALE, AND PANCETTA

SERVES 4 TO 6   TOTAL TIME: 45 MINUTES

WHY THIS RECIPE WORKS Salty pancetta and fresh, sweet peas are a classic combination and make a great base for pasta, which eagerly takes up the pancetta's rich flavors. Add in hearty but quick-cooking baby kale and you have a simple, fresh pasta dish with a meaty backbone. For our pasta, we opted for thick-stranded bucatini, similar to spaghetti but hollow, which allowed the pasta to absorb plenty of flavorful sauce. To build our base, we first rendered the pancetta, reserving the crispy pieces for garnish and using the fat to bloom bright lemon zest and garlic. Then we added white wine, chicken broth, and water to build a savory cooking liquid for our pasta. As the liquid simmered down and our pasta approached doneness, we stirred in baby kale and peas, letting everything finish together. A quick, vigorous stir with the addition of some Parmesan at the end of cooking bound the now-reduced liquid into a cheesy, cohesive sauce. For a flavorful topping and some crunchy contrast, we topped off each serving with a mixture of panko, Parmesan, and lemon zest, as well as the crisped pancetta. You can substitute 1 pound of spaghetti for the bucatini if desired.

½ cup panko bread crumbs, toasted
1½ ounces Parmesan cheese, grated (¾ cup)
1 tablespoon extra-virgin olive oil
1 tablespoon grated lemon zest
Salt and pepper
2 ounces pancetta, cut into ½-inch pieces
2 garlic cloves, minced
½ cup dry white wine
2½ cups water
2 cups chicken broth
1 pound bucatini
5 ounces (5 cups) baby kale
1 cup frozen peas

1 Combine toasted panko, ¼ cup Parmesan, oil, 1 teaspoon lemon zest, ¼ teaspoon salt, and ¼ teaspoon pepper in bowl. Cook pancetta in Dutch oven over medium heat until crisp, 6 to 8 minutes; transfer to paper towel–lined plate.

2 Add garlic and remaining 2 teaspoons zest to fat left in pot and cook until fragrant, about 30 seconds. Stir in wine, scraping up any browned bits, and cook until nearly evaporated, about 3 minutes. Stir in water and broth, scraping up any browned bits.

3 Increase heat to high and bring to boil. Stir in pasta, reduce heat to medium, and simmer vigorously, stirring often, until pasta is nearly tender, 8 to 10 minutes.

4 Stir in kale and peas and continue to simmer until pasta and kale are tender, about 4 minutes. Add remaining ½ cup Parmesan and stir vigorously until pasta is creamy and well coated, about 30 seconds. Season with salt and pepper to taste. Serve, sprinkling individual portions with crisp pancetta and bread-crumb mixture.

TOASTING PANKO BREAD CRUMBS

Toss bread crumbs with oil in shallow dish and season with salt and pepper. Microwave crumbs, stirring often, until crumbs are deep golden brown, 3 to 5 minutes.

MUSSELS MARINARA WITH SPAGHETTI

SERVES 4 TO 6   TOTAL TIME: 1 HOUR

WHY THIS RECIPE WORKS Mussels are made for one-pot meals. They're quick-cooking, flavorful, and relatively inexpensive, and they require minimal prep. Better still, they infuse everything else in the pot with their briny liquid, providing the base for a great sauce. To work these shellfish into a solid meal, we looked to an Italian classic, mussels marinara. Traditionally the mussels are draped in a spicy tomato sauce and served over pasta, but we needed to cook everything together in one pot, preparing both pasta and mussels directly in the sauce. Though "marinara" can suggest a smooth sauce, we thought a chunkier version would make this more of a meal. Pulsing whole canned tomatoes in the food processor did the trick. We gave our sauce plenty of oomph by adding finely chopped onion, lots of garlic, minced anchovy, and red pepper flakes, which would stand up well to the mussels. After trying the sauce, we wanted it to have more seafood character. Substituting some clam juice for some of the water increased the briny profile just enough. As for the mussels, we added them just as the spaghetti was nearing doneness. Within minutes, the shells gently opened and released their liquor, bolstering the briny marinara sauce further. With a glug of olive oil and a sprinkling of parsley, our simple yet sensational mussels marinara was ready. When adding the spaghetti in step 3, stir gently to avoid breaking the noodles; after a minute or two they will soften enough to be stirred more easily. If necessary, add hot water, 1 tablespoon at a time, to adjust the consistency of the sauce before serving. Discard any mussels with an unpleasant odor or a cracked or broken shell. Drizzle with extra-virgin olive oil and serve with crusty bread.

WEEKNIGHT FRIENDLY

2 (28-ounce) cans whole peeled tomatoes
3 tablespoons extra-virgin olive oil
1 onion, chopped fine
6 garlic cloves, minced
1 anchovy fillet, rinsed and minced
½ teaspoon red pepper flakes
2 cups water
1 (8-ounce) bottle clam juice
1 pound spaghetti
2 pounds mussels, scrubbed and debearded
¼ cup minced fresh parsley
    Salt and pepper

1 Working in 2 batches, pulse tomatoes and their juice in food processor until coarsely chopped and no large pieces remain, 6 to 8 pulses; transfer to bowl.

2 Heat 2 tablespoons oil in Dutch oven over medium heat until shimmering. Add onion and cook until softened, about 5 minutes. Stir in garlic, anchovy, and pepper flakes and cook until fragrant, about 30 seconds. Stir in processed tomatoes and simmer gently until tomatoes no longer taste raw, about 10 minutes.

3 Stir in water, clam juice, and pasta, increase heat to high, and bring to boil. Reduce heat to medium, cover, and simmer vigorously, stirring often, for 12 minutes. Stir in mussels, cover, and continue to simmer vigorously until pasta is tender and mussels have opened, 2 to 4 minutes.

4 Uncover, discard any mussels that refuse to open, reduce heat to low, and stir in remaining 1 tablespoon oil and parsley. Cook, tossing pasta gently, until well coated with sauce, 1 to 2 minutes. Season with salt and pepper to taste and serve.

LEMONY LINGUINE WITH SHRIMP AND SPINACH

SERVES 4 TO 6   TOTAL TIME: 1 HOUR

WHY THIS RECIPE WORKS Sweet shrimp, bright lemon, and tender spinach come together seamlessly in this one-pan interpretation of the Italian classic *spaghetti al limone*. The original is an example of simple Italian cooking at its best, where a few simple ingredients create an intensely flavored dish. Following suit, we knew the key to making our pasta sing was to coax maximum flavor out of each ingredient. Thinking resourcefully, we saved the shrimp shells and made a quick shrimp broth by simmering them with white wine for just 5 minutes, and then enhanced this with clam juice. We used this flavorful liquid to poach our shrimp and cook our pasta, which became infused with the shrimp's briny flavor as the liquid reduced. We found the flat, wide strands of linguine stood up better to the shrimp and spinach than did more traditional spaghetti. Baby spinach wilted immediately when stirred into the warm pasta along with our shrimp. To add plenty of lemon flavor, we whisked up a lemon-Parmesan dressing, using the citrus's zest as well as its juice, and poured this over the still-hot pasta to maximize absorption and create a nutty, creamy sauce. Finally, we finished the dish with a healthy pat of butter and a sprinkle of fresh basil, rounding out and balancing the sauce and accenting it with a hit of sweet, herbal flavor. For instructions on how to devein shrimp, see page 219.

5 tablespoons extra-virgin olive oil

2 teaspoons grated lemon zest plus ¼ cup juice (2 lemons)

1 garlic clove, minced
  Salt and pepper

1 ounce Parmesan cheese, grated (½ cup)

1 pound jumbo shrimp (16 to 20 per pound), peeled and deveined, shells reserved

2½ cups dry white wine

2½ cups water

1 (8-ounce) bottle clam juice

1 pound linguine

5 ounces (5 cups) baby spinach

¼ cup shredded fresh basil

2 tablespoons unsalted butter, softened

1 Whisk ¼ cup oil, lemon zest and juice, garlic, and ½ teaspoon salt together in bowl, then stir in Parmesan until thick and creamy; cover and set aside.

2 Heat remaining 1 tablespoon oil in Dutch oven over medium heat until shimmering. Add shrimp shells and cook, stirring frequently, until beginning to turn spotty brown, 2 to 4 minutes. Stir in wine and simmer until reduced slightly, about 5 minutes. Strain mixture through colander set over large bowl; discard shells.

3 Return reduced wine mixture to pot, add water and clam juice, and bring to gentle simmer over medium heat. Stir in shrimp and cook until just opaque throughout, about 2 minutes. Using slotted spoon, transfer shrimp to separate bowl.

4 Add pasta to liquid left in pot, increase heat to high, and bring to boil. Reduce heat to medium and simmer vigorously, stirring often, until pasta is tender, 12 to 14 minutes.

5 Off heat, stir in spinach and cooked shrimp and let sit until spinach is wilted and shrimp are warmed through, about 30 seconds. Stir in lemon sauce, basil, and butter until butter is melted and pasta is well coated. Season with salt and pepper to taste and serve.

THE CASSEROLE DISH

WEEKNIGHT
FRIENDLY

Hands-Off Spaghetti and Meatballs

The Casserole Dish Going Way Beyond Potluck

For many, this humble dish conjures up memories of, well, casseroles: cheesy, meaty, and loaded with homey, comforting flavors but also a lot of highly processed convenience items. We set out to breathe new life into this standby dish, filling it with layer upon layer of fresh, modern flavors and textures, covering everything from classic lasagna to baked quinoa.

Wondra-ful Thickening

While testing our recipes, we found that dishes we'd hoped would have lush, creamy sauces fell flat because the casserole dish was not conducive to thickening liquids quickly enough. That's when we discovered the power of Wondra—a finely ground, low-protein flour that is able to dissolve instantly (and with very few lumps) in hot and cold liquids alike. It proved a game changer.

Grease Is NOT the Word

Greasy, soggy, wet: These were all complaints raised during our early recipe tests. Since evaporation happens more slowly in a casserole dish, these recipes required lean, low-moisture ingredients that wouldn't create pools of grease or a mushy texture. Swapping in a cottage cheese–based sauce for béchamel, using a drier cheese like Parmesan, or working with precisely measured liquids delivered rich flavor without gooping up the dish.

Finish with a Blast of Heat

Like other one-pot pasta and rice dishes, these casseroles rely on the moisture in the surrounding sauce or liquid to cook through. To get the ingredients to heat thoroughly, we often sealed everything under a layer of aluminum foil, trapping steam for speedier cooking. But we always finished these dishes uncovered—you need that blast of dry heat to melt and brown a cheesy topping or create a crisp crust. We also used this final stage as an opportunity to add a topping that served the recipe best by being barely cooked, like chopped basil or fresh tomatoes.

Frozen's Just Fine

Old-school casseroles are often maligned for their reliance on convenience items (think plasticky cheese sauces or canned soup), but when it came to our one-dish dinners, we didn't hesitate to look in the freezer aisle. While nothing beats farm-fresh vegetables, frozen, canned, or jarred produce offers guaranteed success year-round. Opting for these easy (and inexpensive) ingredients meant we could serve up recipes with fresh-tasting okra, tomatoes, artichokes, or spinach at any time of year. Likewise, store-bought puff pastry and Boursin cheese tasted great and kept prep to a minimum.

Equipping Your Kitchen

Casserole Dishes
The Not-So-Basic Basics

There's more to these dishes than meets the eye. Depending on the recipe, we rotated through three different casserole dishes: The classic tempered glass rectangle, its squared-off cousin, and a modern broiler-safe take on the original. It's wise to have all three on hand. The square and rectangular tempered glass dishes are great for many uses—we turned to the former for big-batch dinners and to the latter for richer meals that didn't fare as well as leftovers. Unfortunately, their manufacturer, Pyrex, has discovered that abrupt changes in temperature can cause unexpected cracking or shattering, making them unsafe for broiling. So, for casseroles that demand some extra browning, we tested porcelain dishes of the same rectangular dimensions and keep our winning model at the ready.

Our favorites: **Pyrex Bakeware 9x13 Baking Dish** ($8.99), **Pyrex 8-Inch Square Glass Baking Dish** ($9.00), and **HIC Porcelain Lasagna Baking Dish** ($37.49).

GOOD TO GO

Unlike meals made in heavy Dutch ovens, or time-sensitive stir-fries, casserole dish dinners are perfectly suited to packing up and bringing to a potluck party, and insulated food carriers make it easy to arrive with your casserole still piping hot. Our go-to carrier keeps food hot for more than 3 hours and expands to fit two 13 by 9-inch dishes. Our favorite: **Rachel Ray Expandable Lasagna Lugger** ($26.95).

VEGETABLE AND ORZO TIAN

SERVES 4 AS A MAIN DISH OR 6 AS A SIDE DISH   TOTAL TIME: 1 HOUR

WEEKNIGHT FRIENDLY

WHY THIS RECIPE WORKS For a Mediterranean-inspired vegetable casserole pairing creamy orzo and the summery flavors (and striking colors) of zucchini, summer squash, and tomatoes, we sought out a relatively hands-off approach. The challenge was getting pasta and vegetables to finish cooking simultaneously without sacrificing taste or texture. While most recipes first cook orzo separately in a pot, we achieved perfectly cooked pasta by tightly shingling the vegetables on the orzo's surface, trapping the moisture within the confines of the casserole dish. Swapping out water for vegetable broth as our cooking liquid reinforced the vegetables' flavor, and shallots and garlic mixed into the orzo provided aromatic depth and sweetness. Stirring in some Parmesan gave the orzo a creamy texture, and a combination of oregano and red pepper flakes contributed floral, spicy notes to this otherwise mild meal. To our delight, the pasta and vegetables were close to perfection after 20 minutes in a hot oven. More Parmesan cheese sprinkled on top of the vegetables before a few minutes under the broiler made for an appealing presentation, and chopped basil made for a fresh, bright finish. When shopping, look for squash, zucchini, and tomatoes with similar-size circumferences so that they are easy to shingle into the dish.

3 ounces Parmesan cheese, grated (1½ cups)

1 cup orzo

2 shallots, minced

3 tablespoons minced fresh oregano
  or 1 teaspoon dried

3 garlic cloves, minced

⅛ teaspoon red pepper flakes
  Salt and pepper

1 zucchini, sliced ¼ inch thick

1 yellow summer squash, sliced ¼ inch thick

1 pound plum tomatoes, cored and sliced ¼ inch thick

1¾ cups vegetable broth

1 tablespoon extra-virgin olive oil

2 tablespoons chopped fresh basil

1 Adjust oven rack to middle position and heat oven to 425 degrees. Combine ½ cup Parmesan, orzo, shallots, oregano, garlic, pepper flakes, and ¼ teaspoon salt in bowl. Spread mixture evenly into broiler-safe 13 by 9-inch baking dish. Alternately shingle zucchini, squash, and tomatoes in tidy rows on top of orzo.

2 Carefully pour broth over top of vegetables. Bake until orzo is just tender and most of broth is absorbed, about 20 minutes.

3 Remove dish from oven, adjust oven rack 9 inches from broiler element, and heat broiler. Drizzle vegetables with oil, season with salt and pepper, and sprinkle with remaining 1 cup Parmesan. Broil until nicely browned and bubbling around edges, about 5 minutes.

4 Remove dish from oven and let rest for 10 minutes. Sprinkle with basil before serving.

SHINGLING SLICED VEGETABLES

Shingle slices of zucchini, summer squash, and tomatoes tightly on top of uncooked orzo in tidy, attractive rows.

SPICY SHRIMP SKEWERS WITH CHEESY GRITS

SERVES 4 TO 6   TOTAL TIME: 1 HOUR 30 MINUTES

WHY THIS RECIPE WORKS Lowcountry-style shrimp and creamy grits doesn't immediately conjure up a casserole dish, but we thought this vessel had the potential to turn out a hands-off version of this comfort classic. A baking dish was certainly big enough to cook grits for a small crowd, and across its low sides we could perch rows of seasoned shrimp suspended on skewers. So we stirred up dry grits with bold flavorings, chicken broth, and milk right in our casserole dish, covered it, and baked until the grits were tender. Adding in cheddar cheese at that point (rather than at the start of baking) kept it from breaking down into an oily mess. Meanwhile, we tossed the shrimp with melted butter and chili powder, threaded them on skewers, and balanced them on the casserole. After 10 more minutes, the shrimp emerged tender and spicy above the now-thickened grits. Since we hadn't sautéed the shrimp in a sauce, we mixed a simple fragrant mixture of butter, chili powder, and smoky chipotle chile powder to dollop over our meal, tying the whole thing together. Chopped scallions and lime wedges finished the dish with a burst of fresh brightness. The grits' cooking time in step 1 will depend on the brand of grits. You will need eight 12-inch metal or bamboo skewers for this recipe. For instructions on how to devein shrimp, see page 219.

4½ cups chicken broth
1½ cups old-fashioned grits
¾ cup whole milk
3 scallions, white parts minced, green parts sliced thin on bias
2 garlic cloves, minced
    Salt and pepper
1½ pounds jumbo shrimp (16 to 20 per pound), peeled and deveined
4 tablespoons unsalted butter, melted
2 teaspoons chili powder
6 ounces sharp cheddar cheese, shredded (1½ cups)
1 teaspoon chipotle chile powder
    Lime wedges

1 Adjust oven rack to middle position and heat oven to 350 degrees. Spray 13 by 9-inch baking dish with vegetable oil spray. Combine broth, grits, milk, scallion whites, garlic, and ¼ teaspoon salt in prepared dish, cover tightly with aluminum foil, and bake until grits are tender, 50 to 75 minutes.

2 Pat shrimp dry with paper towels and toss in bowl with 1 tablespoon melted butter, 1 teaspoon chili powder, ¼ teaspoon salt, and ¼ teaspoon pepper.

Working with 1 shrimp at a time, thread tail onto one 12-inch skewer, and head onto second 12-inch skewer. Repeat with remaining shrimp, alternating direction of heads and tails, packing 6 to 8 shrimp tightly onto each pair of skewers.

3 Remove grits from oven and increase oven temperature to 450 degrees. Stir cheddar into grits and season with salt and pepper to taste. Lay shrimp skewers widthwise across baking dish so that shrimp hover over grits. Continue to bake grits and shrimp until shrimp are opaque throughout and grits have thickened slightly, about 10 minutes.

4 Meanwhile, microwave remaining 3 tablespoons melted butter, remaining 1 teaspoon chili powder, chipotle chile powder, and ⅛ teaspoon salt until fragrant, about 20 seconds.

5 Carefully remove dish from oven and transfer shrimp skewers to plate. Stir grits thoroughly, then portion into serving bowls. Remove shrimp from skewers and place on top of grits. Drizzle with spice butter, sprinkle with scallion greens, and serve with lime wedges.

CURRIED CHICKEN WITH COCONUT RICE AND LIME YOGURT SAUCE

SERVES 4   TOTAL TIME: 1 HOUR 15 MINUTES

WHY THIS RECIPES WORKS Chicken and rice casseroles can be dreary and bland. We wanted to give this dinner staple a complete makeover, in the process streamlining some of the steps in order to get great results from one pan. To liven things up, we looked to the warm, complex flavors associated with Indian curries. We cooked our rice in coconut milk, right in the baking dish, stirring in carrots to ensure they would become tender. We sliced the chicken thin and tossed it with bold spices—a mix of curry powder and minced garlic bloomed in the microwave. Because we cut the chicken into small pieces, all we had to do was fold it into the rice, along with some peas, for the last 10 minutes of cooking for tender, juicy results. Our robust casserole was done, but we thought a few simple accompaniments were necessary to give it the complex flavor we were looking for. We whisked up a light and tangy yogurt sauce seasoned with lime zest and juice and cilantro. A sprinkle of scallions provided a fresh, savory bite, and toasted almonds added a crunchy contrast to the tender rice. We prefer the richer flavor of whole-milk yogurt here; however, low-fat or nonfat yogurt can be substituted. For an accurate measurement of boiling water, bring a full kettle of water to a boil and then measure out the desired amount.

1 cup plain whole-milk yogurt
2 tablespoons minced fresh cilantro or mint
1 teaspoon grated lime zest plus 1 tablespoon juice
   Salt and pepper
2 cups boiling water
1⅓ cups long-grain white rice
¾ cup canned coconut milk
3 carrots, peeled and cut into ¼-inch pieces
2 tablespoons extra-virgin olive oil
2 garlic cloves, minced
1 tablespoon curry powder
1 pound boneless, skinless chicken breasts, trimmed, halved lengthwise, and sliced thin
1 cup frozen peas
⅓ cup sliced almonds, toasted
2 scallions, sliced thin

1 Adjust oven rack to middle position and heat oven to 450 degrees. Combine yogurt, cilantro, lime zest and juice, and ¼ teaspoon salt in bowl; cover and refrigerate until serving.

2 Combine boiling water, rice, coconut milk, carrots, and ½ teaspoon salt in 13 by 9-inch baking dish. Cover tightly with aluminum foil and bake until rice is nearly tender, 25 to 30 minutes.

3 While rice bakes, combine oil, garlic, curry powder, 1 teaspoon salt, and ¼ teaspoon pepper in large bowl and microwave until fragrant, about 30 seconds. Let mixture cool slightly, then stir in chicken.

4 Remove rice from oven, fluff gently with fork, and gently stir in chicken and peas. Re-cover tightly with foil and continue to bake until rice is tender and chicken is cooked through, 10 to 15 minutes.

5 Remove dish from oven, let cool for 10 minutes, then fluff rice gently with fork. Serve, drizzling individual portions with yogurt sauce and sprinkling with almonds and scallions.

DEVILED PORK CHOPS WITH SCALLOPED POTATOES

SERVES 4   TOTAL TIME: 1 HOUR 30 MINUTES

WHY THIS RECIPE WORKS   Could we improve on deviled pork chops served with scalloped potatoes by baking the chops on top of the potatoes for a hands-off one-pan meal? It was too tempting not to try. We had to be sure the chops would get a crisp, crackling coating while staying moist within, so we boosted the crumb coating's flavor with Parmesan cheese and made sure it clung by mixing Dijon mustard, mayonnaise, and hot sauce into a spicy upgrade from the usual egg wash. To ensure the scalloped potatoes underneath finished cooking with the chops, we parcooked thinly sliced spuds in the microwave with chicken broth, rosemary, and onion and garlic powders. Scalloped potatoes require a lush sauce, and we made quick work of it by stirring in cream and Wondra flour. We baked the potatoes for 30 minutes (which gave us enough time to dredge and bread the chops), and then placed the chops right on top of the potatoes. Soon our tender potatoes were bathed in their sauce, and the pork boasted a golden-brown crust. You can substitute an equal amount of all-purpose flour for the Wondra flour, if necessary; however, the sauce will have a pasty, slightly gritty texture. For instructions on how to toast panko, see page 194.

2   pounds russet potatoes, peeled and sliced ¼ inch thick

¾   cup chicken broth

1½ teaspoons minced fresh rosemary or ½ teaspoon dried

½   teaspoon onion powder

¼   teaspoon garlic powder
    Salt and pepper

¾   cup heavy cream

2   tablespoons Wondra flour

1½ ounces Parmesan cheese, grated (¾ cup)

1   cup panko bread crumbs, toasted

1   tablespoon Dijon mustard

1½ teaspoons mayonnaise

1½ teaspoons hot sauce

4   (6- to 8-ounce) boneless pork chops, ¾ inch thick, trimmed

1   tablespoon minced fresh parsley

1 Adjust oven rack to middle position and heat oven to 400 degrees. Combine potatoes, broth, rosemary, onion powder, garlic powder, and ½ teaspoon salt in large bowl, cover, and microwave until edges of potatoes are translucent and pliable, about 8 minutes.

2 Stir cream, Wondra, and ¼ teaspoon pepper into hot potato mixture. Transfer mixture to 13 by 9-inch baking dish and press into even layer. Cover with aluminum foil and bake until potatoes are nearly tender, about 30 minutes.

3 While the potatoes bake, combine ¼ cup Parmesan and panko in shallow dish. Whisk mustard, mayonnaise, and hot sauce together in small bowl. Cut 2 slits, about 2 inches apart, through fat on edges of each chop. Pat chops dry with paper towels and season with salt and pepper.

4 Working with 1 chop at a time, brush 1 side with mustard mixture, then press chop, mustard side down, into panko mixture, pressing gently to adhere. Lay chop, coated side up, on large plate.

5 Remove potatoes from oven and sprinkle evenly with remaining ½ cup Parmesan. Place chops, coated side up, on top of potatoes in dish. Bake, uncovered, until pork registers 135 degrees, 10 to 15 minutes.

6 Remove dish from oven and let rest until pork registers 145 degrees, about 10 minutes. Sprinkle with parsley and serve.

BAKED COD WITH ARTICHOKES, OLIVES, AND SUN-DRIED TOMATOES

SERVES 4 TOTAL TIME: 1 HOUR

WHY THIS RECIPE WORKS Wanting to infuse baked cod with fresh Mediterranean flavors, we set our sights on cod baked with artichokes, olives, and tomatoes. To streamline this recipe, we swapped out fresh tomatoes for sun-dried and used the tomatoes' packing oil to infuse the dish with plenty of bright, rich flavor. We tossed artichoke hearts (frozen, for extra convenience) in some of that oil and roasted them to build some browning. Next, we mixed in the sun-dried tomatoes along with kalamata olives and lemon zest, stirring some of the savory packing oil into the vegetables. We brushed more of that same oil on our cod fillets before baking them atop the vegetables. The fish was perfectly cooked in just 15 minutes, and a drizzle of lemon juice and a sprinkling of fresh basil provided the perfect finish. You can substitute haddock or halibut for the cod. To thaw the frozen artichokes quickly, microwave them, covered, for 3 to 5 minutes, then drain them thoroughly in a colander.

1 pound frozen artichoke hearts, thawed and patted dry

¾ cup oil-packed sun-dried tomatoes, drained, ¼ cup oil reserved

Salt and pepper

1 teaspoon grated lemon zest plus 1 tablespoon juice

½ cup pitted kalamata olives, chopped

4 (6-ounce) skinless cod fillets, 1 to 1½ inches thick

2 tablespoons chopped fresh basil

1 Adjust oven rack to middle position and heat oven to 450 degrees. Toss artichokes with 2 tablespoons tomato oil in bowl and season with salt and pepper. Spread into 13 by 9-inch baking dish and roast until lightly browned, about 15 minutes.

2 Stir lemon zest, olives, sun-dried tomatoes, and 1 tablespoon tomato oil into artichokes in dish. Pat cod dry with paper towels, then nestle into artichoke mixture. Brush tops of fish with remaining 1 tablespoon tomato oil and season with salt and pepper. Bake until fish flakes apart when gently prodded with paring knife and registers 140 degrees, 15 to 18 minutes.

3 Remove dish from oven. Drizzle fish with lemon juice, sprinkle with basil, and serve.

TUCKING THE TAIL

For pieces of fish of uneven thickness, tuck thinner end under before cooking so all pieces will cook at same rate.

BAKED QUINOA WITH KALE AND CHICKPEAS

SERVES 4 TOTAL TIME: 45 MINUTES

WHY THIS RECIPE WORKS Quinoa makes a stellar side dish, but we wanted this healthy grain to be the center of attention in a robust vegetarian casserole with layers of flavor and a cheesy feta topping. We started with a simple combination of quinoa, chickpeas, lemon zest, and scallions, pouring hot water over the mixture and baking it until the quinoa had absorbed all of the liquid. The resulting dish lacked heft, but hearty kale proved to be the perfect solution. Roasted kale seemed a surefire way to bulk up the dish, but we found the extra step of roasting the leaves too fussy for this quick one-pan supper. Turning to the microwave, we decided to steam the kale to tenderize the leaves. Our quinoa bake was taking on a distinctly Mediterranean flavor profile, so we decided to swap out the scallions for chopped tomatoes and a splash of fresh lemon juice, ensuring our dish was bright-tasting and colorful. A generous sprinkling of tangy feta cheese finished this simple casserole off with perfect savory complexity. We like the convenience of prewashed quinoa. If you buy unwashed quinoa (or if you are unsure if it's washed), be sure to rinse it before cooking to remove its bitter protective coating.

WEEKNIGHT FRIENDLY

5 ounces (5 cups) baby kale
½ cup water plus 1 tablespoon water
1 cup prewashed white quinoa
1 (15-ounce) can chickpeas, rinsed
  Salt and pepper
2 teaspoons grated lemon zest plus 1 tablespoon juice
2 tablespoons extra-virgin olive oil
2 plum tomatoes, cored and finely chopped
6 ounces feta cheese, crumbled (1½ cups)

1 Adjust oven rack to middle position and heat oven to 450 degrees. Combine kale and 1 tablespoon water in bowl, cover, and microwave until slightly wilted, 1 to 2 minutes. Transfer to colander and let drain, pressing with back of spoon to remove as much moisture as possible.

2 Combine wilted kale, quinoa, chickpeas, ½ teaspoon salt, and ¼ teaspoon pepper in 8-inch square baking dish. Combine remaining ½ cup water and 1 teaspoon lemon zest in bowl, cover, and microwave until just steaming, about 1 minute. Pour lemon-water mixture evenly into dish and cover tightly with aluminum foil. Bake until quinoa is tender and no liquid remains, 20 to 30 minutes.

3 Meanwhile, whisk oil, lemon juice, remaining 1 teaspoon lemon zest, ½ teaspoon salt, and ¼ teaspoon pepper together in bowl.

4 Remove dish from oven and fluff quinoa with fork. Gently fold in tomatoes and lemon vinaigrette. Sprinkle with feta and continue to bake, uncovered, until feta is warmed through, 3 to 5 minutes. Serve.

BAKED SCALLOPS WITH COUSCOUS, BRAISED LEEKS, AND TARRAGON-ORANGE VINAIGRETTE

SERVES 4   TOTAL TIME: 1 HOUR

WEEKNIGHT FRIENDLY

WHY THIS RECIPE WORKS We wanted a simple way to prepare sea scallops that was guaranteed to get them tender and infused with sophisticated flavors. Cooking them on a bed of Israeli couscous, leeks, and white wine seemed easy and would allow the pearls of pasta to absorb the scallops' briny liquid. To ensure our scallops finished cooking at the same time as the rest of the dish, we jump-started the leeks and couscous in the microwave, adding garlic and a pinch of saffron to subtly perfume the dish. We stirred in wine and boiling water, which started the dish off hot and shortened the cooking time. Using a very hot oven and sealing the pan with foil promised perfectly (and efficiently) cooked scallops that steamed atop the couscous. A quick tarragon-orange vinaigrette to drizzle over the finished dish provided an appealing accent that complemented the scallops and leeks without overpowering them. We recommend buying "dry" scallops, which don't have chemical additives and taste better than "wet." Dry scallops will look ivory or pinkish; wet scallops are bright white. For an accurate measurement of boiling water, bring a full kettle of water to a boil and then measure out the desired amount.

1 pound leeks, white and light green parts only, halved lengthwise, sliced thin, and washed thoroughly
1 cup Israeli couscous
5 tablespoons extra-virgin olive oil, plus extra for serving
4 garlic cloves, minced
Salt and pepper
Pinch saffron threads (optional)
¾ cup boiling water
¼ cup dry white wine
1½ pounds large sea scallops, tendons removed
2 tablespoons minced fresh tarragon
1 tablespoon white wine vinegar
½ teaspoon Dijon mustard
½ teaspoon grated orange zest plus 1 tablespoon juice

1 Adjust oven rack to middle position and heat oven to 450 degrees. Combine leeks, couscous, 2 tablespoons oil, garlic, ½ teaspoon salt, ¼ teaspoon pepper, and saffron, if using, in bowl, cover, and microwave, stirring occasionally, until leeks are softened, about 6 minutes. Stir in boiling water and wine, then transfer mixture to 13 by 9-inch baking dish.

2 Pat scallops dry with paper towels and season with salt and pepper. Nestle scallops into couscous mixture and cover dish tightly with aluminum foil. Bake until couscous is tender, sides of scallops are firm, and centers are opaque, 20 to 25 minutes.

3 Meanwhile, whisk remaining 3 tablespoons oil, tarragon, vinegar, mustard, orange zest and juice, and ⅛ teaspoon salt together in bowl.

4 Remove dish from oven. Drizzle vinaigrette over scallops and serve, passing extra oil separately.

WASHING LEEKS

1 Trim and discard root and dark green leaves. Halve lengthwise and slice thin.
2 Rinse cut leeks thoroughly to remove dirt and sand using salad spinner or bowl of water.

CAJUN-STYLE RICE WITH ANDOUILLE, SHRIMP, AND OKRA

SERVES 4 TOTAL TIME: 1 HOUR 15 MINUTES

WHY THIS RECIPE WORKS Jambalaya is a Cajun favorite that can require a lot of standing at the stove. We decided to take jambalaya's spicy, bold flavors and apply them to a simple rice dish that could be baked in the oven. Blooming a full tablespoon of Cajun seasoning in the microwave with onion, garlic, and celery brought the flavors to life before we combined the mixture with rice. Using chicken broth as our cooking liquid promised rice with rich flavor, and adding in canned diced tomatoes delivered some juicy brightness to the dish. Once everything was combined in the casserole dish, we covered it tightly with aluminum foil to ensure gently steamed grains. Toward the end of cooking we added our Cajun heavy hitters—andouille sausage, shrimp, and okra—and allowed them to cook and warm through in the last 10 minutes of baking. Finished with a sprinkling of scallions and a hit of hot sauce, this proved a true Cajun feast. Spiciness will vary between the different brands of Cajun seasoning and andouille sausage.

2 celery ribs, chopped fine
1 onion, chopped fine
3 garlic cloves, minced
1 tablespoon extra-virgin olive oil
1 tablespoon Cajun seasoning
1 teaspoon salt
¼ teaspoon pepper
1⅓ cups long-grain white rice
1 (14.5-ounce) can diced tomatoes, drained
2¾ cups chicken broth
12 ounces medium-large shrimp (31 to 40 per pound), peeled and deveined
12 ounces andouille sausage, sliced ¼ inch thick on bias
1½ cups frozen sliced okra, thawed
2 scallions, sliced thin
Hot sauce

1 Adjust oven rack to middle position and heat oven to 450 degrees. Combine celery, onion, garlic, oil, Cajun seasoning, salt, and pepper in bowl and microwave, stirring occasionally, until vegetables are softened, about 5 minutes. Transfer vegetables to 13 by 9-inch baking dish and stir in rice and tomatoes.

2 Microwave broth in covered bowl until steaming, about 3 minutes, then pour over mixture in dish. Cover dish tightly with aluminum foil and bake until rice is nearly tender, 25 to 30 minutes.

3 Remove foil, fluff rice with fork, and gently stir in shrimp, andouille, and okra. Cover tightly with foil and continue to bake until rice is tender, sausage and okra are warmed through, and shrimp is opaque throughout, 10 to 15 minutes.

4 Remove dish from oven and let cool for 10 minutes. Fluff rice gently with fork, sprinkle with scallions, and serve with hot sauce.

DEVEINING SHRIMP

1 After removing shell, use paring knife to make shallow cut along back of shrimp, exposing vein.
2 Use tip of knife to lift vein out. Discard vein by wiping blade against paper towel.

MEXICAN-STYLE SPAGHETTI SQUASH CASSEROLE

SERVES 4   TOTAL TIME: 2 HOURS

WHY THIS RECIPE WORKS Spaghetti squash makes for a great pasta replacement or a fun side dish, but we wanted to showcase this versatile vegetable's ability to work as a casserole by jazzing it up with bright Mexican flavors. We roasted the oblong yellow squash in the traditional method, simply halving it and roasting until the sweet strands could be easily shredded from the skins with a fork. While the squash roasted, we built a flavorful base for our casserole by blooming minced garlic, smoked paprika, and cumin in the microwave. Incorporating black beans, corn, and tomatoes turned the spiced squash into a true meal while reinforcing the Mexican flavors. Scallions lent a subtle oniony flavor without overpowering the sweet squash, as well as nice pop of color. Minced jalapeño gave just the right amount of gentle heat. We sampled a variety of toppings, but creamy avocado and mellow, slightly briny queso fresco won us over. We also enjoyed serving our squash with a squeeze of lime juice. To make this dish spicier, reserve and add the jalapeño chile seeds to the filling.

1   (2½– to 3-pound) spaghetti squash, halved lengthwise and seeded
3   tablespoons extra-virgin olive oil
    Salt and pepper
2   garlic cloves, minced
½   teaspoon smoked paprika
½   teaspoon ground cumin
1   (15-ounce) can black beans, rinsed
1   cup frozen corn
6   ounces cherry tomatoes, halved
6   scallions (4 minced, 2 sliced thin)
1   jalapeño chile, stemmed, seeded, and minced
1   avocado, halved, pitted, and cut into ½-inch pieces
2   ounces queso fresco, crumbled (½ cup)
    Lime wedges (optional)

1 Adjust oven rack to middle position and heat oven to 375 degrees. Spray 8-inch square baking dish with vegetable oil spray. Brush cut sides of squash with 1 tablespoon oil and season with salt and pepper. Place squash, cut side down, in prepared dish (squash will not sit flat in dish) and roast until just tender, 40 to 45 minutes. Flip squash cut side up and let sit until cool enough to handle, about 20 minutes.

2 While squash roasts, combine remaining 2 tablespoons oil, garlic, paprika, cumin, and ¾ teaspoon salt in large bowl and microwave until fragrant, about 30 seconds. Stir in beans, corn, tomatoes, minced scallions, and jalapeño until well combined.

3 Using fork, scrape squash into strands in bowl with bean mixture. Stir to combine, then spread mixture evenly in dish and cover tightly with aluminum foil. Bake until warmed through, 20 to 25 minutes.

4 Remove dish from oven. Sprinkle with avocado, queso fresco, and sliced scallions. Serve with lime wedges, if using.

SHREDDING SPAGHETTI SQUASH

Holding roasted squash half with clean dish towel over large bowl, use fork to scrape squash flesh from skin, shredding flesh into fine pieces.

CHICKEN, SPINACH, AND ARTICHOKE POT PIE

SERVES 4   TOTAL TIME: 1 HOUR

WHY THIS RECIPE WORKS We love spinach and artichoke dip so much that it inspired this modern spin on chicken pot pie. Mixing thawed frozen spinach with jarred artichokes and Boursin cheese gave us a flavorful, creamy base. Shredded carrots and capers upped the ante, introducing contrasting texture and a briny zing. To create a lush sauce, we stirred in broth, cream, and, for instant thickening, Wondra flour. We then sliced our chicken thinly, tossed it with lemon zest for brightness, and placed the slices atop the vegetables, a surefire way to keep the meat from drying out. A buttery sheet of puff pastry made the perfect top to our updated pot pie. The result had wonderful vegetable flavor and a creaminess that had tasters reaching for more. We prefer jarred artichoke hearts, labeled "baby" or "cocktail," that are 1½ inches or shorter in length. Larger artichoke hearts tend to have fibrous leaves. If you are using larger hearts, trim the top ¼ to ½ inch from the leaves. Do not use marinated or oil-packed artichoke hearts. To thaw frozen puff pastry, let it sit either in the refrigerator for 24 hours or on the counter for 30 minutes to 1 hour. You can substitute an equal amount of all-purpose flour for the Wondra flour, if necessary; however, the sauce will have a pasty, slightly gritty texture.

1¼ pounds frozen spinach, thawed and squeezed dry
1 (5.2-ounce) package Boursin Garlic & Fine Herbs cheese
1 cup jarred whole artichoke hearts packed in water, halved
2 carrots, peeled and shredded
¾ cup chicken broth
½ cup heavy cream
¼ cup capers, rinsed
1 tablespoon Wondra flour
12 ounces boneless, skinless chicken breast, trimmed and sliced thin
1 teaspoon grated lemon zest
   Salt and pepper
1 (9½ by 9-inch) sheet puff pastry, thawed
1 large egg, lightly beaten with 2 tablespoons water

1 Adjust oven rack to middle position and heat oven to 425 degrees. Spray 8-inch square baking dish with vegetable oil spray. Combine spinach, Boursin, artichokes, carrots, broth, cream, capers, and Wondra together in bowl, then transfer to prepared dish.

2 Toss chicken with lemon zest in separate bowl, season with salt and pepper, and spread in even layer over spinach mixture. Cut puff pastry into 8-inch square and place over top of chicken. Cut four 2-inch slits in center of dough, then brush dough with egg mixture.

3 Bake until crust is golden brown and filling is bubbling, 30 to 35 minutes, rotating pan halfway through baking. (Assembled pot pie can be refrigerated for up to 24 hours; bake as directed.)

4 Remove pot pie from oven and let cool for 10 minutes before serving.

SAVORY BREAD PUDDING WITH TURKEY SAUSAGE AND KALE

SERVES 4 TO 6   TOTAL TIME: 2 HOURS

WHY THIS RECIPE WORKS For a savory spin on comforting bread pudding, we turned to earthy kale and meaty, spiced sausage. Our first attempts at this dish left us with unappealing pools of grease, so we had to take a closer look at our ingredients. Cutting back on cheese and swapping in leaner (but still flavorful) turkey sausage for pork were easy ways to lighten this casserole. Microwaving the kale with some aromatics and oil jump-started its cooking and eliminated excess water in our finished dish. Since soggy bread is the downfall of any bread pudding, we toasted torn baguette slices to enrich their flavor and give the bread some custard-withstanding crispness. We stirred the toasted bread into our simple custard, prepared with 3 parts cream to 2 parts milk, which made it rich but not over the top. To prevent curdling, we stabilized the custard by using just yolks rather than the traditional whole eggs. Once the bread had absorbed some of the custard and the kale was mixed in, we assembled the bread pudding, layering the custard-bread mixture with sausage and topping it off with Parmesan. From there, all we had to do was bake it, covered at first to set the filling, then uncovered for the last 20 minutes to generate some appealing browning.

1 (18- to 20-inch) baguette, torn or cut into 1-inch pieces (10 cups)
1 pound kale, stemmed and chopped
4 shallots, sliced thin
2 garlic cloves, minced
1 teaspoon extra-virgin olive oil
3 cups heavy cream
2 cups whole milk
8 large egg yolks
1 tablespoon Dijon mustard
1 pound turkey sausage, casings removed
¼ cup grated Parmesan cheese
2 tablespoons minced fresh chives

1 Adjust oven rack to middle position and heat oven to 450 degrees. Arrange bread in even layer in 13 by 9-inch baking dish. Bake, stirring occasionally, until bread is crisp and browned, about 12 minutes; let cool for 10 minutes. Reduce oven temperature to 400 degrees.

2 Meanwhile, combine kale, shallots, garlic, and oil in bowl and microwave, stirring occasionally, until kale is wilted, about 5 minutes. Wrap kale mixture in clean dish towel and wring tightly to squeeze out as much liquid as possible.

3 Whisk cream, milk, egg yolks, and mustard together in large bowl. Stir in toasted bread and drained kale mixture until well combined.

4 Spray now-empty baking dish with vegetable oil spray. Pour half of bread mixture into prepared dish. Crumble half of sausage into ½-inch pieces over top. Top with remaining bread mixture and remaining sausage. Sprinkle with Parmesan.

5 Cover tightly with greased aluminum foil and bake for 45 minutes. Uncover and continue to bake until custard is just set and top is browned, about 20 minutes.

6 Remove dish from oven and let cool for 10 minutes. Sprinkle with chives before serving.

SPICY CHORIZO AND POBLANO ENCHILADAS

SERVES 4 TO 6   TOTAL TIME: 1 HOUR 15 MINUTES

WHY THIS RECIPE WORKS From making the sauce and cooking the filling to rolling the tortillas, preparing enchiladas can be a time-consuming, labor-intensive endeavor. We set out to streamline this dish so we could serve boldly flavored enchiladas any night of the week. Although canned enchilada sauce is passable, we decided to create our own alternative, fresh-tasting sauce, combining canned tomato sauce with chili powder, cumin, sugar, salt, and pepper. Powdered onion and garlic elevated the flavor and kept the sauce smooth, no pureeing needed. We next turned to the filling, avoiding anything that required prior cooking or excessive prep. Thin slices of Spanish-style chorizo provided meaty, authentic taste and texture and fit nicely inside the rolled tortillas. For some fresh, bright flavor, we mixed in chopped poblano and minced cilantro. Smooth-melting Monterey Jack cheese bound the filling together. After spreading some of the sauce over the bottom of our casserole dish, we filled our corn tortillas (warmed to make them more pliable) and arranged them in the dish. After we spread on the remaining sauce and sprinkled on some extra cheese for a bubbly topping, our nearly effortless enchiladas were ready for baking to meaty, cheesy perfection. Be sure to use Spanish-style chorizo, which is sold precooked.

2 (8-ounce) cans tomato sauce
3 tablespoons chili powder
2 teaspoons ground cumin
2 teaspoons sugar
½ teaspoon onion powder
¼ teaspoon garlic powder
¼ teaspoon salt
¼ teaspoon pepper
8 ounces Monterey Jack cheese, shredded (2 cups)
8 ounces Spanish-style chorizo sausage, halved lengthwise and sliced thin
1 poblano chile, stemmed, seeded, and chopped fine
3 tablespoons minced fresh cilantro
12 (6-inch) corn tortillas, warmed
2 tablespoons vegetable oil
  Lime wedges

1 Adjust oven rack to middle position and heat oven to 450 degrees. Whisk tomato sauce, chili powder, cumin, sugar, onion powder, garlic powder, salt, and pepper together in bowl. In separate bowl, combine 1 cup Monterey Jack, chorizo, poblano, and 2 tablespoons cilantro.

2 Spread ½ cup sauce over bottom of 13 by 9-inch baking dish. Brush both sides of tortillas with oil. Stack tortillas, wrap in damp dish towel, and place on plate; microwave until warm and pliable, about 1 minute.

3 Working with 1 warm tortilla at a time, spread ¼ cup cheese-chorizo filling across center. Roll tortilla tightly around filling and place seam side down in baking dish; arrange enchiladas in 2 columns across width of dish. Pour remaining 1½ cups sauce over top to cover completely and sprinkle remaining 1 cup Monterey Jack down center of enchiladas.

4 Cover dish tightly with greased aluminum foil, and bake until enchiladas are heated through and cheese is melted, 20 to 25 minutes. Remove dish from oven and let cool for 10 minutes. Sprinkle with remaining 1 tablespoon cilantro and serve with lime wedges.

BEEF TACO BAKE

SERVES 4 TO 6   TOTAL TIME: 1 HOUR

WHY THIS RECIPE WORKS Taco night often leaves the home cook with a litany of prep steps and a mountain of dishes to clean afterward. Deconstructing the traditional taco and layering its components in a casserole dish seemed like a fun way to lighten that load. Beans are a favorite taco topping, so we combined the canned refried variety with spicy Ro-tel tomatoes and minced cilantro and spread the creamy mixture into our dish as the first layer. For a rich, cheesy layer, we sprinkled on Colby Jack cheese—a variety that promised even melting and minimal grease. To incorporate that classic taco shell crunch, we broke shells into pieces and scattered them over the cheese. For the meat, we opted for 90 percent lean ground beef, again to preempt any crunch-diminishing grease. Stirring chopped onion, garlic, chili powder, and oregano into the beef and microwaving the mixture kept the texture crumbly and bloomed the seasonings. We livened the beef layer by stirring in more Ro-tel tomatoes, cider vinegar for tang, and brown sugar for subtle sweetness. After adding the beef mixture to the dish, we topped it off with more cheese and shell pieces before baking. Finished with a sprinkling of fresh sliced scallions, this unique casserole delivered all the taco flavors we love, and cleanup was a snap. If you can't find Ro-tel tomatoes, substitute one 14.5-ounce can diced tomatoes, drained, and one 4-ounce can chopped green chiles, drained. Colby Jack cheese is also known as CoJack; if unavailable, substitute Monterey Jack cheese. Serve with your favorite taco toppings such as shredded lettuce, sour cream, salsa, and avocado.

1 pound 90 percent lean ground beef
1 onion, chopped fine
4 garlic cloves, minced
2 tablespoons chili powder
1½ teaspoons minced fresh oregano or ½ teaspoon dried
   Salt and pepper
2 teaspoons apple cider vinegar
1 teaspoon packed brown sugar
2 (10-ounce) cans Ro-tel Diced Tomatoes & Green Chilies, drained
1 (16-ounce) can refried beans
¼ cup minced fresh cilantro
8 ounces Colby Jack cheese, shredded (2 cups)
12 taco shells, broken into 1-inch pieces (2 cups)
2 scallions, sliced thin

1 Adjust oven rack to middle position and heat oven to 375 degrees. Combine beef, onion, garlic, chili powder, oregano, ½ teaspoon salt, and ¼ teaspoon pepper in bowl and microwave, stirring occasionally and breaking up meat, until most of beef is cooked (some pink will remain), about 5 minutes. Stir in vinegar, sugar, and half of tomatoes.

2 Combine remaining tomatoes, refried beans, and cilantro in separate bowl, and spread evenly into 8-inch square baking dish. Sprinkle with ½ cup cheese and scatter 1 cup broken taco shells over top. Crumble beef mixture into dish and sprinkle with ½ cup cheese. Top with remaining 1 cup broken taco shells and remaining 1 cup cheese.

3 Bake until filling is bubbling and cheese is melted and spotty brown, about 25 minutes. Remove dish from oven and let cool for 10 minutes. Sprinkle with scallions and serve.

REUBEN STRATA

SERVES 4 TO 6   TOTAL TIME: 3 HOURS

WHY THIS RECIPE WORKS Reubens are a deli counter classic—layers of rye bread, warm corned beef, and melted Swiss cheese are always a good thing. In turning this sandwich into a gooey, crowd-pleasing strata that would feed the whole gang, we needed to make it taste like the iconic sandwich as much as possible. Using seeded rye bread proved very important in giving us a strong rye flavor. We also used a whole pound of corned beef. Layering the two with some Swiss cheese and then bathing everything in a simple custard delivered a creamy texture that really hit home. You can't have a Reuben without sauerkraut, but adding this zingy ingredient before baking muted its flavor. Instead, sprinkling it (along with some extra cheese) on top after baking and then broiling to finish kept its picklelike tang intact. The brunch-worthy result had all the comforting flavor of the original sandwich.

8 slices seeded rye bread, toasted
1 pound thinly sliced deli corned beef, chopped
8 ounces Swiss cheese, shredded (2 cups)
3 large eggs
1½ cups whole milk
1 teaspoon salt
½ teaspoon pepper
12 ounces sauerkraut, rinsed and squeezed dry
2 tablespoons minced fresh chives

1 Spray 8-inch square baking dish with vegetable oil spray. Arrange half of bread in prepared dish. Sprinkle half of corned beef over bread, then top with ⅔ cup Swiss. Repeat with remaining bread, remaining corned beef, and ⅔ cup cheese to make second layer.

2 Whisk eggs, milk, salt, and pepper together in bowl, then pour evenly over top. Cover dish tightly with plastic wrap, pressing it flush to surface. Weigh strata down and refrigerate for at least 1 hour or up to 24 hours.

3 Adjust oven rack to upper-middle position and heat oven to 325 degrees. Meanwhile, let strata sit at room temperature for 20 minutes. Unwrap strata and bake until edges and center are puffed and edges have pulled away slightly from sides of dish, about 50 minutes, rotating dish halfway through baking.

4 Remove dish from oven, adjust oven rack 8 inches from broiler element, and heat broiler. Sprinkle sauerkraut over top of strata, then sprinkle with remaining ⅔ cup cheese. Broil until cheese is melted and golden, about 5 minutes.

5 Remove dish from broiler and let cool for 10 minutes. Sprinkle with chives and serve.

WEIGHING DOWN STRATA

Cover surface with plastic wrap, pressing it flush to surface, and weigh strata down using a zipper-lock bag full of sugar or dried beans.

BACON-CHEESEBURGER PASTA

SERVES 4 TOTAL TIME: 1 HOUR

WEEKNIGHT FRIENDLY

WHY THIS RECIPE WORKS For a stick-to-your-ribs pasta bake with almost zero prep work, we combined ground beef, pickles, American cheese, bacon, and chopped onion with macaroni for a casserole that delivered all the bright, tangy, meaty flavors of our favorite burger. Tomato sauce, with its smooth texture and long-cooked flavor, provided the perfect base for our sauce, which we seasoned with Worcestershire sauce and dry mustard. Combining chopped dill pickles with brown sugar gave the sauce the same sweetly pungent flavor of pickle relish but with more crunch. Slices of American cheese, bits of crispy bacon (precooked in the microwave), and a sprinkling of chopped onion made the perfect toppings. To preserve the flavor and texture of the bacon and onions, we didn't add our toppings until just before the end. Make sure to crumble the beef into pieces that measure ½ inch or smaller in step 1.

12 ounces (3 cups) elbow macaroni
 1 pound 85 percent lean ground beef
    Salt and pepper
 3 cups water
 1 (15-ounce) can tomato sauce
⅓ cup chopped dill pickles
 2 teaspoons Worcestershire sauce
 2 teaspoons dry mustard
 1 teaspoon packed brown sugar
½ teaspoon garlic powder
 4 slices bacon
 6 slices American cheese
½ cup finely chopped onion (optional)

1 Adjust oven rack to middle position and heat oven to 475 degrees. Spray 13 by 9-inch baking dish with vegetable oil spray. Spread macaroni into prepared dish, crumble beef into ½-inch pieces over top, and season with salt and pepper.

2 Whisk water, tomato sauce, pickles, Worcestershire, mustard, sugar, garlic powder, ½ teaspoon salt, and ½ teaspoon pepper together in bowl. Pour into dish with macaroni and stir gently to combine. Cover tightly with aluminum foil and bake for 25 minutes.

3 Meanwhile, microwave bacon on plate until crisp, about 5 minutes. Transfer to paper towel–lined plate to drain, then crumble into ½-inch pieces.

4 Remove dish from oven and stir macaroni thoroughly, scraping sides and bottom of dish. Lay cheese slices over top and sprinkle with crisped bacon. Return uncovered dish to oven and continue to bake until macaroni is tender and cheese is melted, 5 to 8 minutes.

5 Remove dish from oven and let cool for 10 minutes. Sprinkle with onion, if using, before serving.

HANDS-OFF SPAGHETTI AND MEATBALLS

SERVES 4   TOTAL TIME: 1 HOUR 15 MINUTES

WHY THIS RECIPE WORKS An entirely hands-off dinner of spaghetti and meatballs sounds like a dream: no long wait for the water to boil, no tedious browning of the meatballs, no sink full of dirty dishes to clean. We kept this dish supersimple, paring it down to the basics to deliver the nostalgic, satisfying meal of our childhoods. An easy combination of ground beef, store-bought pesto, and panko bread crumbs yielded meatballs with tons of flavor. We wanted the pasta to cook right in the sauce, so we spread spaghetti in a casserole dish and covered it with jarred marinara sauce. Thinning the sauce with a bit of water ensured there would be enough moisture to properly cook the strands. We then nestled the meatballs into the sauce and let everything cook covered in a very hot oven for 30 minutes. These conditions simulated boiling on the stovetop, enabling our pasta to cook in the sauce and absorb the flavors surrounding it. Once our pasta was al dente, we uncovered it, gave it a stir, and let the meatballs brown and the sauce thicken for the last few minutes of baking. A simple sprinkling of Parmesan and basil completed our dish. Our favorite jarred marinara sauce is Victoria Marinara Sauce.

12 ounces spaghetti, broken in half
 1 (24-ounce) jar marinara sauce
 2 cups water, plus extra hot water as needed
 1 pound 90 percent lean ground beef
 ¾ cup panko bread crumbs
 ⅓ cup prepared basil pesto
    Salt and pepper
 2 tablespoons chopped fresh basil
    Grated Parmesan cheese

1 Adjust oven rack to middle position and heat oven to 475 degrees. Spray 13 by 9-inch baking dish with vegetable oil spray. Spread pasta into prepared dish. Pour marinara sauce and water over pasta and toss gently with tongs to coat.

2 Using hands, combine beef, panko, pesto, 1 teaspoon salt, and ¼ teaspoon pepper in bowl until well combined. Pinch off and roll mixture into 1½-inch meatballs (about 15 meatballs). Place meatballs on top of pasta in dish. Cover dish tightly with aluminum foil and bake for 30 minutes.

3 Remove dish from oven and stir pasta thoroughly, scraping sides and bottom of dish. Return uncovered dish to oven and continue to bake until pasta is tender and sauce is thickened, 5 to 8 minutes.

4 Remove dish from oven. Toss to coat pasta and meatballs with sauce, adjusting sauce consistency with extra hot water as needed. Let cool for 10 minutes. Season with salt and pepper to taste, sprinkle with basil, and serve with Parmesan.

EASY BAKED MAC AND CHEESE

SERVES 4   TOTAL TIME: 1 HOUR

WHY THIS RECIPE WORKS The test kitchen has no shortage of macaroni and cheese recipes, but could we create an ultraconvenient one-dish version that was as easy as starting from the boxed stuff, but without the pot of boiling water (and with superior cheesy flavor)? To make things totally simple, we wanted to be able to cook the pasta without having to heat up the water or toast the macaroni. Cooking the pasta at a relatively moderate temperature in a mixture of water and evaporated milk helped us do just that while also establishing a creamy base for the cheese sauce. Stirring in a meltable blend of shredded cheddar and American cheeses at the end of baking gave us perfectly and evenly cooked pasta in a lush, smooth sauce. And panko bread crumbs, browned in the microwave and sprinkled on before serving, provided irresistible crunch. For instructions on how to toast panko, see page 194.

12 ounces (3 cups) elbow macaroni
2½ cups water
1 (12-ounce) can evaporated milk
½ teaspoon dry mustard
   Salt and pepper
6 ounces sharp cheddar cheese, shredded (1½ cups)
6 ounces American cheese, shredded (1½ cups)
½ cup panko bread crumbs, toasted

1 Adjust oven rack to middle position and heat oven to 375 degrees. Spray 13 by 9-inch baking dish with vegetable oil spray. Spread macaroni into prepared dish. Whisk 2 cups water, evaporated milk, dry mustard, 1 teaspoon salt, and ½ teaspoon pepper together in bowl. Pour into baking dish and stir gently to combine.

2 Cover tightly with aluminum foil and bake, stirring occasionally, until macaroni is nearly tender and most liquid has been absorbed, about 30 minutes.

3 Remove dish from oven and stir macaroni thoroughly, scraping sides and bottom of dish. Stir in remaining ½ cup water, cheddar cheese, and American cheese. Cover dish with foil and return to oven to bake until macaroni is tender and cheese is melted, 5 to 8 minutes.

4 Remove dish from oven. Stir to coat pasta evenly in sauce, and let cool for 10 minutes. Sprinkle with toasted panko before serving.

SAUSAGE LASAGNA WITH SPINACH AND MUSHROOMS

SERVES 4   TOTAL TIME: 1 HOUR 30 MINUTES

WHY THIS RECIPE WORKS For an easy creamy lasagna that could serve a family of four, we needed to do some streamlining. Instead of making the usual laborious béchamel and tomato sauces on the stovetop, we opted for a quick and flavorful no-cook cheese sauce and a jar of our favorite marinara. For the cheese sauce, we chose cottage cheese as our base, as it proved more flavorful than ricotta and turned creamy (instead of grainy) when cooked. To bump up the cheesy flavor without adding excess moisture, we mixed in Parmesan. For the filling, we chose the supersavory combination of Italian sausage, cremini mushrooms, and baby spinach. To speed up the prep, we microwaved the filling, allowing the sausage to cook through, the spinach to wilt, and the mushrooms to shed their moisture. After pressing out any of the filling's excess moisture, we began layering. Working in an 8-inch square dish—just the right size for four servings—we layered the marinara, no-boil noodles, sausage filling, cheese sauce, and some shredded mozzarella. We repeated these layers once more and topped the lasagna off with plenty of mozzarella for a bubbly, cheesy crust. We prefer the flavor of whole-milk cottage cheese here, but low-fat cottage cheese can be substituted; do not use nonfat cottage cheese. Our favorite jarred marinara sauce is Victoria Marinara Sauce.

4   ounces (½ cup) whole-milk cottage cheese
2   ounces Parmesan cheese, grated (1 cup)
1   garlic clove, minced
    Salt and pepper
12 ounces hot or sweet Italian sausage, casings removed, sausage crumbled into ½-inch pieces
8   ounces cremini mushrooms, trimmed and sliced thin
5   ounces (5 cups) baby spinach
1   (24-ounce) jar marinara sauce
6   no-boil lasagna noodles
8   ounces whole-milk mozzarella cheese, shredded (2 cups)

1 Adjust oven rack to middle position and heat oven to 425 degrees. Combine cottage cheese, Parmesan, garlic, and ¼ teaspoon pepper in bowl.

2 Combine sausage, mushrooms, ¼ teaspoon salt, and ¼ teaspoons pepper in bowl, cover, and microwave, stirring occasionally, until sausage is no longer pink and mushrooms have released their liquid, about 9 minutes. Stir in spinach and microwave until wilted, about 1 minute. Transfer mixture to colander and let drain for 5 minutes, pressing on mixture with back of spoon to remove as much moisture as possible.

3 Grease 8-inch square baking dish. Spread 1 cup marinara sauce into prepared dish and lay 2 noodles on top (noodles may overlap slightly). Top with half of sausage mixture, half of cottage cheese mixture, and ½ cup mozzarella. Repeat layering with 2 noodles, 1 cup marinara sauce, remaining sausage mixture, remaining cottage cheese mixture, and ½ cup mozzarella. Lay remaining 2 noodles on top, cover with remaining marinara sauce, and sprinkle with remaining 1 cup mozzarella. (Assembled lasagna can be refrigerated for up to 24 hours; increase covered baking time in step 4 to 45 minutes.)

4 Cover dish tightly with greased aluminum foil and bake until bubbling around edges, about 30 minutes. Remove foil and continue to bake until cheese is spotty brown, 10 to 15 minutes, rotating dish halfway through cooking. Remove dish from oven and let cool for 15 minutes before serving.

CHEESY BUTTERNUT SQUASH AND SWISS CHARD LASAGNA

SERVES 4   TOTAL TIME: 1 HOUR 45 MINUTES

WHY THIS RECIPE WORKS It's a shame how often vegetable lasagnas end up a flavorless mass of mushy vegetables and limp noodles. To create the ideal vegetarian lasagna— with a crisp, browned crust, tender noodles, and perfectly cooked vegetables bathed in a rich sauce—we started from the bottom up. We began with a creamy no-cook sauce (creamier than ricotta, way less effort than béchamel) by combining cottage cheese, Parmesan, cream, and cornstarch, plus fresh sage for its savory notes. To keep this a one-pot meal, we chose no-boil noodles. For our vegetables, butternut squash and Swiss chard paired well, and adding lemon zest, garlic, and nutmeg gave the veggies a refined flavor profile. To avoid a waterlogged lasagna, we microwaved the vegetables to help them release excess liquid. For a dish this rich, we went with our smaller 8-inch square casserole dish, which would satisfy four people. To assemble, we layered the sauce, noodles, and vegetables, topping it off with shredded mozzarella. After 30 minutes of baking under an aluminum foil cover, we finished it off uncovered for a bubbly browned top. We prefer the flavor of whole-milk cottage cheese here, but low-fat cottage cheese can be substituted; do not use nonfat cottage cheese.

10 ounces (1¼ cups) whole-milk cottage cheese
 2 ounces Parmesan cheese, grated (1 cup)
 1 cup heavy cream
 1 tablespoon minced fresh sage or 1 teaspoon dried
 1 teaspoon cornstarch
   Salt and pepper
 1 pound butternut squash, peeled, seeded, and cut into ½-inch pieces (3 cups)
 1 pound Swiss chard, stemmed and cut into 1-inch pieces
 1 tablespoon extra-virgin olive oil
 2 garlic cloves, minced
 1 teaspoon grated lemon zest
 ⅛ teaspoon ground nutmeg
 6 no-boil lasagna noodles
 4 ounces whole-milk mozzarella cheese, shredded (1 cup)

1 Adjust oven rack to middle position and heat oven to 425 degrees. Whisk cottage cheese, Parmesan, cream, sage, cornstarch, ¼ teaspoon salt, and ¼ teaspoon pepper together in bowl.

2 Combine squash, chard, oil, garlic, lemon zest, nutmeg, ¼ teaspoon salt, and ⅛ teaspoon pepper in bowl, cover, and microwave until chard is wilted and butternut squash is just tender, about 7 minutes. Transfer mixture to colander and let drain for 5 minutes.

3 Grease 8-inch square baking dish. Spread 1 cup cheese sauce into prepared dish and lay 2 noodles on top (noodles may overlap slightly). Top with half of squash mixture and half of cheese sauce. Repeat layering with 2 noodles, remaining squash mixture, and ½ cup cheese sauce. Lay remaining 2 noodles on top, cover with remaining cheese sauce, and sprinkle with mozzarella. (Assembled lasagna can be refrigerated for up to 24 hours; increase covered baking time in step 4 to 45 minutes.)

4 Cover dish tightly with greased aluminum foil and bake until bubbling around edges, about 30 minutes. Remove foil and continue to bake until cheese is spotty brown, 10 to 15 minutes, rotating dish halfway through cooking.

5 Remove dish from oven and let cool for 15 minutes before serving.

THE ROASTING PAN

WEEKNIGHT
FRIENDLY

Twin Roast Chickens with Root Vegetables
and Tarragon Vinaigrette

The Roasting Pan Not Just for the Holidays

Of all the major vessels in the home kitchen, the roomy roasting pan probably gets the least mileage. Rather than keeping this versatile, durable pan in storage until November, we wanted to explore its strengths and applicability to year-round cooking. Ideal for serving a crowd (or for folks who love leftovers), this sturdy standby has more to offer than just roasting large cuts of meat. Working to turn out a full meal from this full-size vessel taught us a few things along the way.

Draw Upon Those Drippings

Many of our roasting pan recipes have you propping the protein on a bed of potatoes or even placing it on a roasting rack, and for good reason: Elevating poultry and meat maximizes its exposure to the oven's dry heat, encouraging even browning as the fat renders. We used those flavorful juices to our advantage, picking sides that benefited from a bit of fat (think hearty bread stuffing or tender fingerling potatoes).

Stovetop Sear and Simmer

It's easy to forget that the roasting pan works on the stovetop as well as in the oven, and the former proved adept at imparting that deep sear needed to bring a roast to the next level. Most pans are large enough to straddle two stovetop burners, but even when this is not the case, a good roasting pan will still conduct the heat needed to bloom spices, brown potatoes, simmer a broth, or build up a fond.

Give It a Rest

Whether we're cooking a pork tenderloin or a large beef roast, we always let meat rest after roasting. Resting allows the meat fibers—which contract when hot—to relax and reabsorb any juices they've squeezed out, and we've found that the hotter the oven and the bigger the roast, the longer the waiting time needed. So, much as we wanted to start carving when we pulled a roast from the oven, it paid to wait.

Bring Some Zing

Roasting pan dinners are, by nature, heavy. Laden with hefty cuts of meat, savory herbs, and hearty root vegetables, these meals pack a lot of goodness onto every plate. The easiest way to prevent these dishes from being too rich is to introduce a bright, buzzy sauce. Whether sweet and fruity or tangy and acidic, an easy stir-together sauce is the surest way to bring some lightness to the table.

Equipping Your Kitchen

Roasting Pan
The Heavy Hitter

Handsome, heavy-duty, and ready to take on everything from herb-flecked chicken breasts to a showstopping holiday roast, the roasting pan is a true kitchen icon. In this book, we encourage you to pull out this versatile vessel more than once a year, but we still find it hard to justify spending $300 (or more) for this pan. After roasting mountains of potatoes and a barrage of hefty roasts, we determined that our ideal pans are made of stainless steel and aluminum for even heating. Lightweight pans with roomy handles make maneuvering a breeze, even when using oven mitts. Our favorite: **Calphalon Contemporary Stainless Roasting Pan with Rack** ($99.99).

Roasting Rack
The Best Supporting Actor

A good roasting rack securely holds a roast, a whole chicken (or two), or a turkey, elevating the meat so it doesn't sit in fat while cooking. The rack should allow hot air to circulate around the meat—key for accurate cooking and a perfectly rendered exterior. We dislike many of the racks that come bundled with roasting pans (even our winning pan's rack is slightly unstable), so we keep a good rack at the ready. When in doubt, we go for the biggest rack available, the larger sizes winning us over for stability, capacity, and 360-degree air circulation. (Small racks skitter around because they're not broad enough to brace themselves, and short-legged racks cause steaming rather than roasting.) U- and V-shaped racks are best for cradling the roast, and a good set of handles makes safe work of lifting the food out of the pan for carving. Our favorite: **All-Clad Nonstick Large Rack** ($24.95).

ROASTED CHICKEN BREASTS WITH GARLICKY FINGERLING POTATOES

SERVES 8   TOTAL TIME: 1 HOUR 30 MINUTES

WHY THIS RECIPE WORKS Cooking for a crowd can be overwhelming, but the utter simplicity of a roasting pan filled with bone-in chicken breasts and fingerling potatoes all but guarantees a table of satisfied guests. We played around with ways to elevate the dish, trying compound butters, spice rubs, and tangy sauces, but simply brushing bone-in breasts with oil and seasoning them with salt and pepper won us over. Timing the cooking just right gave us juicy, flavorful chicken with crisp browned skin. We also loved the ease of creamy fingerlings roasted in the chicken juices. By roasting ten garlic cloves along with the potatoes, we made an unctuous sweet garlic paste that we tossed with the spuds and some fresh chives for a simple side. Even without the crowd, leftovers would be delicious. This dish is best served with lemon wedges.

2½ pounds fingerling potatoes, unpeeled, halved lengthwise
10 garlic cloves, peeled
¼ cup extra-virgin olive oil
Salt and pepper
8 (12-ounce) bone-in split chicken breasts, trimmed
¼ cup minced fresh chives
Lemon wedges

1 Adjust oven rack to middle position and heat oven to 500 degrees. Spray bottom of 16 by 12-inch roasting pan with vegetable oil spray. Toss potatoes, garlic, 2 tablespoons oil, 1 teaspoon salt, and ½ teaspoon pepper in bowl, then spread evenly into prepared pan. Roast for 20 minutes.

2 Brush chicken with remaining 2 tablespoons oil and season with salt and pepper. Lay chicken, skin side up, on top of potatoes. Roast until chicken registers 160 degrees and skin has started to crisp, about 30 minutes.

3 Remove pan from oven. Adjust oven rack 8 inches from broiler element and heat broiler. Broil until chicken skin is golden brown, 3 to 5 minutes.

4 Remove pan from oven. Transfer chicken to platter, tent with aluminum foil, and let rest 10 minutes. Transfer garlic to bowl and mash into paste with fork. Add mashed garlic and chives to potatoes and toss together. Serve with lemon wedges.

TRIMMING BONE-IN BREASTS

Using kitchen shears, trim off rib section from each breast, following vertical line of fat from tapered end of breast up to socket where wing was attached.

HERBED PORK TENDERLOIN WITH FENNEL, TOMATOES, ARTICHOKES, AND OLIVES

SERVES 4 TO 6   TOTAL TIME: 1 HOUR

WHY THIS RECIPE WORKS A roasting pan isn't just for special occasions and hulking cuts of meat. Its broad area easily accommodated two pork tenderloins and an assortment of vegetables for a low-fuss meal that—seasoned properly—transported us to Provence. This is the kind of recipe that works as well for company as it does for a weeknight dinner. Cooking the tenderloins until buttery-smooth was key, and roasting them atop a bed of vegetables buffered the heat to ensure juicy meat all the way through. Rather than searing the meat, we rubbed it with herbes de Provence, salt, and pepper. The Mediterranean seasoning inspired our selection of vegetables: sweet, delicately flavored fennel, earthy artichoke hearts (frozen, to keep things easy), and briny olives. After softening the fennel in the microwave, we tossed it with the other vegetables and olive oil, and spread the mixture into the roasting pan, placing the tenderloins on top. The vegetables were nearly cooked when the pork was done, so we removed the meat, added in juicy halved cherry tomatoes and lemon zest, and let the vegetables finish in the oven. After 10 minutes, the fennel was tender, the tomatoes had softened and begun to release their juice, and the bright aroma of lemon filled the kitchen. Be sure to thoroughly thaw and pat dry the frozen artichokes; otherwise their moisture will inhibit the browning of the roasted vegetables. Herbes de Provence, a blend of dried herbs such as rosemary, basil, marjoram, bay leaves, thyme, and lavender, is available in the spice aisle of supermarkets.

WEEKNIGHT
FRIENDLY

2 (12- to 16-ounce) pork tenderloins, trimmed
2 teaspoons herbes de Provence
   Salt and pepper
2 large fennel bulbs, stalks discarded, bulbs halved, cored, and cut into ½-inch-thick strips
12 ounces frozen artichoke hearts, thawed and patted dry
½ cup pitted kalamata olives, halved
3 tablespoons extra-virgin olive oil
18 ounces cherry tomatoes, halved
1 tablespoon grated lemon zest
2 tablespoons minced fresh parsley

1 Adjust oven rack to lower-middle position and heat oven to 450 degrees. Pat pork dry with paper towels and season with herbes de Provence, ½ teaspoon salt, and ¼ teaspoon pepper.

2 Combine fennel and 2 tablespoons water in bowl, cover, and microwave until softened, about 5 minutes; drain well. Toss drained fennel, artichokes, olives, and oil together in bowl and season with salt and pepper.

3 Spread vegetables into 16 by 12-inch roasting pan and lay pork on top. Roast until pork registers 140 to 145 degrees, 25 to 30 minutes, turning tenderloins over halfway through roasting.

4 Remove pan from oven. Transfer pork to cutting board, tent loosely with aluminum foil, and let rest for 10 minutes. Meanwhile, stir cherry tomatoes and lemon zest into vegetables and continue to roast until fennel is tender and tomatoes have softened, about 10 minutes.

5 Remove pan from oven. Stir parsley into roasted vegetables. Slice pork into ½-inch-thick slices and serve with vegetables.

BEEF TENDERLOIN WITH SMOKY POTATOES AND PERSILLADE RELISH

SERVES 6 TO 8   TOTAL TIME: 1 HOUR 30 MINUTES

WHY THIS RECIPE WORKS For special occasions, few cuts top a beef tenderloin. This elegant roast cooks quickly and serves a crowd, and its rich, buttery slices are fork-tender. We found that a hot oven delivered rich, roasted flavor and perfectly rosy meat without overcooking this lean cut. Tying the roast helped to ensure even cooking. The roast needed company, and small whole red potatoes were a perfect pairing. To punch up the flavor, we tossed the potatoes with smoked paprika, which added a pleasant smokiness to complement our meat, along with garlic and scallions for a deep, flavorful backbone. The tender meat needed a sauce, so we made a simple yet bold persillade relish, which featured parsley, capers, and cornichons. Use extra-small red potatoes measuring less than 1 inch in diameter. Center-cut beef tenderloin roasts are sometimes sold as Châteaubriand.

Beef and Potatoes

1 (3-pound) center-cut beef tenderloin roast, trimmed
¼ cup extra-virgin olive oil
Salt and pepper
3 pounds extra-small red potatoes, unpeeled
5 scallions, minced
4 garlic cloves, minced
1 tablespoon smoked paprika
⅓ cup water

Persillade Relish

¾ cup minced fresh parsley
½ cup extra-virgin olive oil
6 tablespoons minced cornichons plus
    1 teaspoon brine
¼ cup capers, rinsed and chopped coarse
3 garlic cloves, minced
1 scallion, minced
1 teaspoon sugar
¼ teaspoon salt
¼ teaspoon pepper

1 For the beef and potatoes Adjust oven rack to middle position and heat oven to 425 degrees. Pat roast dry with paper towels, coat with 2 tablespoons oil, and season with salt and pepper. Tie roast with kitchen twine at 1½-inch intervals; set aside at room temperature.

2 Heat remaining 2 tablespoons oil in 16 by 12-inch roasting pan over medium-high heat (over 2 burners, if possible) until shimmering. Add potatoes, scallions, garlic, paprika, ½ teaspoon salt, and ¼ teaspoon pepper and cook until scallions are softened, about 1 minute. Off heat, stir in water, scraping up any browned bits. Transfer roasting pan to oven and roast potatoes for 15 minutes.

3 Remove roasting pan from oven, stir potato mixture, and lay beef on top. Return pan to oven and roast until beef registers 120 to 125 degrees (for medium-rare), 35 to 50 minutes.

4 For the persillade relish While beef roasts, combine all ingredients in bowl.

5 Remove pan from oven. Transfer roast to carving board, tent with aluminum foil, and let rest 15 minutes. Cover potatoes left in pan with foil to keep warm. Remove twine from roast, slice into ½-inch-thick slices, and serve with potatoes and persillade relish.

PERUVIAN ROAST CHICKEN WITH SWISS CHARD AND SWEET POTATOES

SERVES 6   TOTAL TIME: 2 HOURS 45 MINUTES

WHY THIS RECIPE WORKS One of the world's great roast chickens, *pollo a la brasa* boasts a bronzed exterior seasoned with a robust paste of garlic, spices, lime juice, chile, and mint. Lacking the spit traditionally used to roast the bird whole, we instead figured, why not use leg quarters? They fit neatly in our roasting pan and yielded more bronzed skin coated in a tasty paste. We smeared the paste over and under the skin before letting the chicken rest for at least an hour to allow the flavors to meld. We used our roasting pan to brown a side of sweet potatoes before arranging the chicken on top and roasting both together, allowing the chicken drippings to baste the potatoes as they became tender. We then removed the chicken and potatoes to rest while we cooked 4 pounds of chard in the delicious juices left behind, ensuring there was plenty to go around. Some leg quarters are sold with backbone attached; removing it (with a heavy chef's knife) before cooking makes the chicken easier to serve.

¼ cup fresh mint leaves

10 garlic cloves (5 chopped, 5 sliced)

¼ cup extra-virgin olive oil

1 tablespoon ground cumin

1 tablespoon honey

2 teaspoons smoked paprika

2 teaspoons dried oregano

2 teaspoons grated lime zest plus ¼ cup juice (2 limes), plus lime wedges for serving
   Salt and pepper

1 teaspoon minced habanero chile

6 (10-ounce) chicken leg quarters, trimmed

3 pounds sweet potatoes, peeled, ends squared off, and sliced into 1-inch-thick rounds

4 pounds Swiss chard, stemmed and cut into 1-inch pieces

2 tablespoons minced fresh cilantro

1 Adjust oven rack to middle position and heat oven to 425 degrees. Process mint, chopped garlic, 1 tablespoon oil, cumin, honey, paprika, oregano, lime zest and juice, 2 teaspoons pepper, 1 teaspoon salt, and habanero in blender until smooth, 20 seconds.

2 Using your fingers, gently loosen skin covering thighs and drumsticks and spread half of paste directly on meat. Spread remaining half of paste over exterior of chicken. Place chicken in 1-gallon zipper-lock bag and refrigerate for at least 1 hour or up to 24 hours.

3 Toss potatoes with 1 tablespoon oil and ½ teaspoon salt in bowl. Heat remaining 2 tablespoons oil in 16 by 12-inch roasting pan over medium-high heat (over 2 burners, if possible) until shimmering. Add potatoes, cut side down, and cook until well browned on bottom, 6 to 8 minutes.

4 Off heat, flip potatoes. Lay chicken, skin side up, on top. Roast until thighs and drumsticks register 175 degrees and potatoes are tender, 40 to 50 minutes, rotating pan halfway through roasting.

5 Remove pan from oven. Transfer potatoes and chicken to platter, tent loosely with aluminum foil, and let rest 10 minutes. Being careful of hot pan handles, pour off all but ¼ cup liquid left in pan. Add sliced garlic and cook over high heat (over 2 burners, if possible) until fragrant, about 30 seconds. Add chard and ¼ teaspoon salt and cook, stirring constantly, until chard is wilted and tender, about 8 minutes; transfer to serving bowl.

6 Sprinkle cilantro over chicken and potatoes and serve with chard and lime wedges.

ROAST PORK LOIN WITH SWEET POTATOES AND CILANTRO SAUCE

SERVES 6   TOTAL TIME: 3 HOURS 15 MINUTES

WHY THIS RECIPE WORKS Mild pork paired with a cilantro sauce and sweet potatoes seemed like a great way to ease into fall with a little of summer's brightness. To ensure the lean boneless roast emerged from the oven juicy and well seasoned, we brined the pork and cooked it at a moderate 375 degrees. A mixture of ground coriander, cumin, salt, and pepper gave the pork's exterior color and flavor, and complemented the lively cilantro sauce. For a side, we tossed sweet potato chunks with some oil and a pinch of cayenne pepper and roasted them along with the pork. By the time the pork was done, the vegetables were tender but a little pale, so we set the pork aside to rest, then turned up the heat and returned the roasting pan to the oven to give them some caramelization. A ¼-inch-thick layer of fat on top of the roast is ideal; if your roast has a thicker fat cap, trim it back accordingly. If the pork is enhanced (injected with a salt solution), do not brine in step 1 but season with salt in step 2. This sauce uses two entire bunches of cilantro, including the stems.

Pork and Potatoes

- ½ cup sugar
- Salt and pepper
- 1 (3-pound) boneless center-cut pork loin roast, trimmed
- 1 teaspoon ground coriander
- 1 teaspoon ground cumin
- 3 pounds sweet potatoes, peeled, quartered, and cut into 2-inch pieces
- 3 tablespoons vegetable oil
- ⅛ teaspoon cayenne pepper

Cilantro Sauce

- 2½ cups fresh cilantro leaves and stems, trimmed (2 bunches)
- ½ cup extra-virgin olive oil
- 4 teaspoons lime juice
- 2 garlic cloves, minced
- ½ teaspoon sugar
- Salt and pepper

1 For the pork and potatoes Dissolve sugar and ½ cup salt in 2 quarts cold water in large container. Submerge pork in brine, cover, and refrigerate for 1½ to 2 hours.

2 Adjust oven rack to lower-middle position and heat oven to 375 degrees. Remove pork from brine and pat dry with paper towels. Season pork with coriander, cumin, and pepper, and tie with kitchen twine at 1½-inch intervals.

3 Toss sweet potatoes in bowl with oil and cayenne, season with salt and pepper, and spread evenly into 16 by 12-inch roasting pan. Lay pork, fat side up, on top of potatoes. Roast until pork registers 140 to 145 degrees, 50 to 70 minutes, turning pork over halfway through roasting.

4 For the cilantro sauce Meanwhile, pulse all ingredients together in food processor until cilantro is finely chopped, 10 to 15 pulses, scraping down bowl as needed. Season with salt and pepper to taste.

5 Remove pan from oven. Transfer pork to carving board, tent loosely with aluminum foil, and let rest for 15 minutes. While pork rests, increase oven temperature to 450 degrees and continue to roast potatoes until nicely browned, about 10 minutes. Remove twine from pork, slice into ¼-inch-thick slices, and serve with potatoes and cilantro sauce.

SPICED PORK LOIN WITH WARM POTATO, CELERY ROOT, AND FENNEL SALAD

SERVES 6 TO 8   TOTAL TIME: 3 HOURS

WHY THIS RECIPE WORKS A roast pork loin surrounded by roasted root vegetables is always impressive. Season the pork with a salt–brown sugar spice rub (essentially a dry brine), toss the vegetables with a mustard vinaigrette (creating a German-style salad), and add a bright parsley-basil relish, and you have a company-worthy meal. Roasting the pork fat side down allowed the fat to render into the vegetables for added flavor. Once the pork reached 135 degrees, we flipped it fat side up to broil along with the vegetables for even more browning. A ¼-inch-thick layer of fat on top of the roast is ideal; if your roast has a thicker fat cap, trim it accordingly.

2 tablespoons plus ½ teaspoon packed brown sugar
2 teaspoons ground fennel
2 teaspoons ground coriander
  Salt and pepper
1 (3- to 4-pound) boneless center-cut pork loin roast, trimmed
3 pounds red potatoes, unpeeled, cut into ¾-inch pieces
1 celery root (14 ounces), peeled and cut into ¾-inch pieces
1 fennel bulb, stalks discarded, bulb halved, cored, and cut into ¾-inch pieces
6 garlic cloves, minced
¾ cup plus 2 tablespoons extra-virgin olive oil
1¾ cups fresh parsley leaves
½ cup fresh basil leaves
½ cup apple cider vinegar
¼ cup capers, rinsed
1 tablespoon whole-grain mustard

1 Combine 2 tablespoons sugar, fennel, coriander, 1½ teaspoons salt, and ¼ teaspoon pepper in bowl. Pat pork dry with paper towels, rub thoroughly with sugar mixture, and tie roast with kitchen twine at 1-inch intervals. Wrap roast tightly with plastic wrap and refrigerate for at least 1 hour or up to 24 hours.

2 Adjust oven rack to middle position and heat oven to 375 degrees. Combine potatoes, celery root, fennel, half of garlic, 2 tablespoons oil, and 1 teaspoon salt in 16 by 12-inch roasting pan. Roast vegetables for 20 minutes.

3 Stir vegetables and push to edges of pan to clear space in center for pork. Unwrap pork and place, fat side down, in center of pan. Roast until pork registers 135 degrees and vegetables are tender, 40 to 50 minutes.

4 Meanwhile, pulse 1¼ cups parsley, basil, ¼ cup vinegar, capers, remaining garlic, and 1 teaspoon salt in food processor until coarsely chopped, about 10 pulses, scraping down sides of bowl as needed. Transfer mixture to bowl and whisk in ½ cup oil; set relish aside for serving. In large bowl, whisk mustard, remaining ½ cup parsley, remaining ¼ cup vinegar, remaining ¼ cup oil, remaining ½ teaspoon sugar, ½ teaspoon salt, and ¼ teaspoon pepper together; set aside for roasted vegetables.

5 Remove pan from oven and turn roast fat side up. Adjust oven rack 8 inches from broiler element and heat broiler. Broil until top of roast is golden brown, 5 to 10 minutes.

6 Remove pan from oven. Transfer roast to carving board, tent loosely with aluminum foil, and let rest for 15 minutes. Transfer vegetables to bowl with mustard-parsley vinaigrette, toss to combine, and season with salt and pepper to taste. Remove twine from roast, slice into ½-inch-thick slices, and serve with vegetables and parsley-basil relish.

TWIN ROAST CHICKENS WITH ROOT VEGETABLES AND TARRAGON VINAIGRETTE

SERVES 6 TO 8   TOTAL TIME: 2 HOURS

WHY THIS RECIPE WORKS Cooking two whole chickens together is as simple as cooking one, provided your roasting pan is large enough (see our winner, page 245). We sat them side by side on a V-rack to allow maximum air circulation for even cooking and browning. We also started the birds breast side down to get a jump-start on browning while protecting the white meat from overcooking. We then flipped them to finish cooking, giving the birds an allover golden hue. Underneath the rack we scattered a mix of root vegetables—carrots, parsnips, shallots, and potatoes—and let them soak up all the chicken drippings, turning them brown and tender, almost like a confit. While the chicken was resting, we carefully lifted our roasting pan to the stovetop and continued to cook the vegetables to glaze them with the pan drippings. With all these roasted flavors, a bright herb was necessary to provide contrast. Tarragon added a classy French touch. Half went under the skin, providing a nice hint of flavor without overpowering the chicken. We used the rest in an herb-heavy vinaigrette, which gave our vegetables punchy flair.

6   shallots, peeled and halved
1½ pounds red potatoes, unpeeled, cut into 1-inch pieces
1   pound carrots, peeled and cut into 1-inch pieces
1   pound parsnips, peeled and cut into 1-inch pieces
5   tablespoons extra-virgin olive oil
    Salt and pepper
2   (4-pound) whole chickens, giblets discarded
6   tablespoons minced fresh tarragon
⅓   cup minced fresh parsley
2   tablespoons sherry vinegar
1   teaspoon Dijon mustard

1 Adjust oven rack to middle position and heat oven to 475 degrees. Toss shallots, potatoes, carrots, parsnips, 1 tablespoon oil, ½ teaspoon salt, and ½ teaspoon pepper together in bowl. Spread vegetables evenly into 16 by 12-inch roasting pan. Spray V-rack with vegetable oil spray and nestle into pan with vegetables.

2 Pat chickens dry with paper towels, tie legs together with kitchen twine, and tuck wingtips behind back. Using fingers, gently loosen skin covering breasts and thighs. Spread 3 tablespoons tarragon under skin of chickens, directly onto meat.

3 Season exterior of chickens with salt and pepper. Place chickens, breast side down, in prepared V-rack. Roast for 20 minutes.

4 Flip chickens breast side up and continue to roast until breasts register 160 degrees and thighs register 175 degrees, 50 to 60 minutes.

5 Remove pan from oven. Transfer chicken to carving board, tent loosely with aluminum foil, and let rest for 15 minutes. Being careful of hot pan handles, place pan over medium-high heat on stovetop (over 2 burners, if possible) and cook vegetables, stirring gently, until lightly browned and glistening, 8 to 10 minutes.

6 Whisk remaining ¼ cup oil, remaining 3 tablespoons tarragon, parsley, vinegar, and mustard together in small serving bowl. Carve chickens and serve with vegetables and vinaigrette.

BACON-WRAPPED PORK LOIN WITH ROASTED RED POTATOES AND PEACH SAUCE

SERVES 8   TOTAL TIME: 3 HOURS 45 MINUTES

WHY THIS RECIPE WORKS What's the best part of roasting a bacon-wrapped pork loin over potatoes? Is it how the bacon guarantees a juicy, tender piece of meat (both flavoring and basting the roast), or how it infuses the potatoes with smoky, bacony taste? If only all recipes prompted such questions. To add extra flavor and juiciness, we applied a rub of sugar and thyme to the pork loin first and let it chill for at least an hour. Laying out and overlapping bacon slices and then wrapping them around the roast worked perfectly to encase the meat—and made for a beautiful presentation. Cooking the roast in a low oven to start rendered some of the fat, and then cranking the oven to 475 degrees helped to crisp the bacon. As the pork roasted, the potatoes cooked in the roasting pan below—with the smoky bacon drippings deeply flavoring the tender potatoes. An easy peach chutney–like sauce, made by quickly microwaving peaches, white wine, vinegar, sugar, and whole-grain mustard, offered a tangy, sweet complement to our smoky pork and potatoes. Use small red potatoes measuring 1 to 2 inches in diameter. A ¼-inch-thick layer of fat on top of the roast is ideal; if your roast has a thicker fat cap, trim it accordingly.

1 (3½-pound) boneless center-cut pork loin roast, trimmed
3 tablespoons sugar
2 teaspoons minced fresh thyme or ¾ teaspoon dried
 Salt and pepper
3 pounds small red potatoes, unpeeled, halved
1 small shallot, minced
1 tablespoon extra-virgin olive oil
12 ounces bacon
10 ounces frozen peaches, thawed and cut into 1-inch pieces
¼ cup dry white wine
1 tablespoon apple cider vinegar
2 teaspoons whole-grain mustard

1 Rub pork with 1 tablespoon sugar and 1 teaspoon thyme, and season with salt and pepper. Wrap in plastic wrap and refrigerate for at least 1 hour or up to 24 hours.

2 Adjust oven rack to middle position and heat oven to 250 degrees. Combine potatoes, shallot, oil, remaining 1 teaspoon thyme, ½ teaspoon salt, and ¼ teaspoon pepper in 16 by 12-inch roasting pan.

3 Arrange bacon slices parallel to counter's edge on cutting board, overlapping as needed to match length of roast. Unwrap roast and place in center of bacon, with longer side of roast perpendicular to counter's edge. Bring ends of bacon up and around sides of roast, overlapping ends of slices as needed. Place bacon-wrapped roast, seam side down, on top of potatoes. Roast pork and potatoes until pork registers 90 degrees, 50 minutes to 1 hour.

4 Remove pan from oven and increase oven temperature to 475 degrees. Continue to roast pork and potatoes until bacon is crisp and browned and meat registers 130 degrees, about 30 minutes.

5 Transfer pork to carving board, tent loosely with aluminum foil, and let rest 15 minutes. Toss potatoes with pan juices, season with salt and pepper, and transfer to platter; cover with foil to keep warm.

6 While pork rests, combine peaches, wine, vinegar, mustard, and remaining 2 tablespoons sugar in bowl and microwave, stirring occasionally, until thickened, 8 to 10 minutes. Slice pork into ½-inch-thick pieces and serve with potatoes and peach sauce.

ROAST BEEF SIRLOIN WITH CARAMELIZED CARROTS AND POTATOES

SERVES 6 TO 8   TOTAL TIME: 2 HOURS

WHY THIS RECIPE WORKS When most people think of a beef roast, prime rib or tenderloin come to mind. And while both are tender and flavorful, they are also expensive. We wanted a comparatively affordable roast paired with root vegetables for an easy but impressive roast beef dinner. Boneless top sirloin roast fit the bill because it offered beefy flavor and had enough marbling to stay tender, but not so much that it would require an extended cooking time to break down its fat. Roasting at a low temperature allowed plenty of time for heat to be conducted through the roast's center for even cooking. Carrots and potatoes were a natural pairing, and zapping them in the microwave for some advanced cooking ensured that they would cook at roughly the same rate as the roast. Searing one side on the stovetop gave us some browning before we added in the parcooked vegetables (tossed with thyme). We left the pan in a 250-degree oven for a good 45 minutes before cranking up the heat for some bonus browning on both the roast and vegetables. At that point, we gave the veggies extra time in the oven for more deeply caramelized flavor. Top sirloin is our favorite beef roast for this recipe, but any boneless roast from the sirloin will work well. If your carrots are very thick, slice them in half lengthwise first to ensure even cooking.

2 pounds carrots, peeled and cut into 2-inch pieces
2 pounds red potatoes, unpeeled, cut into
    1½-inch pieces
¼ cup vegetable oil
1 tablespoon minced fresh thyme or 1 teaspoon dried
    Salt and pepper
1 (3- to 4-pound) boneless top sirloin roast, trimmed

1 Adjust oven rack to lower-middle position and heat oven to 250 degrees. Combine carrots, potatoes, and 3 tablespoons water in bowl, cover, and microwave, stirring occasionally, until vegetables are nearly tender, 15 to 20 minutes. Drain well, then toss with 3 tablespoons oil and thyme and season with salt and pepper.

2 While vegetables microwave, pat beef dry with paper towels, season with salt and pepper, and tie with kitchen twine at 1½-inch intervals. Heat remaining 1 tablespoon oil in 16 by 12-inch roasting pan over medium heat (over 2 burners, if possible) until just smoking. Brown beef well on 1 side, about 3 minutes.

3 Off heat, flip roast browned side up and spread vegetables around meat. Roast beef and vegetables until center of meat registers 110 degrees, 45 minutes to 1 hour.

4 Remove pan from oven and increase oven temperature to 500 degrees. Continue to roast beef and vegetables until center of meat registers 120 to 125 degrees (for medium-rare), 10 to 15 minutes.

5 Transfer beef to carving board, tent loosely with aluminum foil, and let rest for 15 minutes. While beef rests, continue to roast vegetables until nicely browned, 10 to 20 minutes. Remove twine from beef, slice into ¼-inch-thick slices, and serve with vegetables.

ROAST TURKEY BREAST WITH HERB STUFFING AND CRANBERRY SAUCE

SERVES 4 TO 6   TOTAL TIME: 5 HOURS 30 MINUTES

WHY THIS RECIPE WORKS Following a similar strategy to our Roasted Chicken and Stuffing (page 53), we simplified turkey dinner by cooking turkey breast and stuffing in one pan. To start, we sautéed fresh herbs and aromatics right in the roasting pan before placing an herb butter–rubbed turkey breast on top. For the stuffing, we sprinkled bread cubes around the breast so they could toast in the oven and absorb the turkey's juices. Starting at a high temperature allowed the turkey's juices to render for a super-crisp skin; we later lowered the heat to allow the bird to cook through gently. Mere minutes in the microwave were all we needed to make a tangy-sweet cranberry sauce to serve on the side. If using a self-basting turkey breast (such as a frozen Butterball) or kosher turkey, do not brine in step 1, but season with salt after rubbing with butter in step 2.

Salt and pepper
1 (6- to 7-pound) bone-in whole turkey breast, trimmed
5 tablespoons unsalted butter, softened
2 tablespoons minced fresh sage
2 tablespoons minced fresh thyme
1 onion, chopped fine
2 celery ribs, minced
1 pound hearty white sandwich bread, cut into ½-inch cubes
12 ounces (3 cups) frozen cranberries, thawed
1 cup sugar
¼ cup water
1 cup chicken broth, plus extra as needed
1 tablespoon minced fresh parsley

1 Dissolve ½ cup salt in 4 quarts cold water in large container. Submerge turkey in brine, cover, and refrigerate for 3 to 6 hours; remove from brine and pat dry with paper towels.

2 Adjust oven rack to middle position and heat oven to 425 degrees. Mash 3 tablespoons butter, 1 tablespoon sage, 1 tablespoon thyme, 1 teaspoon salt, and ½ teaspoon pepper together in bowl. Using fingers, gently separate skin from meat. Spread half of butter mixture under skin directly onto meat. Spread remaining butter mixture evenly over skin.

3 Melt remaining 2 tablespoons butter in 16 by 12-inch roasting pan over medium heat (over 2 burners, if possible). Add onion, celery, ¼ teaspoon salt, and ¼ teaspoon pepper and cook until vegetables are softened, about 5 minutes. Stir in remaining 1 tablespoon sage and remaining 1 tablespoon thyme and cook until fragrant, about 30 seconds. Off heat, place turkey, skin side up, on top of vegetables and arrange bread around turkey. Roast turkey for 30 minutes.

4 Reduce oven temperature to 325 degrees and continue to roast turkey until breast registers 160 degrees, about 1 hour.

5 While turkey roasts, combine cranberries, sugar, water, and ¼ teaspoon salt in bowl and microwave, stirring occasionally, until cranberries are broken down and juicy, about 10 minutes. Coarsely mash cranberries with fork; set aside for serving.

6 Remove pan from oven. Transfer turkey to carving board, tent loosely with aluminum foil, and let rest 15 minutes. Stir broth and parsley into stuffing left in pan, cover with foil, and let stand 10 minutes; add extra broth if stuffing is dry. Carve turkey and serve with stuffing and cranberry sauce.

CHUCK ROAST DINNER IN FOIL

SERVES 6 TOTAL TIME: 5 HOURS 30 MINUTES

WHY THIS RECIPE WORKS Traditionally, this lazy cook's pot roast involves rubbing a chuck roast with onion soup mix, wrapping it in aluminum foil, and cooking it in the oven until tender. While we liked the ease of this one-pan dish, we weren't fans of its artificial, salty taste. To develop oniony flavor with ease, we started with onion powder and salt, but ditched the monosodium glutamate in favor of soy sauce, which enhanced the roast's beefy flavor. Brown sugar added sweetness and depth, while a surprise ingredient, a little espresso powder, provided toasty complexity. You will need an 18-inch-wide roll of heavy-duty aluminum foil for this recipe.

3 tablespoons cornstarch
4 teaspoons onion powder
2 teaspoons packed light brown sugar
2 teaspoons salt
1 teaspoon pepper
1 teaspoon garlic powder
1 teaspoon instant espresso powder
1 teaspoon dried thyme
½ teaspoon celery seeds
1 (4-pound) boneless beef chuck-eye roast, trimmed
2 onions, peeled and quartered
6 red potatoes, unpeeled, quartered
4 carrots, peeled and cut into 1½-inch pieces
2 bay leaves
2 tablespoons soy sauce

1 Adjust oven rack to lower-middle position and heat oven to 300 degrees. Combine cornstarch, onion powder, sugar, salt, pepper, garlic powder, espresso powder, thyme, and celery seeds together in bowl.

2 Pat roast dry with paper towels. Separate roast into 2 pieces along natural seam and trim fat to ¼-inch thickness. Tie kitchen twine around each roast at 1-inch intervals and coat thoroughly with cornstarch mixture.

3 Crisscross two 30 by 18-inch sheets of heavy-duty aluminum foil inside 16 by 12-inch roasting pan. Place onions, potatoes, carrots, and bay leaves in center of foil and drizzle with soy sauce. Set roasts on top of vegetables. Fold opposite corners of foil toward each other and crimp edges tightly to seal. Transfer pan to oven and cook until meat is completely tender, about 4½ hours.

4 Remove pan from oven and open foil pouch. Transfer roasts to carving board, tent loosely with more foil, and let rest 15 minutes. Using slotted spoon, transfer carrots and potatoes to platter, discarding onions and bay leaves. Strain contents left in roasting pan through fine-mesh strainer into fat separator. Let liquid settle, then pour defatted pan juices into serving bowl.

5 Remove kitchen twine from roasts, slice thinly against grain, and transfer to platter with vegetables. Pour ½ cup defatted pan juices over meat. Serve with remaining pan juices.

SPLITTING AND TYING A ROAST

1 Separate roast into 2 pieces along natural seam.
2 Tie kitchen twine around each piece at 1-inch intervals.

BIG BATCH BEEF STEW

SERVES 12 TO 14   TOTAL TIME: 5 HOURS

WHY THIS RECIPE WORKS Few things are as satisfying as a hearty bowl of old-fashioned beef stew, except perhaps being able to share it with a dozen or so of your closest friends and family. Whether cooking for a party or just to stock the freezer, a roasting pan makes for a supereasy way to turn out classic beef stew with fall-apart meat and tender vegetables draped in a rich brown gravy. We chose chuck-eye roast for its great flavor and abundance of intramuscular fat and connective tissue, which made it well suited for long, slow, moist cooking. We bypassed the need to sear the meat by browning onions to develop fond in the pan on the stovetop. Garlic and tomato paste added a considerable flavor boost. To thicken our stew, we stirred in flour with the aromatics before adding red wine and chicken broth (which provided more complexity compared with beef broth). We seasoned the meat with salt and pepper before placing it in the pan, along with carrots, bay leaves, and thyme, and then we covered the pan and popped it in the oven to give the meat and carrots a head start. After an hour and a half we added potatoes and roasted everything for another 2 hours, ensuring the spuds wouldn't fall apart. We tossed in frozen peas just before serving, as they needed only a few minutes to warm through. A little parsley sprinkled at the end made for a fresh finishing touch. With minimal fuss, we had created a simple but intensely flavored old-fashioned beef stew, with plenty to share.

4 tablespoons unsalted butter

4 onions, chopped coarse

Salt and pepper

5 garlic cloves, minced

2 tablespoons tomato paste

1 cup all-purpose flour

1 cup red wine

4 cups chicken broth

7 pounds boneless beef chuck-eye roast, pulled apart at seams, trimmed, and cut into 1-inch chunks

2 pounds carrots, peeled and sliced 1 inch thick

3 bay leaves

1½ tablespoons minced fresh thyme or 1½ teaspoons dried

3 pounds red potatoes, unpeeled, cut into 1-inch chunks

1 cup frozen peas

½ cup minced fresh parsley

1 Adjust oven rack to lower-middle position and heat oven to 325 degrees. Melt butter in 16 by 12-inch roasting pan over medium-high heat (over 2 burners, if possible). Add onions and 1½ teaspoons salt and cook until onions are softened and lightly browned, 10 to 15 minutes.

2 Stir in garlic and tomato paste and cook until fragrant, about 30 seconds. Stir in flour and cook, stirring constantly, until golden, about 1 minute. Slowly whisk in wine, scraping up any browned bits. Gradually whisk in broth, smoothing out any lumps. Season meat with salt and pepper and add to pan. Add carrots, bay leaves, and thyme.

3 Bring stew to simmer. Off heat, cover roasting pan loosely with aluminum foil. Transfer pan to oven and cook stew for 1½ hours.

4 Stir in potatoes and continue to cook in oven, covered, until meat is tender, 2 to 2½ hours.

5 Remove pan from oven. Discard bay leaves. Stir in peas and let heat through, about 5 minutes. Stir in parsley and season with salt and pepper to taste. Let cool for 15 minutes before serving.

THE SLOW COOKER

WEEKNIGHT
FRIENDLY

Sweet and Tangy Pulled Chicken
Sandwiches with Carolina-Style Coleslaw

The Slow Cooker Dinner Is Done

The appeal of a slow cooker is clear: After a modest investment of up-front effort, you can sit back for a few hours (or even head off to work) confident that you'll have a perfectly cooked, truly hands-off meal by dinnertime. Creating meals with satisfying, complex flavors without lengthy prep work or additional pans proved a great challenge, but these recipes really deliver. They also demonstrate the vessel's versatility, going well beyond soups and stews. All it took were a few tricks.

Speed Up to Slow Down

Believe it or not, the fastest appliance in the kitchen is the slow cooker's greatest ally. Rather than cook aromatics and spices on the stovetop to bloom their flavors (thereby breaking our one-pan rule), we simply microwaved them. We also used the microwave to parcook delicate vegetables before adding them to the slow cooker at the end of cooking to ensure that they remained colorful and crisp-tender.

Don't Skimp on the Aromatics

Because the moist heat environment and long cooking times tend to dull flavors, we call for generous amounts of onions, garlic, herbs, spices, and other flavorful ingredients in our recipes. We used umami-rich ingredients like tomato paste, soy sauce, and anchovies to ramp up the meaty richness of everything from soups and stews to sauces. And to give the recipes a bright flavor boost at the end of the cooking time, we often finished with fresh herbs, lemon or lime juice, or a final sprinkling of cheese.

Finish with Quick-Cooking Ingredients

Certain ingredients need just a short stint in the slow cooker to warm through and meld into the dish, so we saved them until the end. Quick-cooking couscous and delicate vegetables like frozen peas, baby spinach, and chopped tomatoes turned mushy when added at the beginning of cooking, so we waited to add them until the end. It took less than 20 minutes for fresh stir-ins like sliced red bell pepper or baby spinach to soften, or for couscous to turn perfectly tender.

At Your Convenience

The best part of using a slow cooker should be its ease, so we turned to convenience items when standard ingredients took too much time or advance cooking. For instance, we learned that neither instant nor raw rice worked in casseroles, but packaged precooked rice worked perfectly. We also turned to everyday items like frozen artichokes, canned tomatoes, and even store-bought pesto to instantly bring some consistently fresh flavor to these year-round recipes.

Equipping Your Kitchen

Slow Cooker
The Steady Eddy

Here in the test kitchen we've been putting slow cookers through the wringer for years. Though new models are always popping up on the market, we defer to those slow cookers that have clear glass lids (so we can keep an eye on the food's progress), are intuitive to use, and bring the food to a safe cooking temperature quickly. Most slow cookers (including our hands-down favorite) can be programmed to cook for a desired amount of time before switching to a "keep warm" setting, making them convenient for busy home cooks. Six-quart models with roomy, heavy stoneware crocks are expert at cooking food gently and efficiently, producing tender, juicy (not overcooked) food. Our top pick is a real upgrade from old-school models in that its built-in internal sensor monitors and adjusts the cooking temperature automatically, keeping the contents from boiling and ensuring uniform cooking. Our favorite: **KitchenAid 6-Quart Slow Cooker with Solid Glass Lid** ($99.99).

HOLD ON TO YOUR LID

While testing slow cookers we came across **The Lid Pocket** ($9.99), a handy tool that hooks over the edge of the cooker on one end and curves into a cupped slot on the other, creating the perfect place to rest the lid for easier serving. We tried it with several sizes of slow cookers and found it fit all, but not as snugly as we'd like. (Carelessly placed lids flopped too far back and fell out if the cooker was bumped.) Though hardly perfect, it does provide a compact, convenient resting place for lids, freeing up a hand and keeping the counter dry.

LEMONY CHICKEN AND RICE WITH SPINACH AND FETA

SERVES 4 TO 6   COOKING TIME: 4 TO 5 HOURS ON LOW

WHY THIS RECIPE WORKS For a chicken and rice dinner that was big on flavor but light on prep, we looked to the Mediterranean for inspiration and included feta for its briny tang, lemon for brightness, and baby spinach for freshness and color. We started by softening aromatics in the microwave for a quick flavor base, then added our chicken and rice to cook gently in the slow cooker. Once the chicken and rice were done, we stirred in a generous amount of crumbled feta and a few handfuls of baby spinach, plus some half-and-half to make sure our dish was rich and creamy. Using both lemon zest and juice delivered citrusy, but not tart, flavor; adding them at the end ensured the lemon retained its bold, bright notes. Store-bought precooked rice is important to the success of this dish; it consistently remains intact and retains the proper doneness. Do not use freshly made or leftover rice, as it will turn mushy and will blow out in the slow cooker. Don't shred the chicken too finely in step 2; it will break up more as it is stirred back into the casserole. Our favorite brand of store-bought cooked rice is Minute Ready to Serve White Rice.

1 onion, chopped fine
1 tablespoon vegetable oil
3 garlic cloves, minced
2 teaspoons minced fresh oregano or ½ teaspoon dried
4 cups store-bought cooked rice
2 pounds boneless, skinless chicken thighs, trimmed
   Salt and pepper
4 ounces (4 cups) baby spinach
6 ounces feta cheese, crumbled (1½ cups)
½ cup half-and-half
1 teaspoon grated lemon zest plus 2 tablespoons juice

1 Combine onion, oil, garlic, and oregano in bowl and microwave, stirring occasionally, until onion is softened, about 5 minutes; transfer to 5½- to 7-quart slow cooker. Stir in rice. Season chicken with salt and pepper and nestle into rice. Cover and cook until chicken is tender, 4 to 5 hours on low.

2 Transfer chicken to cutting board and let cool slightly. Using 2 forks, shred into bite-size pieces. Gently stir shredded chicken, spinach, 1 cup feta, and half-and-half into slow cooker and let sit until spinach is wilted and casserole is heated through, about 5 minutes.

3 Stir in lemon zest and juice and season with salt and pepper to taste. Sprinkle with remaining ½ cup feta. Serve.

PESTO CHICKEN WITH FENNEL AND TOMATO COUSCOUS

SERVES 4   COOKING TIME: 2 TO 3 HOURS ON LOW

WHY THIS RECIPE WORKS   Pouring a simple sauce of pesto thinned with braising liquid over the chicken just before serving adds a wonderful dimension to this Italian-style dinner. We started by softening fennel in the microwave along with some garlic. Then we set the stage for a flavorful braise by combining the vegetables in our slow cooker with chicken stock and bone-in chicken, also adding some cherry tomatoes for a punch of bright acidity. Once everything had simmered, we used most of the braising liquid, now enriched with the chicken's juices, to cook couscous for a quick and easy side dish. We stirred the remaining liquid into store-bought pesto to make a fresh herbal sauce to pour over our tender chicken. Our favorite brand of store-bought pesto is Buitoni Pesto with Basil.

1 fennel bulb, stalks discarded, bulb halved, cored, and sliced thin
1 tablespoon extra-virgin olive oil
2 garlic cloves, minced
½ cup chicken broth
  Salt and pepper
4 (12-ounce) bone-in split chicken breasts, trimmed
8 ounces cherry tomatoes, halved
1 cup couscous
½ cup prepared basil pesto

1 Combine fennel, oil, and garlic in bowl and microwave, stirring occasionally, until fennel is tender, about 5 minutes; transfer to 5½- to 7-quart slow cooker.

2 Stir in broth, ½ teaspoon salt, and ½ teaspoon pepper. Season chicken with salt and pepper and nestle into slow cooker. Sprinkle tomatoes over chicken, cover, and cook until chicken registers 160 degrees, 2 to 3 hours on low.

3 Transfer chicken to serving dish, remove skin, and tent with aluminum foil. Strain braising liquid into fat separator and let sit for 5 minutes. Reserve strained vegetables and 1½ cups defatted liquid; discard extra cooking liquid. Return 1 cup defatted liquid and vegetables to now-empty slow cooker. Stir in couscous, cover, and cook on high until tender, about 15 minutes.

4 Combine remaining ½ cup reserved liquid and pesto in bowl and season with salt and pepper to taste. Pour sauce over chicken. Fluff couscous with fork and serve.

SPICED PORK TENDERLOIN WITH COUSCOUS

SERVES 4   COOKING TIME: 1 TO 2 HOURS ON LOW

WHY THIS RECIPE WORKS We wanted to make tender pork tenderloin with warm spices and an easy side dish—all in the slow cooker. Since pork tenderloin is so lean, we built flavor in stages. First, we rubbed the pork with garam masala, a fragrant Indian spice blend, to get a complex flavor without needing a laundry list of spices. We then simmered the tenderloin in chicken broth enhanced with plenty of garlic. Once the pork was done, we stirred couscous into the potent cooking liquid along with some raisins and almonds; 15 minutes later we had a richly flavored couscous side. An easy bright parsley vinaigrette rounded out the earthy flavors of both the spiced pork and the couscous. Because they are cooked gently and not browned, the tenderloins will be rosy throughout even once they register 145 degrees. Check the tenderloins' temperature after 1 hour of cooking and continue to monitor until they register 145 degrees. You will need an oval slow cooker for this recipe.

1   cup chicken broth
4   garlic cloves, minced
2   (12- to 16-ounce) pork tenderloins, trimmed
2   teaspoons garam masala
    Salt and pepper
1   cup couscous
½   cup raisins
¼   cup sliced almonds, toasted
½   cup extra-virgin olive oil
½   cup minced fresh parsley
2   tablespoons red wine vinegar

1 Combine broth and half of garlic in 5½- to 7-quart slow cooker. Season pork with garam masala, ½ teaspoon salt, and ¼ teaspoon pepper. Nestle into slow cooker, side by side, alternating thicker end to thinner end. Cover and cook until pork is tender and registers 145 degrees, 1 to 2 hours on low.

2 Transfer pork to cutting board and tent with aluminum foil. Strain cooking liquid into fat separator and let sit for 5 minutes. Reserve 1 cup defatted liquid; discard extra cooking liquid. Stir reserved liquid, couscous, and raisins into now-empty slow cooker. Cover and cook on high until couscous is tender, about 15 minutes. Fluff couscous with fork, then stir in almonds.

3 Whisk oil, parsley, vinegar, and remaining garlic together in bowl and season with salt and pepper to taste. Slice pork and serve with couscous and parsley vinaigrette.

SPANISH CHICKEN AND SAFFRON STEW

SERVES 6 TO 8   COOKING TIME: 4 TO 5 HOURS ON LOW

WHY THIS RECIPE WORKS Craving the rich, saffron-infused flavor of a Spanish stew—but wanting something easy enough for a lazy weeknight—we devised a streamlined take that hit all the key flavors. To start, we microwaved saffron with paprika, onions, and garlic to bloom and intensify their flavor. We added this mixture to the slow cooker along with chicken broth, boneless chicken thighs—a perfect choice for long simmering—and canned diced tomatoes. After hours of cooking, the spices infused the stew with rich flavor. A finishing touch of toasted, chopped almonds and minced parsley mimicked the nutty Spanish *picadas* used to thicken and flavor stews at the last minute. It was a simple touch that brought the perfect complexity to our meal.

2 onions, chopped fine

6 garlic cloves, minced

1 tablespoon extra-virgin olive oil

1 tablespoon paprika

¼ teaspoon saffron threads, crumbled

4 cups chicken broth, plus extra as needed

1 (14.5-ounce) can diced tomatoes, drained

3 tablespoons instant tapioca

4 pounds boneless, skinless chicken thighs, trimmed
   Salt and pepper

¼ cup chopped almonds, toasted

¼ cup minced fresh parsley

1 Combine onions, garlic, oil, paprika, and saffron in bowl and microwave, stirring occasionally, until onions are softened, about 5 minutes; transfer to 5½- to 7-quart slow cooker.

2 Stir in broth, tomatoes, and tapioca. Season chicken with salt and pepper and nestle into slow cooker. Cover and cook until chicken is tender, 4 to 5 hours on low.

3 Using large spoon, skim excess fat from surface of stew. Break chicken into about 1-inch pieces with tongs. (Adjust stew consistency with extra hot broth as needed.) Stir in almonds and parsley and season with salt and pepper to taste. Serve.

SOUTHERN BLACK-EYED PEA SOUP

SERVES 6   COOKING TIME: 9 TO 10 HOURS ON LOW OR 6 TO 7 HOURS ON HIGH

WHY THIS RECIPE WORKS The slow cooker is the perfect environment for incorporating dried beans into a creamy, flavorful soup. We wanted to take advantage of this to make a classic Southern-style black-eyed pea soup. To give our soup plenty of kick, we added Cajun seasoning and kielbasa sausage. We used the microwave to bloom the seasoning for more flavor and to jump-start the kielbasa as well as the onions, then we dumped them into the slow cooker to simmer away with the peas and a combination of chicken broth and water. The only prep the black-eyed peas needed was to be quickly picked over (to remove any small stones or debris) and rinsed. Then we added them right into the slow cooker, where they gently simmered, absorbing the flavors of the sausage, aromatics, and seasonings, until they were perfectly cooked. Collard greens, stirred in during the final 30 minutes of cooking so they'd be just tender, and wild rice added color and heft. Feel free to use leftover wild rice or precooked rice from the supermarket. Kielbasa can be quite salty, so be careful when seasoning the soup with additional salt.

2 onions, chopped fine

8 ounces kielbasa sausage, halved lengthwise and sliced ½ inch thick

3 garlic cloves, minced

1 teaspoon Cajun seasoning

8 ounces (1⅓ cups) dried black-eyed peas, picked over and rinsed

5 cups chicken broth

2 cups water

1 pound collard greens, stemmed and cut into 1-inch pieces

1 cup cooked wild rice

1 teaspoon hot sauce, plus extra for seasoning
   Salt and pepper

1 Combine onions, kielbasa, garlic, and Cajun seasoning in bowl and microwave, stirring occasionally, until onions are softened, about 5 minutes; transfer to 5½- to 7-quart slow cooker. Stir in peas, broth, and water. Cover and cook until beans are tender, 9 to 10 hours on low or 6 to 7 hours on high.

2 Stir in collard greens, cover, and cook on high until tender, 20 to 30 minutes. Stir in wild rice and let sit until heated through, about 5 minutes. Stir in hot sauce and season with salt, pepper, and extra hot sauce to taste. Serve.

SORTING DRIED BEANS

Before cooking dried beans, pick them over for small stones or debris. Spreading beans onto a plate makes debris easier to spot.

CHICKPEA TAGINE

SERVES 6   COOKING TIME: 10 TO 11 HOURS ON LOW OR 7 TO 8 HOURS ON HIGH

WHY THIS RECIPE WORKS This Moroccan-style stew gets its complex flavor from a combination of simple but varied seasonings. We started with a base of paprika and garam masala, along with onions, garlic, and strips of lemon zest, all of which perfumed the sauce with warm, exotic aromas. Dried chickpeas turned rich and creamy during the long cooking and absorbed the sauce's flavors. Since many vegetables would be obliterated after hours in a slow cooker, we opted to stir in softened bell peppers and thawed frozen artichokes at the end, cooking them just to heat through. (Frozen artichokes are generally packaged already quartered; if yours are not, cut the artichoke hearts into quarters before using.) To continue the Moroccan flavor profile, we added kalamata olives and raisins to introduce a salty-sweet counterpoint. But we weren't done: Our final additions of tangy yogurt, sweet honey, fresh cilantro, and aromatic grated lemon zest brought the balanced flavors of this stew into perfect alignment.

WEEKNIGHT
FRIENDLY

2 onions, chopped fine

8 garlic cloves, minced

3 tablespoons extra-virgin olive oil,
   plus extra for serving

4 teaspoons paprika

2 teaspoons garam masala

6 cups chicken broth, plus extra as needed

1 pound (2½ cups) dried chickpeas, picked over
   and rinsed

4 (3-inch) strips lemon zest plus 1 teaspoon
   grated lemon zest

2 red or yellow bell peppers, stemmed, seeded,
   and cut into matchsticks

18 ounces frozen artichokes, thawed

½ cup pitted kalamata olives, chopped coarse

½ cup golden raisins

½ cup whole Greek yogurt

½ cup minced fresh cilantro

2 tablespoons honey
   Salt and pepper

1 Combine onions, garlic, 2 tablespoons oil, paprika, and garam masala in bowl and microwave, stirring occasionally, until onions are softened, about 5 minutes; transfer to 5½- to 7-quart slow cooker.

2 Stir broth, chickpeas, and lemon zest strips into slow cooker. Cover and cook until chickpeas are tender, 10 to 11 hours on low or 7 to 8 hours on high.

3 Discard lemon zest strips. Combine bell peppers with remaining 1 tablespoon oil in bowl and microwave, stirring occasionally, until tender, about 5 minutes. Stir softened bell peppers, artichokes, olives, and raisins into stew, cover, and cook on high until heated through, about 10 minutes.

4 In bowl, combine ¼ cup hot stew liquid with yogurt (to temper), then stir mixture into stew. Stir in cilantro, honey, and grated lemon zest. (Adjust stew consistency with additional hot broth as needed.) Season with salt and pepper to taste and drizzle with extra-virgin olive oil.

STUFFED SPICED EGGPLANTS WITH TOMATOES AND PINE NUTS

SERVES 4 COOKING TIME: 5 TO 6 HOURS ON LOW

WHY THIS RECIPE WORKS When cooked, eggplants turn rich and creamy, losing the bitterness they have when raw. Italian eggplants, which are slightly smaller than the ubiquitous globe eggplants, are the ideal size and shape for stuffing when halved, and two of them fit easily in a slow cooker. Drawn to the flavors of Turkey, where stuffed eggplant is a way of life, we created a simple stuffing with canned diced tomatoes, Pecorino Romano, pine nuts, and aromatics including onion, garlic, oregano, and cinnamon. We nestled the halved eggplants cut side down in this fragrant mixture and let them cook until tender. After removing the eggplants from the slow cooker, we gently pushed the soft flesh to the sides to create a cavity, which we filled with the tomato mixture left behind in the slow cooker. Topped with extra cheese and fresh chopped parsley, these eggplants looked beautiful and were far easier than most traditional versions to make. Be sure to buy eggplants that are no more than 10 ounces; larger eggplants will not fit properly in your slow cooker. You may need to trim off the eggplant stems to help them fit. You will need an oval slow cooker for this recipe.

1 onion, chopped fine
3 tablespoons extra-virgin olive oil
3 garlic cloves, minced
2 teaspoons minced fresh oregano or ½ teaspoon dried
¼ teaspoon ground cinnamon
⅛ teaspoon cayenne pepper
1 (14.5-ounce) can diced tomatoes, drained
2 ounces Pecorino Romano cheese, grated (1 cup)
¼ cup pine nuts, toasted
1 tablespoon red wine vinegar
Salt and pepper
2 (10-ounce) Italian eggplants, halved lengthwise
2 tablespoons minced fresh parsley

1 Combine onion, 1 tablespoon oil, garlic, oregano, cinnamon, and cayenne in bowl and microwave, stirring occasionally, until onion is softened, about 5 minutes; transfer to 5½- to 7-quart slow cooker.

2 Stir in tomatoes, ¾ cup Pecorino, pine nuts, vinegar, and ¼ teaspoon salt. Season eggplant halves with salt and pepper and nestle, cut side down, into slow cooker (eggplants may overlap slightly). Cover and cook until eggplants are tender, 5 to 6 hours on low.

3 Transfer eggplant halves, cut side up, to platter. Using 2 forks, gently push eggplant flesh to sides of each half to make room for filling. Stir remaining 2 tablespoons oil into tomato mixture and season with salt and pepper to taste. Mound tomato mixture evenly into eggplants and sprinkle with parsley and remaining ¼ cup Pecorino. Serve.

PREPARING EGGPLANT

Using two forks, gently push flesh to sides of each eggplant half to make room in center for filling.

GREEK-STYLE STUFFED BELL PEPPERS

SERVES 4 COOKING TIME: 4 TO 5 HOURS ON LOW OR 3 TO 4 HOURS ON HIGH

WHY THIS RECIPE WORKS Traditional versions of stuffed peppers can be problematic, with bland fillings and tough or mushy peppers, so we knew that creating an easy stuffed pepper recipe in the slow cooker would require some tinkering. We also wanted to add everything straight to the slow cooker without spending time pre-cooking the peppers or their filling—we just needed to get the bell peppers to soften in the time it took the meat to cook through. The trick was to add a little water to the slow cooker so the peppers gently steamed until they were just crisp-tender. Precooked white rice was a great timesaver and was readily available at the supermarket. Using meatloaf mix (a combination of ground beef, pork, and veal) as our filling's base added meaty complexity. To give the filling bold Greek flavors, we added crumbled feta cheese, kalamata olives, and garlic, as well as oregano for aroma. We topped the cooked peppers with a slice of provolone cheese and a sprinkling of scallions. Choose peppers with flat bottoms so that they stay upright in the slow cooker. If meatloaf mix is unavailable, use 8 ounces each of 90 percent lean ground beef and ground pork. Our favorite brand of store-bought cooked rice is Minute Ready to Serve White Rice.

4 (6-ounce) red, orange, or yellow bell peppers
1 pound meatloaf mix
3 ounces feta cheese, crumbled (¾ cup)
¾ cup cooked rice
½ cup pitted kalamata olives, chopped fine
3 scallions, sliced thin
3 garlic cloves, minced
2 teaspoons minced fresh oregano or 1 teaspoon dried
1 teaspoon salt
4 slices deli provolone cheese (4 ounces)

1 Trim ½ inch off top of each bell pepper, then remove core and seeds. Finely chop bell pepper tops, discarding stems. Gently mix chopped bell peppers, meatloaf mix, feta, rice, olives, two-thirds of scallions, garlic, oregano, and salt together in bowl with hands until thoroughly combined. Pack filling evenly into cored bell peppers.

2 Pour ⅓ cup water into 5½- to 7-quart slow cooker. Place stuffed bell peppers upright in slow cooker. Cover and cook until bell peppers are tender, 4 to 5 hours on low or 3 to 4 hours on high.

3 Top each bell pepper with 1 slice provolone, cover, and continue to cook on high until cheese is melted, about 5 minutes. Using tongs and slotted spoon, transfer bell peppers to serving dish; discard cooking liquid. Sprinkle with remaining scallions and serve.

CORING BELL PEPPERS

1 Trim ½ inch off top of each bell pepper.
2 Remove core and seeds.

PORK LOIN WITH WARM DIJON POTATO SALAD

SERVES 6 TO 8   COOKING TIME 3½ TO 4½ HOURS ON LOW

WHY THIS RECIPE WORKS A juicy pork loin and potato dinner is a great idea anytime of the week, but achieving one in the slow cooker is tricky. You need to ensure that the potatoes and meat cook through at the same time, and the lean pork can quickly turn overcooked and dry. We seasoned the pork generously with coriander, fennel, salt, and pepper and let it cook unattended for a few hours. Toward the end we monitored its temperature and took it out of the slow cooker as soon as it reached 140 degrees to ensure that it didn't overcook. To get the potatoes to cook at the same rate, we quartered them and gave them a head start in the microwave. While the pork rested, we turned the tender potatoes into a delicious side dish by tossing them with a simple zesty dressing flavored with minced shallot, Dijon mustard, and parsley. Look for small red potatoes measuring 1 to 2 inches in diameter; do not substitute full-size red potatoes or they will not cook through properly. A wider, shorter pork loin roast (about 9 inches long) will fit in the slow cooker best. Check the temperature of the pork loin after 3½ hours of cooking and continue to monitor until it registers 140 degrees. You will need an oval slow cooker for this recipe.

3 pounds small red potatoes, quartered
¼ cup extra-virgin olive oil
1 (4-pound) boneless pork loin roast, trimmed
1 teaspoon ground coriander
1 teaspoon ground fennel
  Salt and pepper
2 shallots, minced
3 tablespoons minced fresh parsley
3 tablespoons white wine vinegar
2 tablespoons Dijon mustard

1 Combine potatoes and 1 tablespoon oil in bowl, cover, and microwave, stirring occasionally, until potatoes are almost tender, about 10 minutes; transfer to 5½- to 7-quart slow cooker. Season roast with coriander, fennel, salt, and pepper and nestle, fat side up, into slow cooker. Cover and cook until pork is tender and registers 140 degrees, 3½ to 4½ hours on low.

2 Transfer roast to carving board, tent with aluminum foil, and let rest for 15 minutes. Whisk remaining 3 tablespoons oil, shallots, parsley, vinegar, mustard, and ½ teaspoon salt together in large bowl. Using slotted spoon, transfer potatoes to bowl with dressing and toss to combine; discard cooking liquid. Season with salt and pepper to taste. Slice meat into ¼-inch-thick slices. Serve with potato salad.

SWEET AND TANGY PULLED CHICKEN SANDWICHES WITH CAROLINA-STYLE COLESLAW

SERVES 4 COOKING TIME: 2 TO 3 HOURS ON LOW

WHY THIS RECIPE WORKS A simple spice mixture and a quick-to-assemble homemade barbecue sauce made it easy to turn slow-cooked bone-in chicken into tangy, silky, shredded chicken—perfect for piling onto buns. Microwaving onions with tomato paste, chili powder, paprika, and cayenne softened them and infused them with layers of barbecue flavor while blooming the spices. We simply seasoned the chicken with salt and pepper before nestling the breasts into our quick sauce of ketchup, molasses, and the aromatics. In the cooker's low-and-slow moist heat, the chicken became infused with the rich essence of the sauce. Stirring in vinegar at the beginning of cooking made the sauce too thin and dulled its acidity, but adding 2 tablespoons of vinegar at the end of cooking, along with a small amount of mustard, gave the sauce the perfect consistency and retained its bright flavors. A tangy vinegar-based coleslaw of cabbage and carrots was easily assembled while the chicken cooked so it would be ready for piling on top. Serve on hamburger buns with pickle chips.

1 onion, chopped fine

¼ cup tomato paste

1 tablespoon chili powder

3 tablespoons extra-virgin olive oil

1 teaspoon paprika

⅛ teaspoon cayenne pepper

¼ cup ketchup

2 tablespoons molasses

2 (12-ounce) bone-in split chicken breasts, skin removed, trimmed
   Salt and pepper

4 cups shredded red or green cabbage

1 small carrot, peeled and shredded

¼ cup cider vinegar

2 tablespoons sugar

1 tablespoon minced fresh parsley
   Pinch celery seeds

2 teaspoons Dijon mustard

4 hamburger buns

1 Combine onion, tomato paste, chili powder, 1 tablespoon oil, paprika, and cayenne in bowl and microwave, stirring occasionally, until onion is softened, about 5 minutes; transfer to 5½- to 7-quart slow cooker.

2 Stir in ketchup and molasses. Season chicken with salt and pepper, nestle into slow cooker, and turn to coat with sauce. Cover and cook until chicken registers 160 degrees, 2 to 3 hours on low.

3 While the chicken cooks, toss cabbage and carrot with 1 teaspoon salt in colander and let drain until wilted, about 1 hour. Rinse cabbage and carrot with cold water, then dry thoroughly with paper towels. Whisk 2 tablespoons vinegar, sugar, parsley, celery seeds, and remaining 2 tablespoons oil together in large bowl; add cabbage mixture and toss to combine. Season with salt and pepper to taste and refrigerate until chilled.

4 Transfer chicken to cutting board and let cool slightly. Using 2 forks, shred into bite-size pieces; discard bones. Stir mustard and remaining 2 tablespoons vinegar into sauce left in slow cooker. (Adjust sauce consistency with hot water as needed.) Stir in shredded chicken and season with salt and pepper to taste. Portion chicken onto buns, top with coleslaw, and serve.

MEXICAN-STYLE PULLED PORK TACOS

SERVES 4   COOKING TIME: 9 TO 10 HOURS ON LOW OR 6 TO 7 HOURS ON HIGH

WHY THIS RECIPE WORKS Pulled pork, cooked in a Mexican mole, on a weeknight? In a bold move, we developed a dish that shattered cooking assumptions: first, that heftier meat cuts like pork butt aren't for weeknight meals; second, that a rich mole requires a laundry list of ingredients. Employing a slow cooker to tenderize tough but richly flavored pork butt over the course of a day gave us succulent meat in time for dinner. To give our pulled pork an equally rich sauce, we created a complex mole quickly by deploying just the right pantry staples: chili powder, cumin, chipotle chiles, canned tomato sauce for acidity, and—for just the right sweetness—raisins. Once the pork was cooked through, we removed it and blended the sauce to give it the perfect consistency. A little lime juice and cilantro at the end balanced the flavors and completed the dish. Pork butt roast is often labeled Boston butt in the supermarket. Serve with Chunky Chipotle Guacamole, sour cream, chopped onion, chopped cilantro, thinly sliced radishes, and lime wedges.

1 (15-ounce) can tomato sauce
1 cup raisins
2 tablespoons chili powder
2 tablespoons ground cumin
1 tablespoon minced canned chipotle chile in adobo sauce
3 garlic cloves, peeled
1 (3-pound) boneless pork butt roast, trimmed
  Salt and pepper
½ cup minced fresh cilantro
3 tablespoons lime juice (2 limes)
12 (6-inch) corn tortillas, warmed

1 Combine tomato sauce, raisins, chili powder, cumin, chipotle, and garlic in 5½- to 7-quart slow cooker. Slice pork roast crosswise into 4 equal pieces, trim excess fat, and season with salt and pepper. Nestle pork into slow cooker, cover, and cook until pork is tender, 9 to 10 hours on low or 6 to 7 hours on high.

2 Transfer pork to bowl and let cool slightly. Using 2 forks, shred into bite-size pieces, discarding excess fat. Using large spoon, skim excess fat from surface of mole sauce.

3 Process sauce in blender until smooth, about 1 minute. Stir in cilantro and lime juice, and season with salt and pepper to taste. (Adjust sauce consistency with hot water as needed.) Stir 2 cups sauce into shredded pork. Serve with warm tortillas and remaining sauce.

Chunky Chipotle Guacamole
MAKES 2½ CUPS

3 ripe avocados, halved and pitted
¼ cup minced fresh cilantro
2 tablespoons finely chopped onion
2 tablespoons lime juice
1–2 teaspoons minced canned chipotle chile in adobo sauce
  Salt and pepper

Mash all ingredients together in bowl and season with salt and pepper to taste.

BEEF AND THREE-BEAN CHILI

SERVES 6 TO 8   COOKING TIME: 6 TO 7 HOURS ON LOW OR 4 TO 5 HOURS ON HIGH

WHY THIS RECIPE WORKS For a supereasy, family-friendly slow-cooker chili, we zeroed in on the essential aromatics: onions, chili powder, and oregano. Ground beef was convenient, but it had a tendency to turn gritty after hours of slow cooking. The solution was to microwave it for a few minutes first so that it became firm enough to break into coarse crumbles that did not turn grainy. Canned tomatoes and beans—we chose a mix of black, pinto, and kidney beans for more complex flavor and visual appeal—eliminated prep work and were full of flavor after hours of gentle simmering with the spices and aromatics. Along with the ground beef, we also microwaved onions and spices before adding them to the slow cooker to ensure that the onions cooked through in time and to bring out the flavor of the chili powder and oregano. Serve with your favorite chili garnishes.

2   pounds 85 percent lean ground beef
2   onions, chopped fine
¼   cup chili powder
1   teaspoon dried oregano
    Salt and pepper
1   (15-ounce) can black beans, rinsed
1   (15-ounce) can pinto beans, rinsed
1   (15-ounce) can kidney beans, rinsed
2   (28-ounce) cans crushed tomatoes
2   tablespoons packed brown sugar

1 Combine ground beef, onions, chili powder, oregano, ½ teaspoon salt, and ½ teaspoon pepper in bowl and microwave, stirring occasionally, until beef is no longer pink, about 10 minutes.

2 Transfer mixture to 5½- to 7-quart slow cooker, breaking up any large pieces of beef. Stir in black beans, pinto beans, kidney beans, tomatoes, and sugar. Cover and cook until beef is tender, 6 to 7 hours on low or 4 to 5 hours on high.

3 Using large spoon, skim excess fat from surface of chili. Break up any remaining large pieces of beef with spoon. Season with salt and pepper to taste and serve.

CAJUN TURKEY BREAST WITH RED BEANS AND RICE

SERVES 6 TO 8   COOKING TIME: 5 TO 6 HOURS ON LOW

WHY THIS RECIPE WORKS For a turkey dinner that feeds a crowd—but not an army—bone-in turkey breast is a great option. It requires no prep work apart from a sprinkle of spice; we simply added it to the slow cooker and walked away while the low, gentle heat kept the lean meat tender and moist. To spice up the mild-tasting turkey, we had Cajun flavors in mind; a generous amount of Cajun seasoning plus salt and pepper did the trick. While we were at it, we surrounded the meat with the fixings for a smoky, spicy, side of red beans and rice with sausage. Canned kidney beans were convenient, and sliced andouille sausage added spice and smokiness. We cooked both underneath the turkey so that the beans absorbed the flavors of the rendered juices. Then, while the turkey rested, we stirred cooked wild rice into the beans and sausage to heat through. A splash of red wine vinegar and a hefty addition of scallions before serving provided welcome freshness. You can find precooked wild rice in the pasta aisle of the supermarket. If the turkey breast's backbone and wings are still intact, you may need to remove them to fit the breast in the slow cooker. Check the temperature of the turkey breast after 5 hours of cooking and continue to monitor until it registers 160 degrees. You will need an oval slow cooker for this recipe.

2 (15-ounce) cans dark red kidney beans, rinsed
8 ounces andouille sausage, halved lengthwise and sliced ¼ inch thick
3 garlic cloves, minced
1 (6- to 7-pound) bone-in whole turkey breast, trimmed
1 tablespoon Cajun seasoning
  Salt and pepper
4 cups cooked wild rice
6 scallions, sliced thin
1 tablespoon red wine vinegar, plus extra for seasoning

1 Combine beans, andouille, and garlic in slow cooker. Season turkey with Cajun seasoning, salt, and pepper, and nestle, skin side up, into 5½- to 7-quart slow cooker. Cover and cook until turkey is tender and registers 160 degrees, 5 to 6 hours on low.

2 Transfer turkey to carving board, tent with aluminum foil, and let rest for 20 minutes. Stir wild rice into bean mixture, cover, and cook on high until heated through, about 10 minutes.

3 Stir in scallions and vinegar and season with salt, pepper, and extra vinegar to taste. Carve turkey, discarding skin. Serve with beans and rice.

BRAISED STEAKS WITH HORSERADISH SMASHED POTATOES

SERVES 4   COOKING TIME: 8 TO 9 HOURS ON LOW OR 5 TO 6 HOURS ON HIGH

WHY THIS RECIPE WORKS Steak and smashed potatoes are a classic pairing that we wanted to bring to the slow cooker, spiked with the peppery bite of horseradish. Our biggest challenge would be getting the steak and potatoes to cook through in the same amount of time. The key to success turned out to be an unlikely tool: a steamer basket. Placing the potatoes in the basket on top of the steaks elevated them above the braising liquid and allowed them to steam gently. Once they were fully cooked, we smashed the potatoes with milk, cream cheese, butter, fresh chives, and spicy horseradish. Below the potatoes, we braised blade steaks in a mix of onions, garlic, and tomato paste until they were nearly fall-apart tender. To make the sauce, we simply defatted the braising liquid and served it with the rich steak and creamy, tangy potatoes. Use small red potatoes measuring 1 to 2 inches in diameter; if your potatoes are larger, cut them into 1-inch pieces to ensure that they cook through properly.

2 onions, chopped fine
6 garlic cloves, minced
2 tablespoons tomato paste
1 tablespoon vegetable oil
4 (8-ounce) beef blade steaks, ¾ to 1 inch thick, trimmed
   Salt and pepper
1½ pounds small red potatoes, unpeeled
¾ cup warm milk, plus extra as needed
2 ounces cream cheese, softened
3 tablespoons unsalted butter, melted
3 tablespoons prepared horseradish
2 tablespoons minced fresh chives

1 Combine onions, garlic, tomato paste, and oil in bowl and microwave, stirring occasionally, until onions are softened, about 5 minutes; transfer to 5½- to 7-quart slow cooker.

2 Season steaks with pepper and nestle into slow cooker. Place steamer basket on top of steaks and arrange potatoes in basket. Cover and cook until beef is tender, 8 to 9 hours on low or 5 to 6 hours on high.

3 Transfer potatoes to large bowl. Transfer steaks to serving dish and tent with aluminum foil. Strain sauce into fat separator and let sit for 5 minutes.

4 Meanwhile, break potatoes into large chunks with rubber spatula. Fold in milk, cream cheese, melted butter, horseradish, and chives until incorporated and only small chunks of potato remain. Adjust potatoes' consistency with extra warm milk as needed and season with salt and pepper to taste. Pour defatted sauce over steaks. Serve with potatoes.

CLASSIC POT ROAST WITH CARROTS AND POTATOES

SERVES 6   COOKING TIME: 9 TO 10 HOURS ON LOW OR 6 TO 7 HOURS ON HIGH

WHY THIS RECIPE WORKS The slow, even, moist heat of the slow cooker is perfect for creating a delicious, fork-tender pot roast. We wanted a pot roast that had classic flavors and that was also easy to assemble. We started with a chuck-eye roast—our favorite cut for pot roast because it's well marbled with fat and connective tissue—and tied it around the center to help it cook more evenly. Enhancing our cooking broth with lots of onions gave the braising liquid some serious flavor, and softening them first in the microwave deepened their sweetness. To this base, we added one of the test kitchen's favorite secret ingredients: instant tapioca. This convenience product, along with some dried porcini mushrooms, created a lush braising liquid with built-in flavor. It also ensured that the sauce wouldn't get watered down as the meat released its juices. To make this roast into a hearty meal, we arranged small unpeeled potatoes and carrots on top of the meat before cooking. We cooked the roast until it was perfectly tender and our sauce had great body and complex flavor. Use small Yukon Gold potatoes measuring 1 to 2 inches in diameter; if your potatoes are larger, cut them into 1-inch pieces to ensure that they cook through properly.

3 onions, chopped fine

4 garlic cloves, minced

2 tablespoons unsalted butter

2 teaspoons minced fresh thyme or 1 teaspoon dried
   Salt and pepper

2 tablespoons tomato paste

½ ounce dried porcini mushrooms, rinsed

2 bay leaves

1 tablespoon instant tapioca

1 cup beef broth

1 (3-pound) boneless beef chuck-eye roast, trimmed and tied

2 pounds small Yukon Gold potatoes, unpeeled

1 pound carrots, peeled and halved widthwise, thick ends halved lengthwise

2 tablespoons minced fresh parsley

1 Combine onions, garlic, butter, thyme, and 1 teaspoon salt together in bowl and microwave, stirring occasionally, until onions are softened, about 10 minutes; transfer to 5½- to 7-quart slow cooker. Stir in tomato paste, mushrooms, bay leaves, and tapioca, then whisk in broth.

2 Season beef with salt and pepper and nestle into slow cooker. Place potatoes and carrots on top of roast. Cover and cook until beef is tender, 9 to 10 hours on low or 6 to 7 hours on high.

3 Transfer roast to cutting board, tent with aluminum foil, and let rest for 15 minutes. Transfer vegetables to serving dish and cover tightly with foil. Using large spoon, skim excess fat from surface of sauce, then season with salt and pepper to taste. Remove twine from roast, slice against grain into ½-inch-thick slices, and transfer to platter. Sprinkle with parsley and serve with sauce.

CONVERSIONS AND EQUIVALENTS

Some say cooking is a science and an art. We would say that geography has a hand in it, too. Flours and sugars manufactured in the United Kingdom and elsewhere will feel and taste different from those manufactured in the United States. So we cannot promise that the loaf of bread you bake in Canada or England will taste the same as a loaf baked in the States, but we can offer guidelines for converting weights and measures. We also recommend that you rely on your instincts when making our recipes. Refer to the visual cues provided. If the dough hasn't "come together, in a ball" as described, you may need to add more flour—even if the recipe doesn't tell you to. You be the judge.

The recipes in this book were developed using standard U.S. measures following U.S. government guidelines. The charts below offer equivalents for U.S. and metric measures. All conversions are approximate and have been rounded up or down to the nearest whole number.

EXAMPLE

1 teaspoon = 4.9292 milliliters, rounded up to 5 milliliters

1 ounce = 28.3495 grams, rounded down to 28 grams

VOLUME CONVERSIONS

U.S.	METRIC
1 teaspoon	5 milliliters
2 teaspoons	10 milliliters
1 tablespoon	15 milliliters
2 tablespoons	30 milliliters
¼ cup	59 milliliters
⅓ cup	79 milliliters
½ cup	118 milliliters
¾ cup	177 milliliters
1 cup	237 milliliters
1¼ cups	296 milliliters
1½ cups	355 milliliters
2 cups (1 pint)	473 milliliters
2½ cups	591 milliliters
3 cups	710 milliliters
4 cups (1 quart)	0.946 liter
1.06 quarts	1 liter
4 quarts (1 gallon)	3.8 liters

WEIGHT CONVERSIONS

OUNCES	GRAMS
½	14
¾	21
1	28
1½	43
2	57
2½	71
3	85
3½	99
4	113
4½	128
5	142
6	170
7	198
8	227
9	255
10	283
12	340
16 (1 pound)	454

CONVERSION FOR COMMON BAKING INGREDIENTS

Baking is an exacting science. Because measuring by weight is far more accurate than measuring by volume, and thus more likely to produce reliable results, in our recipes we provide ounce measures in addition to cup measures for many ingredients. Refer to the chart below to convert these measures into grams.

INGREDIENT	OUNCES	GRAMS
Flour		
1 cup all-purpose flour*	5	142
1 cup cake flour	4	113
1 cup whole-wheat flour	5½	156
Sugar		
1 cup granulated (white) sugar	7	198
1 cup packed brown sugar (light or dark)	7	198
1 cup confectioners' sugar	4	113
Cocoa Powder		
1 cup cocoa powder	3	85
Butter†		
4 tablespoons (½ stick, or ¼ cup)	2	57
8 tablespoons (1 stick, or ½ cup)	4	113
16 tablespoons (2 sticks, or 1 cup)	8	227

* U.S. all-purpose flour, the most frequently used flour in this book, does not contain leaveners, as some European flours do. These leavened flours are called self-rising or self-raising. If you are using self-rising flour, take this into consideration before adding leavening to a recipe.

† In the United States, butter is sold both salted and unsalted. We generally recommend unsalted butter. If you are using salted butter, take this into consideration before adding salt to a recipe.

OVEN TEMPERATURES

FAHRENHEIT	CELSIUS	GAS MARK
225	105	¼
250	120	½
275	135	1
300	150	2
325	165	3
350	180	4
375	190	5
400	200	6
425	220	7
450	230	8
475	245	9

CONVERTING TEMPERATURES FROM AN INSTANT-READ THERMOMETER

We include doneness temperatures in many of the recipes in this book. We recommend an instant-read thermometer for the job. Refer to the above table to convert Fahrenheit degrees to Celsius. Or, for temperatures not represented in the chart, use this simple formula:

Subtract 32 degrees from the Fahrenheit reading, then divide the result by 1.8 to find the Celsius reading.

EXAMPLE

"Roast chicken until thighs register 175 degrees."

To convert:
175°F − 32 = 143°
143° ÷ 1.8 = 79.44°C, rounded down to 79°C

Note: Page references in *italics* indicate photographs.

P